A WONDERFUL CAREER IN CRIME

CONFLICTING WORLDS
New Dimensions of the American Civil War

T. MICHAEL PARRISH, SERIES EDITOR

A WONDERFUL CAREER IN CRIME

**CHARLES COWLAM'S MASQUERADES
IN THE CIVIL WAR ERA & GILDED AGE**

FRANK W. GARMON JR.

LOUISIANA STATE UNIVERSITY PRESS   BATON ROUGE

Published by Louisiana State University Press
lsupress.org

Copyright © 2024 by Louisiana State University Press
All rights reserved. Except in the case of brief quotations used in articles or reviews, no part of this publication may be reproduced or transmitted in any format or by any means without written permission of Louisiana State University Press.

DESIGNER: Barbara Neely Bourgoyne
TYPEFACE: Garamond Premier Pro

COVER IMAGE: Carte de visite of an unidentified man matching descriptions of Charles Cowlam. Courtesy of the Charles Family Photographs, South Caroliniana Library, University of South Carolina.

LIBRARY OF CONGRESS CATALOGING-IN-PUBLICATION DATA

Names: Garmon, Frank W., Jr., author.
Title: A wonderful career in crime : Charles Cowlam's masquerades in the Civil War era and Gilded Age / Frank W. Garmon Jr.
Description: Baton Rouge : Louisiana State University Press, [2024] | Series: Conflicting worlds: new dimensions of the American Civil War | Includes bibliographical references and index.
Identifiers: LCCN 2024001031 (print) | LCCN 2024001032 (ebook) | ISBN 978-0-8071-8216-1 (cloth) | ISBN 978-0-8071-8265-9 (epub) | ISBN 978-0-8071-8266-6 (pdf)
Subjects: LCSH: Cowlam, Charles, 1837– | Swindlers and swindling—United States—Biography. | Crime—United States—History—19th century.
Classification: LCC HV6692.C69 G37 2024 (print) | LCC HV6692.C69 (ebook) | DDC 364.16/3092 [B]—dc23/eng/20240524
LC record available at https://lccn.loc.gov/2024001031
LC ebook record available at https://lccn.loc.gov/2024001032

In memory of my father, Frank Warren Garmon,
1950–2016

CONTENTS

PREFACE & ACKNOWLEDGMENTS ix

INTRODUCTION 1

ONE   CONVICT 14

TWO   SPY 33

THREE   DETECTIVE 51

FOUR   CANDIDATE 85

FIVE   SWINDLER 112

SIX   VETERAN 129

EPILOGUE 145

NOTES 153

BIBLIOGRAPHY 193

INDEX 219

Photographs follow page 74

PREFACE & ACKNOWLEDGMENTS

This book is a product of the pandemic. With many of the major research libraries closed, I searched for a project that could be completed remotely with the help of my undergraduate research assistants. Christopher Newport University values collaborative faculty-student research, and every semester I work with a handful of Junior Fellows with the Center for American Studies. My colleague, Jonathan White, recommended that my students and I peruse the digitized pardon records among the Papers of Abraham Lincoln. He explained that the records were filled with incredible stories and that nearly all of them are unpublished. A good story with a connection to Lincoln might lead to a short publication with a student.

One of my students, Nate Hotes, discovered the letter from Lincoln's pardon clerk summarizing Charles Cowlam's case that begins chapter 1. The concluding sentence, describing Cowlam's application as the least meritorious on file in the office, caught his attention. "There must be a story here," Nate exclaimed excitedly. A quick search of the newspaper databases produced a number of results, but each reference seemed to suggest a different scheme, a different city, and almost certainly a different person. When historians seek to verify if two individuals are the same, they look for a common link between the two. A common place of birth, a father's name, or a city and occupation might establish a definitive connection between two sources. Every time I found a new source relating to Cowlam, I would shake my head in disbelief, thinking, "This can't possibly be the same person," and yet in almost every case there would be some clue connecting the two points. We might expect a con artist to sever all links that could connect them to past crimes, but these allusions to past frauds had the effect of creating a ready-made resume. Cowlam advertised his previous employment, whereabouts, or connections as a

PREFACE AND ACKNOWLEDGMENTS

way of signaling trust and establishing reputation. The previous con served as a calling card for the next swindle. What began as an idea for a short article with a student quickly developed into a book.

A number of archives and libraries have been extraordinarily accommodating in supplying me with photocopies or assisting me in tracking down this elusive and transient charlatan. Special thanks to Bruce Kirby at the Library of Congress, Paul Harrison at the National Archives in Washington, D.C., David Castillo and Tab Lewis at the National Archives in College Park, Maureen Hill at the National Archives in Atlanta, Michel Brideau at the Library and Archives of Canada, Fran Baker at the Chatsworth Archives in the United Kingdom, Joshua L. Goodman and Kimberly Atkins at the State Library and Archives of Florida, Annakathryn Welch at the Archives of Michigan, Tere Elizalde at the Bentley Historical Library at the University of Michigan, Wendi Goen at the Arizona State Library, Ryan P. Semmes at the Mississippi State University Library for sharing items from the Ulysses S. Grant Collection, Karen King and Carolyn Wilson at the Earl Gregg Swem Special Collections Research Center at the College of William and Mary, Karen J. Johnson at the U.S. District Court in Norfolk for the Eastern District of Virginia, and the staff at the Library of Virginia and the Virginia Museum of History and Culture.

Several individuals made it possible to access materials that might otherwise be inaccessible. Matthew Kidd photographed a collection of letters related to Cowlam's employment with the British government at the Chatsworth Archives. Joel Kropf combed the manuscript collections at the Library and Archives of Canada in search of Cowlam's detective work for the Canadian government. Matthew Slaboch generously helped me by photographing a collection at the Arizona State Library. James E. Arsenault, a rare book and manuscript dealer, graciously shared images of Cowlam's pardon from Lincoln and a letter from William Seward to the governor of Virginia, now in the private collection of a California collector. Susan Gehrman, of Battle Creek, Michigan, shared a photograph of Charles's younger sister Elizabeth.

In piecing together Cowlam's life, I contacted several descendants of one of his sisters, Mariette Cowlam, and his brother, George B. Cowlam. Genealogist Melanie Whitt shared her research on Cowlam's mother, Isabella Hays Cowlam, and assisted me in locating the descendants of Mariette Cowlam.

Descendants Stuart Hay Chamberlain Jr., Sarah Dolley, Steve Kasperick-Postellon, Mary Postellon, and Lynn Moffat Winston generously shared what they knew of the family history, and Sarah Dolley went above and beyond in sharing genealogical notes and family correspondence from her late father, Daniel Postellon.

It has been a pleasure working with the Louisiana State University Press. Mike Parrish has challenged me with his incisive recommendations, and Rand Dotson has been supportive throughout the publication process. My colleague Jonathan White read and critiqued the whole manuscript, and provided consistent feedback as the project developed. Robert Colby offered valuable insights after reading the introduction and first chapter. Elizabeth D. Leonard carefully examined the entire book and proposed numerous helpful revisions. Derik Shelor provided thoughtful recommendations as he copy edited the text. Their suggestions have been invaluable and have improved the book immeasurably.

Among the benefits of working at my alma mater is the ability to interact with past mentors and longtime friends. To name everyone individually who fits this description would fill many pages. My colleagues in the Department of Leadership and American Studies at Christopher Newport University supported this project through their steadfast mentorship and encouragement. I am grateful to Elizabeth Kaufer Busch and Nathan Busch for supporting my research as co-directors of the Center for American Studies. William Connell, in the Department of History, shared his expertise on Latin American history to illuminate Cowlam's adventures in Central America. Jesse Spencer, the interlibrary loan specialist at CNU's Paul and Rosemary Trible Library, located numerous odd and unusual requests. The Provost's Office, the College of Social Sciences, the Department of Leadership and American Studies, the Center for American Studies, and the Office of Undergraduate Research and Creative Activity all supported this project at various stages. A faculty development grant allowed me to make multiple trips to the National Archives and Library of Congress. I presented early versions of the introduction and chapter 2 at College of Social Sciences Research Workshops, including one where visiting scholar Barbara Kellerman of Harvard University offered feedback. Friends in other departments at CNU, especially the Department of History and the Department of Economics, inspired me to pursue a Ph.D. in history

PREFACE AND ACKNOWLEDGMENTS

at the University of Virginia, and together with my graduate mentors have helped me become the scholar I am today.

Collaboration with CNU students has made this book possible. The Junior Fellows program with the Center for American Studies and the Summer Scholars program organized through the Office of Undergraduate Research and Creative Activity have helped me immensely. CNU students have assisted with transcribing primary sources, searching newspaper databases, proofreading chapters, and organizing the bibliography. Special thanks to Nathan Hotes for discovering the letter that inspired the project, along with Sarah Badertscher, Grace Cook, Claira Cooper, Dylan Frederick, Christopher Lubinski, Andrew Ramseur, Michael Sparks, and Lucy Vick for their research assistance. A unit on confidence men in my American Entrepreneurship course in the spring of 2022 offered insightful ways of thinking about the literature on swindlers and fraud.

My wife, Katy, has supported me throughout. Her love and encouragement have sustained me and kept me focused on the task at hand. She has accompanied me on research trips and motivated me to complete the book. Our daughter, Victoria, arrived as the project reached the finishing stages. My parents, Warren and Martha Garmon, fostered my interest in the past. Although they both studied engineering, they spent a lifetime together collecting antiques. I dedicate this book to the memory of my father, who would have enjoyed reading it.

A WONDERFUL CAREER IN CRIME

INTRODUCTION

From the shrugged shoulders, titters, whispers, wonderings of the crowd, it was plain that he was, in the extremest sense of the word, a stranger.
—HERMAN MELVILLE, *The Confidence Man: His Masquerade* (1857)

The middle decades of the nineteenth century in the United States witnessed an extraordinary number of young men migrating to urban centers. Among the most popular advice manuals from the era were guides that instructed these enterprising youths in finding employment and navigating the transition to city life. Many of these young men had been raised in a free labor ideology that trusted that economic independence could be achieved through hard work and entrepreneurship. The freedom of working for wages on a contract embodied the opportunities and flexibility that northern workers enjoyed, and served as the first step toward property ownership and independence. Whigs and Republicans alike extolled the virtues of independent laborers by emphasizing the contrast between the growing industrial northern economy built by free laborers and the perceived languishing economy in the South built by slaves. The free labor worldview reflected the aspirations of middle-class northerners, who saw self-employment as the best path to wealth and the surest means of guaranteeing equality of opportunity for all.[1]

At the same time, the idea of working for wages as a step toward economic independence did not hold universal appeal. Pulling one's self up by one's bootstraps was difficult, time-consuming, and could feel insurmountable. In catering to the demands of an employer, some young men equated contract labor with surrendering independence rather than preserving it. Working for someone else seemed to contradict the image of the self-made man. The transition to urban life could also be disorienting. The fast pace of city life was foreign to those who had spent their formative years in the countryside, and working for wages exposed workers to the uncertainties of the market and the vicissitudes of the business cycle. In this sense the middle of the nineteenth century presented a crisis of self-ownership. Mystified by the rise of impersonal, distant causality at the expense of the individual, young men searched for alternatives to the free labor ideal. In his transcendentalist work, *Walden*, Henry David Thoreau described his desire "not to live in this restless, nervous, bustling, trivial Nineteenth Century, but stand or sit thoughtfully while it goes by." Thoreau, like many of his contemporaries, wished to declare independence by engaging in a new sort of entrepreneurship. Where Thoreau's Transcendentalism represented one way forward, many young urbanites sought to forge their own path in rejecting the promises of free labor.[2]

The world of confidence men, imposters, and charlatans offered another avenue for rejecting the free labor ethos. Historians have traditionally attributed the rise of nineteenth-century confidence men to the legacy of republican ideology and puritanical religious influence. The revolutionary generation idealized republican principles of independence, order, and industriousness as safeguards against corruption. Calvinist preachers fixated on declension, worrying constantly about moral degeneration. The first half of the nineteenth century challenged the structures that had governed earlier generations. The transition from local to regional, and ultimately national, markets meant that family farms were no longer self-sufficient. Young men migrated to towns and cities in search of work, removed from their parents' watchful supervision. A series of religious revivals sweeping over the country culminated in the Second Great Awakening, which spawned new denominations and circulated new ideas, some of which blurred the lines between propriety and humbug. Swindlers thrive in periods of transformation and rapid change. When traditional ways of looking at the world are no longer sufficient, the swindler creates room for new ones.[3]

Because confidence men first made their appearances in urban areas, historians have typically presented them as an eastern phenomenon, overlooking examples of scoundrels in the South and Midwest. The Midwest urbanized faster than any other region in the nineteenth century. Whereas less than 4 percent of midwesterners lived in urban areas in the census of 1840, nearly a third of them did so by the census of 1890. Chicago emerged as the fastest

INTRODUCTION

growing city in the world, maturing from a small town of a couple thousand in 1840 to a booming metropolis fifty years later, with a population of more than a million. The development of the smaller cities and towns that dotted the Midwest paralleled the growth of the metropole. Detroit ballooned from nine thousand to more than two hundred thousand over the same span of time. Rapid urbanization created a world of strangers. Many of the new arrivals were transient or seasonal. The continual inflow and outflow of migrants made it difficult to establish trust and evaluate the backgrounds of new acquaintances. Letters from mutual connections could only go so far, and the likelihood of having associates in common diminished in a nation on the move. The stories men told about their past lives substituted in their place, and young men practiced their personal narratives for hasty interviews. It was easy to start a new life in a nineteenth-century city.[4]

Charles Cowlam was a chameleon. He possessed a remarkable talent for blending into new surroundings and ingratiating himself with the leading power brokers. His career as a convict, soldier, secret agent, revenue detective, congressional candidate, adventurer, and con artist spanned the Civil War, Reconstruction, and the Gilded Age. Historians have overlooked him due to his elusive nature. In his adult life he rarely remained in the same city for more than a year unless he was incarcerated. Each change of venue offered Cowlam the opportunity to reinvent himself. He changed his name almost as frequently as he changed his story. One newspaper reported that "he has as many *aliases* as there are letters in the alphabet."[5] Some of Cowlam's aliases were simply misspellings of his last name, which he encouraged throughout his life by changing the pronunciation of his surname to distance himself from past associations. In other cases, his aliases were more elaborate, such as Charles Cushman, William E. Burlick, or Colonel Livingston Grahame.

Cowlam is the only person known to have been pardoned by both Abraham Lincoln *and* Jefferson Davis during the Civil War. Although he was born in Michigan, he was arrested in Portsmouth, Virginia, in 1857 after pilfering the contents of several letters while working as a post office clerk. Charles was only nineteen years old at the time of his arrest, yet he received a ten-year sentence for mail robbery. His older sister and a freshman congressman from his home district took up his cause, and Lincoln agreed to pardon him one month after Virginians voted to secede from the Union. When the governor of Virginia refused to release him, Cowlam appealed to Jefferson Davis, presenting himself as a loyal Confederate who eagerly wished to prove himself on the battlefield. After receiving a pardon from Davis, Cowlam mustered into the Confederate army, but quickly deserted and spent the duration of the conflict as a wartime speculator and drifter. When the war ended, he rushed to Washington with an offer to assist the detectives investigating Lincoln's assassination. He hastened to present himself as a loyal Unionist and to defend the martyred president who had once ordered his release. Naturally he omitted any mention of having previously been incarcerated. For much of the rest of his life he insisted that his time spent in Richmond was all part of an elaborate cover to infiltrate the Confederate Secret Service and spy for the Union.

In the postwar years Cowlam reinvented himself as a detective. He parlayed his peripheral contributions to the Lincoln assassination investigation into stints as a detective for the Internal Revenue Service and a spy for the British government. He also tried unsuccessfully to obtain employment as an investigator for the Canadian government. In a curious twist of fate, the convict was now tasked with investigating crime and gathering intelligence. His record as a detective leaves a mixed impression. Although he uncovered a whiskey smuggling ring and exonerated an African American minister falsely accused of passing counterfeit banknotes, accusations of impropriety always seemed to follow him. The intelligence he gathered was dubious at best, and while working in the Treasury Department he developed a reputation for blackmailing merchants and extorting those accused of violating the revenue laws. Cowlam left the position after little more than a year, likely fleeing for his life. A newspaper article later summarized this chapter in his life by reporting that the "indignation was so intense against him that had he been caught at the time no doubt he would have been lynched."[6]

Reconstruction offered ample opportunities for Cowlam to repackage his identity. The federal government created a wealth of new patronage positions to be filled by those who could demonstrate loyalty to the Union. Northerners who rushed to the South in search of opportunity had limited means of verifying an outsider's credentials. Cowlam benefited from this uncertainty. He partnered with a lame-duck governor who recommended him to President Ulysses S. Grant for appointment as the U.S. marshal for the Northern District of Florida. Grant rescinded his appointment almost immediately

INTRODUCTION

amid a flood of outcry from Florida Republicans. Cowlam then devised a plan to run for Congress under an unsanctioned fusion ticket, and assisted the governor in manipulating the selection of county election commissioners in a desperate effort to rig the election. The scheme collapsed when their machinations failed to affect the outcome.

Having lost the election, Cowlam moved to Manhattan, where he started a fake secret society and newspaper aligned with the Granger and workingmen's movements. There he presented himself as an eligible bachelor despite the fact that he was already married. He soon engaged in a spree of serial bigamy by targeting wealthy widows and disappearing with their fortunes. When the newspapers revealed his frauds, he fled and assumed a new identity. He spent much of the next decade traveling and partaking in various schemes. Cowlam resurfaced again twelve years later, in 1886, at the Central Branch of the National Soldiers' Home in Dayton, Ohio, where he pretended to be a Union colonel under an assumed name. The papers described him as suffering from dementia, and appearing to be about forty years of age with the letters "C.C." tattooed on his arm in India ink. This confused veteran could not remember which unit he had commanded or where he had spent the war. His friends at the soldiers' home initiated a pension inquiry on his behalf only to discover that he had never served.

In piecing together Charles Cowlam's adventures, this book presents a microhistory that illuminates the world of swindlers and intriguers who operated in the shadows of nineteenth-century politics. Microhistory as a methodological technique allows historians to examine closely an episode or character to reveal unfiltered truths that may become obscured in a broader survey of the period.[7] The methodology lends itself well to tracing elusive individuals across sparse records in the pursuit of understanding the larger culture. Microhistory originated out of social and cultural history in an effort to understand everyday life from the ground up rather than through the lens of elite sources. The approach has been more commonly applied to early modern Europe to understand peasant society, culture, and religion, yet microhistory is particularly well suited to elucidating the history of crime and corruption.[8] Most scoundrels like Cowlam would have preferred to have been forgotten, lest their misdeeds be exposed. Their lives appear regularly in the margins of political correspondence, court cases, and sensational newspaper articles, which rarely offer a comprehensive treatment. Cowlam's life typifies what micro-historians call the "exceptional normal," an outlier that stands in as representative for a group of individuals whose experiences might be otherwise lost in the historical record.[9] Such stories appear exotic or unusual because so few records survive attesting to their experiences. If our archives were more complete, however, such narratives might appear less abnormal, and some might even appear commonplace. Cowlam was a remarkable scoundrel, yet there were many like him whose stories are waiting to be discovered.[10]

Cowlam's life reveals a malleability of identity that was particular to the middle decades of the nineteenth century. Verifying credentials, accounting for whereabouts, and cultivating political networks would have all required corroboration and personal connections in other places in time. In a later era, we might expect federal bureaucracies, sharpened by progressive era reforms, to have possessed enhanced capacity for validating information. In an earlier era, Americans would have been more suspicious of Cowlam's transience and he would have struggled to make the intimate connections necessary to obtain letters of introduction. In the Gilded Age, however, his claims to the Union cause and appearance of respectability were all he needed. Cowlam operated in a world where one's network of personal acquaintances could no longer be trusted to evaluate a stranger's qualifications, yet the systems in place for verifying information were rudimentary. When coupled with an increasingly mobile population in the aftermath of the Civil War, the challenges of identifying Americans proved insurmountable. Identification through the means of photographs or fingerprinting were in their infancy, and methods for classifying and cataloging them would not become standardized until the turn of the twentieth century.[11]

The use of aliases presented additional challenges to positive identification. In their report on the American prison system, Alexis de Tocqueville and Gustave de Beaumont noted that in a country where no system of national identification prevailed, "nothing is easier than to change one's name." Aliases allowed criminals to hide their past and conceal their recidivism—so long as they did not return to the same penitentiary where they had previously served or encounter someone who remembered their former existence. The multitude of state and local jurisdictions further complicated efforts to gather information on repeat offenders. Tocqueville and Beaumont emphasized that

INTRODUCTION

"The link that ties the United States together is purely political; there exists no central power to which the police officers might address themselves to obtain information on the past life of the indicted, so that criminal courts *almost always sentence without knowing the true name and still less the history of the guilty.*" The American legal system was a vast treasury of local knowledge. No national registries existed that could have exposed Cowlam's past crimes.[12]

Movement made Cowlam's schemes possible. The legal scholar Lawrence Friedman describes swindling, fraud, and bigamy as "crimes of mobility." In each case, transience made it easier to violate the victim's trust, and easier to disappear after that trust had been violated. An anecdote from Abraham Lincoln's early life illustrates the temptation to start a new life in a new town rather than face consequences. When his business partner died in 1835, saddling him with substantial debts, Lincoln chose to make good on the partnership's obligations. As one biographer observes, "many men in similar circumstances would simply have moved away, left their debts unpaid, and blamed the town for their failure." That Lincoln paid his debts made him exceptional, and launched his reputation as "Honest Abe."[13]

Much of this transience was a byproduct of the Civil War. The war mobilized hundreds of thousands of soldiers and carried them to parts of the country they had never seen before. The scale of the conflict fostered a sense of anonymity, allowing some to cultivate ambiguous identities, or to create new lives entirely. When the hostilities concluded, most veterans returned to the places they had known before the war, but tens of thousands of young men became sidetracked along the way. Carpetbaggers migrated toward new centers of power in the Reconstruction South. Others drifted to cities in search of work or other opportunities. The only points connecting them to their past lives were the stories they told, and each of them had a tale of how they spent the war years. Such narratives contained signposts that connected the narrator to a particular place, situating them in the minds of listeners. When Cowlam described Libby Prison or Union general Benjamin F. Butler's office, he invited listeners to make certain assumptions about him and his connections. The upheaval of the war and its aftermath made it possible for grifters like Cowlam to manufacture new identities for themselves.[14]

Rather than perpetrating frauds against unsuspecting passersby, however, Cowlam reserved his greatest deceptions for the highest levels of government.

In the course of his life he managed to obtain employment in the Treasury Department despite a history of thievery, gain admittance to a National Soldiers' Home without evidence of having ever served, convince politicians in Florida to allow him to run for Congress shortly after arriving in the state, persuade President Grant to appoint him as a U.S. marshal, and receive presidential pardons from Lincoln and Davis. Patronage made these pretenses possible, and Cowlam's intrigues reveal how the patronage system worked. Eric Foner argues that the Republican Party transitioned in the postwar period "from an ideological to an organizational mode of politics." The dramatic expansion of the state and federal governments multiplied the number of prospective applicants in search of sinecure positions. Patronage flowed from parallel state and federal networks, which could fuel factionalism between those who wielded influence over state and local officeholders, and federal appointees who derived their benefaction from Congress. The Civil War and Reconstruction also disrupted the flow of information that patronage politics relied upon. Politicians were dependent on networks of state and local officials to vet candidates and substantiate their connection to the party. Cowlam understood the key to manipulating these relationships. He made powerful friends everywhere he went, played both sides of the patronage game, and arrived with letters of recommendation in hand.[15]

Whereas historians of capitalism have uncovered the vulnerabilities of an economic system built on trust and personal relationships, Cowlam's life exposes the liabilities of a political system built on the same foundations. Ian Klaus emphasizes that the "qualities that are most necessary for trust in any given era are precisely the qualities a sharp swindler is most likely to fake." Government officials relied on the same trust that underpinned financial markets, and political actors suffered from the same issues of verification that plagued private industry, yet the confidence man in corporate America has been studied more extensively than the confidence man in American politics. New historians of capitalism have only recently considered the role of grifters like Cowlam, who applied their talents to dupe politicians, to complement studies of underground markets and illicit trade. Just as con artists can reveal the inner workings of capitalism by exposing cracks in the system, intriguers like Cowlam can reveal how information circulated within political networks. While the recent history of capitalism literature has succeeded in surveying the major macroeconomic trends that underpinned the American economy, the authors of a recent edited volume argue that "what is needed now are bottom-up social histories of the obscure actors who enabled 'capitalist transformation' at the local level." Cowlam's life story offers one such opportunity.[16]

The close connections that Cowlam cultivated with telegraph operators and newspaper editors created further opportunities for his intrigues. Whereas antebellum newspapers had often served as mouthpieces for political parties, the major metropolitan newspapers in the postwar era insulated themselves with a degree of independence from party bosses. The independent press fostered a friendly rivalry between journalists and politicians, and through their wider coverage it became possible to expose corruption on a larger scale than ever before. Yet the same forces that made reporters the antagonists of elected officials could also align their interests. Correspondents could expose corruption to the public or use that information to engage in intrigues of their own, pilfering privileged communication to gain a politician's confidence, leaking the material to their rivals, or shaking them down for cash or employment.[17] In this sense, Cowlam fit in among the thousands of upwardly mobile, white-collar clerks who occasionally succumbed to the allure of easy money, or the shady detectives who operated on both sides of the law.[18]

In many ways, the confidence man serves as a cultural hero for Americans. We simultaneously admire them for their talents and scorn them for their crimes. In revealing the fluidity of American identity, confidence games probe the limits of social mobility and prey upon the trust that makes moving up the ladder possible. Unlike the trickster, a more universal figure that appears in a variety of world literatures, the confidence man is a prototypically American archetype. Where the trickster seeks to disrupt the social order, the confidence man attempts to blend in, and is therefore a representative rather than a marginal figure. The rise of parlor culture and the Victorian taste for the theatrical almost certainly aided the popularity of the confidence man. Scoundrels fill the pages of Victorian fiction. Many of the most sensational works featured an imposter in the midst of elite society, such as an immoral man using the appearance of refinement to pass off his counterfeit respectability. Even more alarming to middle-class sensibilities was the man with a genuinely good background and education who used his reputation for propriety as a facade to mask his rotten character. Double lives and mistaken identities made compelling plot devices in an era when discerning a stranger's true character proved challenging.[19]

Confidence men make for unreliable narrators. They reveal just enough about themselves to allow the listener to fill in the details with assumptions of their own. Like the narrator in Herman Melville's *The Confidence-Man: His Masquerade,* Charles Cowlam was an untrustworthy, but not always undependable, narrator. There was almost always an ember of truth to be found in his sensational stories and tall tales. Melville was known for his ambiguous use of language. The literary scholar Gary Lindberg notes that if Melville "rarely misinforms us, it is because he so rarely tells us anything definite." The shallow character descriptions and the narrator's overly cautious use of language have led scholars to disagree about even basic elements of the novel's plot.[20] The form that Cowlam's intrigues took reveal as much about himself as they do about the expectations of those who fell for his deceptions. While he never committed a massive fraud or a sensational murder, he mastered the art of self-promotion by constantly exaggerating his credentials and forming close connections with prominent individuals. His stories were extraordinary, yet believable and difficult to authenticate. He excelled at presenting himself exactly the way those who encountered him wanted him to appear. As a convict he fit Lincoln's expectations of a youthful offender deserving of clemency. For Davis he appeared a loyal southerner. To those he encountered after the war he was the experienced detective, the elusive southern Unionist, the well-dressed bachelor, or the decorated war veteran. From the vantage point of observers oblivious to his misdeeds, Cowlam appeared to behave exactly as an upwardly mobile Union veteran navigating the transition to civilian life might have acted.

Cowlam's life reveals how local knowledge traveled between the centers of power and the periphery through intermediaries like him. The first chapter considers how the secession crisis disrupted the flow of information between the North and South, sequestering Abraham Lincoln from evidence that would have impugned Cowlam's character and wrecked his chances of obtaining a pardon. Lincoln's pardon issued after secession offered a test of federal authority in the Confederacy, challenging secessionist governors to either recognize his power or disobey his command. Historians have only recently considered how penitentiary convicts fared during the Civil War, and

INTRODUCTION

the research pales in comparison to the scholarship on prisoners of war. Federal prisoners found themselves trapped behind enemy lines, separated from the evidence that could support their appeal and the only person who could grant them clemency. Introducing Cowlam's early life and family history later in the chapter offers a counterpoint to the representations made in his pardon application and provides context for his subsequent schemes.

Chapter 2 begins with the story Cowlam told to the detectives investigating the Lincoln assassination, before circling back to his appeal to Jefferson Davis for a pardon. Cowlam's testimony attempted to account for his activities during the war, demonstrate his loyalty to the Union cause, and convince the investigators of his usefulness to the investigation. Micro-historians have long noted how pardon tales often take on a literary quality, and the contradictory narratives Cowlam presented are no exception.[21] The particulars of his pardon and the fragmentary evidence of his time in the Confederacy cast doubt on his postwar statements but also explain why he was taken seriously. Cowlam told listeners what they wanted to hear, knowing that the cloud of war would conceal his past and make his claims difficult to verify.

Chapter 3 details Cowlam's postwar career as a detective. After trying unsuccessfully to secure a position with the Canadian government, he managed to obtain a job with the Internal Revenue Service, and later worked for the British government in Ireland. In each case, his access to confidential information floating along the telegraph wires and his association with prominent politicians secured him audiences with the leading power brokers. His position in the Internal Revenue Service afforded him his first experiences in the Reconstruction South, in a district covering Georgia and northern Florida. Once employed, Cowlam appeared proactive and persistent, investigating cases relentlessly, and seemed to be constantly on the move. On the surface he gave every impression of leading an honest life for the first time, yet his lack of scruples always seemed to catch up with him. In pitching his credentials to the Canadian and British authorities, Cowlam boasted of his ability to infiltrate and investigate Irish nationalist organizations plotting assassinations in both countries. Though his claims were unfounded, the threats he identified seemed credible to government ministers.

Chapter 4 offers a close examination of Florida politics in the 1872 election. Cowlam worked closely with the Republican governor, Harrison Reed, in his efforts to swing the state elections for the Democrats, with assurances that Reed's energies would be rewarded with a seat in the U.S. Senate. The race in Florida reveals how the divisions within the Republican Party created opportunities for Cowlam to play the various factions against one another. Grant's reputation as a maverick president who wished to remove himself from the influences of establishment politicians aided Cowlam's efforts. By refusing to consult with Republican officeholders in Florida, Grant isolated himself from sources of information that could have exposed Cowlam's schemes. Ultimately the local knowledge gathered from the patronage system revealed the governor's intrigues and contributed to Cowlam's removal.

Chapter 5 follows Cowlam's time in New York and disappearance after the independent press and a pugnacious attorney exposed his fraudulent secret society and serial bigamy. The chapter emphasizes the Panic of 1873, which commenced shortly after his arrival. The economic depression that resulted galvanized the workingmen's movement and created a feeling of vulnerability among the affluent. Cowlam capitalized on both sentiments, and discovered more lucrative forms of fraud than federal officeholding. The secret society and accompanying newspaper rode the coattails of the burgeoning Granger movement. His bigamy took advantage of the decentralized nature of vital recordkeeping by wooing wealthy women into marriage and disappearing with their fortunes. The chapter illustrates the challenges of verifying identity and tracking fugitives in the transient Gilded Age.

The final chapter finds Cowlam in the Central Branch soldiers' home in Dayton, Ohio, pretending to be a Union colonel. The chapter considers examples of those who claimed to have been soldiers—what today would be called "stolen valor"—in the years after the Civil War. The pension inquiry initiated on Cowlam's behalf reveals the curious working, and growing sophistication, of the federal government in corroborating the identities of its citizens. Without a name, unit, or date of service to work with, officials at the Pension Bureau were able to uncover Cowlam's life story after a four-month investigation. During that time the examiners made inquiries from Canada to Guatemala in search of the amnesic soldier's background.

On a related note, Cowlam's life also reveals the perils of historical quotation. His sensational style of writing has led him to be quoted occasionally by historians unaware of his checkered past. Authors can be forgiven for lending

INTRODUCTION

credibility to Cowlam's fabricated anecdotes, however, as he carefully curated his life story to fit the situation and audience. His letters never fail to offer stunning quotations, and he always placed himself at the center of action and controversy. He wanted to be believed. His ubiquitous misrepresentations have made it difficult for anyone to connect the dots until now. It makes one wonder how many other Charles Cowlams linger in the footnotes of history, waiting to be unmasked.

ONE
CONVICT

The vice of this unfortunate is pardonable. Consider, he lies not out of wantonness.
—HERMAN MELVILLE, *The Confidence Man: His Masquerade* (1857)

On the same day that Confederates in South Carolina attacked Fort Sumter a clerk at the pardon office penned a letter to Attorney General Edward Bates. The clerk summarized the pardon application of Charles Cowlam, who had been convicted of stealing from the mails while working as an assistant in the post office in Portsmouth, Virginia, in November 1857 and sentenced to ten years in prison in Richmond. Cowlam's application had the support of several prominent individuals, including Congressman Francis W. Kellogg and former U.S. Senator Charles E. Stuart, both from Cowlam's home state of Michigan, and from "a large number of other gentlemen whose recommendation is entitled to great respect." His application also included heartfelt letters from his older sister, Sarah, who described the effect that Charles's incarceration had left on her and her orphaned sisters.

"But there is a lion in the path that leads to mercy in this case," the pardon office clerk continued. Although Cowlam had been convicted at the tender age of nineteen, this was not his first offense. The superintendent of the Virginia State Penitentiary informed the pardon office that Cowlam had just finished serving a fifteen-month sentence for a housebreaking in Parkersburg, in what is now West Virginia, only months before his most recent conviction. In the course of his earlier incarceration, moreover, "he was recognized as an acquaintance of men from the Ohio Penitentiary, with whom he had served there." Cowlam had also "pretended to attempt to commit suicide" after his most recent arrest, and he was believed to have other aliases. "If these statements are true," the clerk mused, "Cowlam has run a wonderful career in crime for one so young." He concluded the letter by noting, "I am compelled to say that I regard his application as one of the least meritorious on file in the office." Twelve days later the attorney general marked the application "Refused."[1]

Abraham Lincoln ignored the recommendation of his attorney general. He drafted the pardon on May 8, 1861, and formally signed it on May 28. Unfortunately for Cowlam, the pardon arrived too late. Secessionists in Virginia had voted to leave the Union on April 17, and the delegates signed the Ordinance of Secession on May 23, five days before Lincoln's pardon would be issued. On June 7, Virginia Governor John Letcher's aide-de-camp, S. Bassett French, informed Lincoln that "the Commonwealth of Virginia not being one of the United States of America the power of the chief Executive of that nation is not recognized by the Government of this State." The *Boston Morning Journal* summarized the governor's response to Lincoln, explaining "that functionary don't know A. Lincoln; don't recognize his authority; and don't propose to let Charles Conlan [sic] go until he gets ready."[2]

Despite the obstacles standing in the way of clemency, Cowlam is the only federal prisoner known to have been pardoned by both Abraham Lincoln and Jefferson Davis. His story illustrates the obstacles that inmates convicted of federal crimes in the South faced at the start of the Civil War. The war separated convicts from the evidence that could secure their release, witnesses who could testify on their behalf, and the executive authority that could grant them clemency. Cowlam's case raises an interesting question. What happened to federal prisoners jailed in states that had seceded from the Union? Virtually all of the scholarship on Civil War prisons concerns prisoners of war, not criminals sentenced by the federal courts.[3] The literature on crime and penal systems is often comparative and focused on the postwar growth of the prison system, particularly in the era of progressive reform, to uncover the origins of mass incarceration.[4] Congress did not establish a network of federal prisons until decades after the Civil War. Instead, state and local penitentiaries routinely housed federal inmates. Those individuals would have found themselves in an odd position after secession. Convicted by one government and imprisoned by another, their appeals for clemency would have navigated uncharted territory. Petitions from respectable citizens, now engaged in a war against the United States, would have made for unconvincing pleas to Lincoln. Letters of support from prominent northerners might have been equally unpersuasive for those seeking clemency from Jefferson Davis. Lincoln's pardons also presented a dilemma for southern governors. Carrying out the pardon would have recognized Lincoln's authority. Refusing the pardon meant housing prisoners convicted by a foreign government.

Studies of Lincoln's clemency emphasize his compassion and mercy. Lincoln received more than one thousand pardon requests from federal convicts during the war, and he granted a larger number of nonmilitary pardons than any of his immediate predecessors. Stories of Lincoln's forgiveness often take on a larger-than-life quality. One story describes a congressman waking Lincoln in the middle of the night to issue a last-minute pardon hours before an execution. Other anecdotes reveal Lincoln taking pity on common soldiers who had deserted, or on those who received harsh sentences for minor offenses. Although many of these recollections contain apocryphal elements, the pardon records themselves are overflowing with examples of Lincoln's sympathy for youthful offenders with otherwise unblemished characters, particularly those with supporting letters from widowed mothers or orphaned siblings. A secretary in the pardon office recalled decades later that there was "nothing harder for him to do than to put aside a prisoner's application, and he could not resist it when it was urged by a pleading wife and a weeping child." Scenes of forgiveness and compassion reinforce Lincoln's reputation as a healer of the nation's wounds. Lincoln's lenient treatment of former Confederates offers further testament of his forgiving nature.[5]

But Lincoln also considered petitioners' social standing, and frequently cited the well-known and respectable persons that supported their applications as he issued his pardons. Peter S. Ruckman Jr. and David Kincaid argue that Lincoln occasionally granted pardons strategically, as part of a larger strategy to encourage morale and promote reconciliation. The handful of pardon applications originating from seceded states at the onset of the Civil War suggest that the pardon office considered each application individually on its merits, not as part of a coordinated policy. The pardon office refused to forward applications from several less meritorious southern prisoners, and once the war began the number of applications originating from inmates in the South evaporated. Lincoln only pardoned one other federal prisoner in the South after secession.[6] John A. Willson had been convicted in the Eastern District of Arkansas in 1859 under circumstances similar to Cowlam's.

He had stolen seven packages of stamped envelopes while working as a mail courier between Gainesville and Taylor Creek, and foolishly offered to sell the packets to the postmaster of Gainesville for slightly less than half of their face value. The postmaster reported Willson immediately. Although Willson at first made contradictory statements, he ultimately confessed to the theft. The presiding judge in the case, Daniel Ringo, sentenced him to ten years in prison but later appealed to the pardon office in 1860 and renewed his request for clemency the following year. Willson was illiterate, and Ringo noted that he had complained frequently "that his father would not supply him with money, of which he had little, or none." Attorney General Bates recommended the pardon to Lincoln, who granted it on May 24, 1861, less than three weeks after Arkansas had left the Union. As in the case of Cowlam's pardon, Lincoln cited Willson's youth, noting that "he was not more than eighteen years of age" at the time of his first offense, and that, prior to his commission of the crime, he had demonstrated good character.[7]

For applicants the pardon process was shrouded in mystery. The pardon clerk reviewed the available evidence and summarized cases for the attorney general to consider. Once the attorney general approved a petition, he would present the case to the president. The petitions were not catalogued, however, and applicants received no status updates as their applications made their way to the president's desk. If no action was taken, the application was simply refiled. Petitioners had no way of knowing if their appeal had been denied, or if it still awaited processing. After the war, many petitioners employed pardon brokers to navigate the process and lobby in favor of their case. The evidence that pardon clerks sifted through could be just as opaque. They constantly navigated misrepresentations and falsehoods presented to them by applicants. Prisoners tried to put their best foot forward, and to appear respectable, repenting, and reformed. In fashioning their crimes as youthful indiscretions, these letters often stretched the truth, and pardon applicants almost always employed a bit of performance or fiction to make their case compelling.[8]

Secession could also separate inmates from evidence that might lead to their release. Faustin Guillot appealed to Lincoln on July 15, 1861, noting that he did not "know how I could lay before you any evidence that you could consult, as I was tried in Key West, Florida, and several gentlemen who had interested themselves in my behalf seem to have ceased their relations with the

U.S government, owing to a difference of political opinion." Guillot had been convicted, along with Alezandro Career, in early December 1859 for murdering Captain Beciente A. Morantes aboard the schooner *Enterprise*. Although Guillot had been sentenced to be executed on January 9, 1860, President James Buchanan commuted Guillot's sentence to seven years in the District of Columbia penitentiary after Guillot's supporters presented evidence that he had cooperated with the prosecution and had only participated in the crime out of fear that his coconspirators might turn on him. Guillot claimed in his letter to Lincoln that both the judge and U.S. attorney in his case supported his efforts for clemency. Yet the judge's comments at his sentencing suggest otherwise. After sentencing Guillot to death, Judge William Marvin noted that the "President of the United States has authority ... to pardon you or to commute your sentence ... but it is my duty to inform you, lest you should be beguiled by false hopes, that you have no reasonable ground to expect his interposition in your behalf." Perhaps the pardon office saw through Guillot's charade. His application was not forwarded to Lincoln.[9]

The secession crisis created a sense of urgency surrounding Cowlam's application. Petitioners urged the president to act swiftly, lest Virginia secede and young Cowlam be trapped in the Confederacy. Despite his past indiscretions, his family and friends rallied behind him with renewed effort. The circumstances of his early life offer important context for considering Cowlam's claims. His family was upstanding and well connected among Michigan Republicans. These connections opened the door for prominent politicians to shepherd his application to Lincoln after the pardon clerk and attorney general had already dismissed it. The pressure they applied was essential in moving Cowlam's application forward. It was necessary to appeal to the president outside of official channels. The pardon clerk and attorney general would have never recommended clemency so long as the letter from the superintendent of the Virginia State Penitentiary sullied Cowlam's file.

EARLY LIFE

Charles Cowlam was born in Saline, Michigan, about ten miles south of Ann Arbor. Although he lied about his age several times in the course of his life, the birthdate he provided on his passport application, November 3, 1837, is the most credible, as that date aligns with his age in the census of 1850, when he was twelve years old. The family spent time in the nearby townships of York and Putnam before moving to Battle Creek in his youth. Battle Creek was an emerging frontier town, situated along the northern branch of the Kalamazoo River, which allowed farmers in the region to send their grain to St. Joseph for transshipment across Lake Michigan, and, from there, around the Great Lakes to the Erie Canal. By the 1840s the region had become a Free Soil stronghold and a haven for eccentrics. The town served as a stopover point for the Underground Railroad in a corridor along the Michigan Central Railroad connecting Chicago to Detroit and ultimately Ontario, Canada. The Quaker merchant Erastus Hussey, who opened the station at Battle Creek, encouraged Sojourner Truth to relocate there in 1857. The town would later emerge as a center for spiritualism and provide the location for John Harvey Kellogg's sanitarium and his eponymous cereal company. Kellogg's followers at the Battle Creek Sanitarium believed that adhering to a vegetarian diet, abstaining from alcohol and tobacco, and partaking in regular enemas would simultaneously cleanse the body of toxins and rid the mind of impure thoughts that might lead to sexual arousal.[10]

Charles's father, Charles Cowlam, was born in the tiny hamlet of Market Rasen, in Lincolnshire, England, in 1810 to a family of Roman Catholics. English Catholics remained a small minority at the turn of the nineteenth century despite a measure of toleration extended in the preceding decades.[11] It is not clear when he emigrated, but by all indications the elder Charles harbored strong antislavery sympathies. He served on the executive committee of the Livingston County Bible Society in 1843, as an officer of the Michigan State Antislavery Society in 1844, and ran for the state House of Representatives in Livingston County for the Liberty Party in 1846. It is not clear if the Cowlams harbored fugitive slaves in their home, but one historian of the Underground Railroad in Michigan notes that many officers in the antislavery society also served as agents who offered safe houses along the railroad's routes.[12] A letter from the period offers an indication of his political sentiments while recounting the Fourth of July celebrations in Saline in 1840. The note describes a day filled with celebratory gunfire, the erection of a liberty pole, the playing of "the Star-Spangled Banner," a reading of the Declaration of Independence, and evening fireworks. In the afternoon a crowd of five or six hundred residents enjoyed an outdoor banquet that began with a series of thirteen toasts offered by prominent citizens. Cowlam's father gave the third toast, exclaiming, "may the day soon arrive when we will all be free."[13]

Before settling in Michigan, the elder Charles lived for a time in Ontario, Canada. It was there that he met his first wife, Elizabeth Amelia Cushman, and the couple married on June 19, 1832, at the present site of Brantford. At that time the settlement was known as Mohawk Village, or Brant's Ford, having been founded more than a generation earlier by Joseph Brant, who led the Mohawks to Ontario after their removal from New York following the American Revolution. Their short-lived marriage produced one daughter, whom they named "Elsie," a Scottish diminutive for Elizabeth, in 1833.[14] Tragedy struck the family the following summer when five members of the Cushman clan succumbed to cholera in August 1834, including Charles's wife, Elizabeth, a sister, a brother, and both of her parents. With five members of the family dead in five days, the calamity led Elizabeth's brother, Henry Josiah Cushman, to leave the Presbyterian Church and join the Baptist faith. In the context of the Second Great Awakening, it was quite common for frontier settlers to cast aside the Calvinism of their forefathers in favor of converting to the Baptist or Methodist faiths. Charles likely followed his brother-in-law in joining the Baptist Church at that time, and he would soon follow Henry when he migrated to Michigan in 1837.[15] It is not clear if their decision to leave Ontario had anything to do with the Upper Canada Rebellion brewing that same year. The Panic of 1837 had forced many Canadian banks to suspend payments that summer, and hard times brought civil unrest that led many Canadians to immigrate to the United States and others to take up arms in revolt.[16]

Charles remarried in Ontario a year after the death of his first wife to Isabella Hays, an emigrant from Scotland. Almost nothing is known about Isabella. The wedding was a civil ceremony, as there was no minister or parson in the area who could perform the service. Their marriage record describes the couple as living in Wilmot, located thirty-five miles northeast of Brantford. After the birth of their first child, Sarah, in 1836, the newlyweds followed Henry J. Cushman to Michigan, where their son Charles was born the following year. The Cowlams and the Cushmans arrived in southern Michigan at a time when the region had only recently opened to American settlers after the Treaty of Chicago removed the Potawatomi from the area. The young couple was received "by letters" into the First Baptist Church of Saline, indicating that they had been active in the Baptist Church elsewhere.[17] Cushman shared Charles's aversion to slavery, and in Michigan he established himself as a prominent millwright, constructing one of the three flouring mills in Battle Creek.[18] The elder Charles probably assisted him in the mill's construction, and learned the trade firsthand. In Battle Creek the family grew to include Elizabeth, born in 1841, George B., born in 1844, and Mariette, born in 1847.[19]

Cowlam's father helped to erect the first steam-powered grist mill in Waukegan, Illinois, situated along Lake Michigan on the north shore of Chicago, in 1849. He was crushed by a piece of equipment while unloading materials for the mill and died soon after from typhus. In a will written shortly before his death, he was unable to sign his name due to the seriousness of his injuries and could only manage to leave a shaky X for his mark. The family possessions recorded in his probate inventory included two stoves, two dining tables, eleven chairs, four feather beds with bedding and bed stands, three clothes chests, a trunk, one secretary desk with books, a clock, a looking glass, and two maps of the United States. Although the value of this personal property totaled $288.60, the family's debts exceeded the value of the estate. Henry Cushman served as executor and presented a note pledged to him in the amount of $184.11. Cushman noted also that he had provided food, clothing, and other necessities for the family totaling $43.77, and had incurred additional expenses in administering the estate. In 1848 Cushman and Cowlam had purchased five town lots in Battle Creek for $900, with the partners agreeing to pay one-third of the money up front and the remaining balance in annual installments with interest over the next two years. The balance of the mortgage remained unpaid at the time of Cowlam's death, and the probate judge granted Cushman's request to allow him to liquidate the town lots in an effort to settle the estate.[20]

The free labor ideology that captivated antebellum northerners idolized the independence and self-reliance of mechanics like Cowlam's father.[21] His father's death exposed the precariousness of this system, however, as his passing left the family dependent on relatives and friends to support them. At the time of his father's death, his mother was pregnant with his youngest sister, Isabella, who went by Isabel and was born in Illinois in 1850. Descendants of the Cowlam line remember that his mother nearly died when Isabel was born.[22]

The family did not remain in Illinois for long, and returned to Michigan shortly after the estate was settled, where the family remained close with the Cushmans.[23] The death of his father at such a young age undoubtedly left an impression on Charles, and his troubles with the law began during his teenage years. Whether stemming from teenage rebelliousness, the death of his father, or the family's diminished financial circumstances, he was first arrested in Calhoun County, Michigan, in 1853. Charles pled guilty to one count each of burglary and larceny, and he was sentenced to thirty days in jail and ordered to pay a $1 fine. He would have been fifteen years old.[24] With no local paper in Battle Creek at the time or a surviving case file with the county court, the details of the case are sparse. A newspaper article published decades later suggests that he was associated with a teenage gang that called themselves the "Red Rangers," known for stealing from orchards and hen roosts. The group soon escalated to breaking into and robbing stores, and it is in this context that Cowlam probably served his first stint in jail.[25]

His second arrest came a year later, in November 1854, in Coolville, Ohio. Working with an accomplice, John Allen, Cowlam broke into and robbed John Johnson's house in Parkersburg, Virginia, before fleeing across the Ohio border to avoid detection. It is not clear why Charles ventured east to Virginia. It is possible that he ran away from home, or he may have simply migrated in search of work in the months before his arrest. When Cowlam was arrested he gave his name as Charles Cushman, his first alias derived from his connections to the Cushman family. While awaiting transfer to Virginia from the jail in Athens, Ohio, Cowlam and his accomplice escaped, but they were quickly recaptured and taken to Parkersburg for trial before the Wood County Circuit Court. Charles received a sentence of fifteen months in the state penitentiary in Richmond, and was released on September 21, 1856.[26]

Soon after his release Cowlam somehow managed to secure a position in the post office in Portsmouth, Virginia, as an assistant or deputy postmaster. Unfortunately, no records survive from the Post Office Department to explain how he could have obtained such a post, given his recent incarceration. Just nine months after his release from the state penitentiary, Cowlam was arrested a third time, on June 22, 1857, after a sting operation exposed his habit of pilfering the contents of letters. Three packages containing more than $2,200 left Baltimore on May 9 and disappeared before reaching Raleigh. On June 6 three more packages, this time containing $1,800 and following the same route, also disappeared. At this point postal agent James L. Maguire identified the Portsmouth, Virginia, post office as the missing link. He prepared three packages with a similar appearance to those that had disappeared, this time addressed to Wilmington, North Carolina. Maguire enclosed three genuine $5 bills among $2,800 of counterfeit currency. After inspecting the mails before and after depositing them at Portsmouth, Maguire proceeded to arrest Cowlam, who, the newspapers reported, "at first stoutly denied his guilt, but finally confessed his crime." Upon searching the contents of Cowlam's trunk, the detective recovered $2,200 of the $4,000 in stolen money, along with the counterfeit notes from the latest delivery. The *Charlotte Democrat* reported that "the Banks in this place have lost a pretty large sum in that direction, and it is fair to assume that Cowlan is the chap who got it."[27]

The trial took place on the second floor of the Norfolk City Hall, in what is now the MacArthur Memorial. U.S. Attorney John Munford Gregory, who had served as the acting governor of Virginia from 1842 to 1843, prosecuted the case against Cowlam. Tazewell Taylor, the bursar of the College of William and Mary, defended him. John Kearns Cooke, the postmaster at Portsmouth, and George S. Allen, a mail agent at Baltimore, were prepared to testify as witnesses to the thefts. At his trial the defendant "arose, as pale as death, and for some time his lips were sealed." Cowlam then entered his plea, remarking, "Gentleman of the jury, I plead guilty. In an unguarded moment I committed the act, and would afterwards have given the world had I never have done it. All I can ask, gentleman, is, that, as I am young, it may go in some way in mitigating my punishment." Cowlam's attorney, Tazewell Taylor, then offered some "feeling remarks" in his support. The local paper reported that the "court, jury, and bar seemed much affected, and many tears were shed." The jury was so moved by Cowlam's plea, newspapers reported, that after finding him guilty the jurors drafted a petition to President Buchanan to release him.[28]

In delivering the sentence, Judge James D. Halyburton described it as a "most unpleasant and painful duty" but added that "the law which imposes it upon me, is wise, just and necessary." He noted that the punishment for those entrusted with the care of the mails was double that of ordinary citizens who robbed a post office. The justification for the severity of the sentence was that postal employees who embezzled letters had greater opportunities for theft and faced a lower likelihood of discovery. Accordingly, the law prescribed a sentence of between ten and twenty-one years imprisonment. Judge Halyburton quoted from Proverbs, emphasizing that "the way of the transgressor is hard," suggesting that Cowlam's feelings of remorse would not excuse his crimes. He ordered Cowlam to serve ten years at hard labor.[29]

That evening Cowlam returned to the jail in Norfolk, where he would await transfer to the state penitentiary in Richmond, and attempted to commit suicide. He used an old knife that he found in his cell and cut two severe gashes in his left arm. Newspaper accounts of the event are conflicted in explaining how the suicide attempt was thwarted. One reported that "his intentions were discovered in time to frustrate them," but another suggested that "the weapon was too dull to enable him to accomplish his object." If the blade was dull, that would explain why the penitentiary superintendent later claimed that Cowlam had "pretended" to commit suicide in his letter to President Buchanan. The next morning U.S. Marshal John F. Wiley and Henry Myers, the superintendent of the City Hospital in Richmond, and two others escorted the prisoner aboard the steamer *Glen Cove,* arriving in Richmond in the evening. The superintendent of the penitentiary, Colonel Charles S. Morgan, recognized Cowlam immediately upon his arrival. The *Richmond Dispatch* reported that "Charles Cowlam is an old prison bird," who admitted to using the alias Charles Cushman during his earlier incarceration.[30]

The Virginia State Penitentiary was a three-story building laid out in a symmetrical horseshoe pattern and surrounded by an imposing brick wall. The structure was designed with solitary confinement in mind, to encourage prisoners to reflect on their misdeeds and reform their behavior through solitude and prayer. Prison rules required inmates to work in complete silence, and the door to each cell was solid to stifle conversation. Cowlam would have had limited means to communicate with the outside world. Prisoners received their mail once every three months. Visits from friends and family were forbidden. Each of the 168 cells was twelve feet long and six and a half feet wide, with nine-foot-tall arched ceilings. The cells were unheated, and the inmates received a "coarse and spare diet." Prison rules dictated that inmates must remain cleanshaven and could not grow the hair on their head longer than three-quarters of an inch. Unsanitary conditions prevailed. Prison physicians complained regularly of the bad air and odors permeating the building. A bathing pool constructed in the summer of 1859, nearly two years after Cowlam's arrival, permitted inmates to bathe regularly for the first time.[31]

Few records survive from the penitentiary that attest to the time Cowlam would have been housed there. Most of the surviving records are receipts detailing the bushels of cornmeal and peas, pounds of beef and bacon, and other foodstuffs purchased by the prison to be consumed by prisoners. Federal convicts like Cowlam were uncommon, but the state profited from his incarceration, receiving 30 cents per day of confinement while paying only 18 cents per day on average for his maintenance. Only seven federal inmates had arrived in the preceding five years. When Cowlam arrived at the prison he was the only prisoner convicted of stealing from the mails, and the only inmate from Michigan. At nineteen years old, he would have been one of the youngest men in the penitentiary.[32]

The prison was already overcrowded before the war began. Even when two inmates were housed in cells designed for solitary confinement, the complex could only accommodate 250 prisoners. Yet the prison regularly jailed more than three hundred. With two or three prisoners sleeping in each room, the features designed to encourage solitary confinement interfered with the guards' ability to supervise the prison population and allowed inmates to share stories and plot escapes. In an effort to combat overcrowding, the state legislature passed a law in June 1858 that authorized prison officials to hire out Black inmates to work on construction projects. Black prisoners erected the Tazewell County Courthouse, a lunatic asylum west of the Alleghanies, and would build railroads and manufacture iron during the Civil War. Despite this temporary relief from overcrowding, the penitentiary remained so packed that the superintendent warned that temporary sheds would need to be constructed in the prison yard if the African American convicts who had been hired to work outside the prison returned.[33]

Pardoning inmates who had served a majority of their sentence offered another avenue to reduce overcrowding. In the absence of a parole system to allow prisoners the chance of early release, governors routinely pardoned between one-sixth and one-half of all inmates before their sentences had concluded. The proportion of those pardoned increased during the Civil War years. Superintendent Morgan complained regularly about the effects of excessive pardoning, noting that "the most unworthy or importune are pardoned, leaving better men behind, and exciting in them inquietude, and hopes but to be disappointed."[34]

THE PARDON

Before the ink was dry on Cowlam's sentence, Charles S. Morgan, the superintendent of the Virginia State Penitentiary, wrote to President Buchanan to warn him of a pardon application that would soon make its way to him. He deemed it his duty to report the character of the young man who had been convicted of stealing money from letters at the post office in Portsmouth. Morgan did not believe Cowlam's pretenses for one moment. He noted that "the circumstances of his youth and intelligence and his protestations of this being his first crime, made a most powerful impression upon the sympathies of the jury and others present, and added to this, he pretended to open the arteries of one arm to commit suicide to thereby give greater confidence in the former purity of character." While contemporaries often described suicide as originating out of a sense of spiritual failing, antebellum observers sometimes interpreted prison suicides as evidence of excessive or unjustified sentences.[35] Morgan believed the effort was a stunt intended to draw sympathy. "We know him well in this institution," Morgan continued. Although the local papers described a petition initiated by the jurors who convicted him, no such petition survives among the documents in Cowlam's case file at the National Archives. Morgan's letter may have arrived before any appeal on Cowlam's behalf could materialize, or Cowlam may have requested the petition be returned to him after the governor of Virginia refused to acknowledge his pardon from Lincoln.[36]

Cowlam's older sister, Sarah, initiated his pardon application to James Buchanan in the summer of 1859, more than two years after his arrest. Sarah explained that "we felt as though we could look up to him, as the one destined to once more make a home for us, for our Father died ten years ago, and since then we have seemed to be the recipients of every grief which fate could give." Just when the cloud of sorrow seemed to be passing away "this last and greatest grief of all came upon us." Their mother had died the previous fall, while Charles had been incarcerated, and her last moments were burdened by "the thought that her eldest son was, a disgraced criminal."[37] With Charles in prison and their mother deceased, the Cowlam children were unable to fend for themselves. One story that has passed down through the family is that after her death the children were parceled out among families close to them.[38] Sarah lived in the household of Leonard H. Stewart, a lawyer and former postmaster, who had previously joined fifty-three other signers from Battle Creek in a spiritualist petition to Congress encouraging the appointment of a scientific committee to investigate the nature of certain physical and mental phenomena of questionable origin.[39] Charles's younger brother, George, went to Woodstock, Ontario, where he lived with the Izard family and trained as a telegraph operator.[40] It is not clear where the other children lived, but presumably they were placed with other families in the vicinity of Battle Creek.

Sarah urged Buchanan to pardon Charles, noting that she could not bear the thought that Charles should "die in a 'prison' and die he shortly must or become a *maniac,* for I received a letter from him a few days since which shocked me more than I can tell by its grief and despair." She included a poem that Charles had written to illustrate the depths of his despondency. Reprinted below, the poem captures his mental state after more than two years of captivity. The verses make clear his feelings of hopelessness and isolation, and emphasize his present humanity despite his past crimes.

> He is somebody's Brother!
> Speak not thus, such words are bitter
> Always, but now doubly so
> Even though he had deserved them
> Hath he not enough of woes
> Many reasons could I give you,
> Each would all unkindness smother
> Listen, though almost a ruin
> Still, is he not someone's Brother?
>
> Poor, and wretched, and forsaken
> Broken in body, heart, and mind.
> Misery hath scarcely left him.
> One small trace of human kind.

> Past-life dead and present bitter.
> Dare he hope the future other!
> Ah! Tis this that keeps life burning
> Some dear heart says "still my brother"
>
> When you feel the harsh words rising
> Against thy erring fellow man
> Pause, and ask am I quite perfect?
> *Then* speak harshly if you can!
> Lenient look on little failings
> Strive to hear with one and other,
> Harsh words harden, kind words soften.
> *God* hath said he is *thy* Brother!![41]

Sarah concluded by noting that it would be the happiest moment of her life when she could write to her brother and inform him of his release. She enclosed part of a letter from Charles so that Buchanan could "see for yourself how he feels about it."[42]

The letter from Charles struck a morose, almost suicidal tone. Although the first page of the letter was not forwarded, the first line of the second page alluded to a plan, perhaps even the plan to obtain his release. Charles noted mischievously, "tis the best way that remains to us, and if properly done, would, I am sure, have a good result. If something is not done—well words would be idle." The letter alternated between frankness with touches of humility, to cheerless desperation. Charles added that he believed that all of the members of the "'Cowlam Tribe' had sense enough (except me) and even our enemies (if we have any, which I doubt,) would allow that much in our favor." He then inquired about each of his siblings, wishing especially to hear from George, who he believed would "be a good man, and a smart man, for I consider that he has talents enough to enable him to rise in the world." His two youngest sisters, "Minnie and Belle, will if they live and I live, be well educated, and refined, intelligent girls. Pretty too, Sammie, as an offset to 'our sister Sammie, and our Brother Charles.'" He described the youngest child, Isabel, as "an odd chicken, and though so unlike Minnie, she will be, I have no doubt, a most beautiful woman. That child's face haunts me while I write." Charles indicated that he expected to die in prison, and prayed that his soul might be spared so that he could see Isabel and all of the other children again in heaven. He suggested that his time in prison would have done him much good if he were allowed a life after it. He encouraged Sarah to "look at my portrait and remember me as I *was* . . . I am not all bad, Sammie, there are good germs of truth and love in my heart yet."[43]

Sarah initiated a renewed push for clemency in the spring of 1860. She wrote again to Buchanan, reiterating many of the themes of her note the previous summer, but focusing on Charles's rehabilitation. She noted that "my brother has, I am painfully aware, committed a great wrong, but if he has *sinned,* he has *suffered.*" She believed Charles to be truly penitent and that, if released, he would lead an honorable life. In emphasizing the burdens that Charles's incarceration had placed on the family, she noted that her two youngest sisters, Mariette and Isabel, did not yet know that Charles was in prison.[44] A petition from Michigan soon followed containing the signatures of former U.S. Senator Charles E. Stuart, five current or former postmasters, and Underground Railroad conductor Erastus Hussey, along with the mayor, sheriff, and county prosecutor from Battle Creek. The petition noted that Charles had "been unable to do any kind of work for the past year, that he is fast gaining into the consumption, and unless he can be pardoned his days are numbered for this world." The petitioners emphasized Cowlam's youth and ill health, contending that clemency would be the only means of saving his life. The petition concluded, "if die he must, it may be in the armes of his friends." The close family friend Henry J. Cushman provided the last signature on the petition, and he likely assisted Sarah in gathering the signatures.[45]

Michigan congressman Francis W. Kellogg appealed to Buchanan's secretary of state, Lewis Cass, asking him to intercede on Cowlam's behalf. Kellogg noted that he had been informed that the judge who presided over his trial, the jury that found him guilty, and the postmasters of Norfolk and Portsmouth had all signed a petition urging Cowlam's release. "His friends inform me he has been troubled with bleeding of the lungs & has not been able to do much work for a year past and they think he will die with the consumption," Kellogg added. Pardon cases that pleaded clemency on medical grounds often contained a letter from a prison physician attesting to the prisoner's poor health. Cowlam's application contained no such letter. Kellogg mentioned that Cowlam "has four sisters all younger than himself," suggesting that Kellogg had not known the family long, as Sarah was older than Charles (their older half-sister Elsie had died in 1856). Kellogg disavowed any personal connection to the case, noting, "I have no interest in the matter & have undertaken this because his relatives live in my district & his sister has written some affecting letters imploring my assistance."[46]

Francis William Kellogg was born in Massachusetts in 1810 and moved to Columbus, Ohio, as a young man. His eastern upbringing and early years in the West gave him, in the words of one contemporary, "the intelligence of the one and the roughness of the other." Although he described his father as a Jeffersonian Democrat, the names of two of his younger brothers, Alexander Hamilton and Charles Carroll Kellogg, suggest Federalist sympathies in the family. His first engagement with politics appears to have been in 1840, when he stumped for Whig candidate William Henry Harrison. In the years that followed, Kellogg lectured frequently on the temperance and antislavery circuits, even traveling to England and Scotland in 1852 to give a series of lectures. In his public addresses he was known for the rapid pace of his delivery. He spoke eloquently, and often from memory. He had a booming voice and he frequently moved his hands excitedly in exaggerated gestures. One contemporary described him as honest and genial, sentimental and poetical, possessing genuine sympathy toward his fellow man, and "impulsive, but not at the expense of prudence." He eventually settled in Grand Rapids, Michigan, in 1855, where he entered the lumber business with his brother, George Ward Kellogg. Francis supported the Republican Party from its inception. He campaigned for John C. Fremont in the Republican Party's first presidential bid in 1856. That election also carried Kellogg to the Michigan state legislature, where he served two terms before his election to the U.S. House of Representatives. Kellogg represented Michigan in Congress from 1859 until 1865, and would have been a recent arrival in Michigan when he and Cowlam were first introduced.[47]

Lincoln's inauguration presented new opportunities to plead Cowlam's case after Buchanan refused to take action. Congressman Kellogg took up the charge, sending several letters to Lincoln and Attorney General Bates. In his first letter to Lincoln, Kellogg described Cowlam as an "intelligent & sprightly youth" whose "wit & genius making him a favorite in the best circles of society he found it impossible to keep up with his associates in appearances on his slender salary & in an evil hour robbed some letters of their contents." In listing reasons for clemency, Kellogg emphasized Cowlam's youth and the severity of his sentence, indicated that Cowlam had "thoroughly repented," and noted his failing health in confinement. He added that "thousands would have signed the petition but I did not think it was necessary." Kellogg also mentioned that his old friend John R. Kellogg had already written to Secretary of State William Seward on Cowlam's behalf.[48]

Sarah took the opportunity to draft an updated petition to Lincoln signed by fifty-seven Michiganders, including three of the four Cowlam sisters. By 1861, presumably Mariette, age fourteen, and Isabel, age eleven, had learned of Charles's imprisonment. The petition attested to the respectability of the Cowlam family and the burdens his incarceration placed on them, noting that the family "has always, and still do occupy a respectable position in society, and have never been disgraced but by the act of Charles as above mentioned."[49]

In the aftermath of the attack on Fort Sumter, Kellogg followed his first letter to Lincoln with two additional letters to Attorney General Bates reiterating Cowlam's case. He noted again that John R. Kellogg had lobbied Seward for Cowlam's release, and that Missouri congressman Francis Blair promised to meet with Bates to discuss the matter. He emphasized that "Virginia will secede too & why keep this poor fellow longer there." Kellogg expressed his desire to return home to Michigan the following day. He penned the second letter to Bates from Cleveland three days later, informing him, "I shall return to Washington soon as they write me. I *must* exhaust all means to secure his pardon." One wonders why Kellogg so doggedly pursued Cowlam's case. Such persistent activists are not uncommon among the pardon case files. Perhaps Sarah Cowlam's appeal left an impression on him, or possibly one or more of the signers of the petitions lobbied the congressman on Charles's behalf.[50]

Edward Bates instructed William Seward to issue a warrant with the text of Cowlam's pardon on May 27, just over a month after Virginia seceded from the Union. Among the reasons listed for granting the pardon, Lincoln mentioned the intercession of Zachariah Chandler, a U.S. senator representing Michigan. That no letter from Chandler is found among the papers in Cowlam's pardon file suggests that Chandler met personally with the president to plead the case. On the same day that Lincoln issued the pardon, Francis Kellogg wrote a congratulatory letter to Charles from Washington, explaining that after long delay he had finally secured his release. He added that "your friends have not sent me any money but may have sent to you. If you are short and can get to this city—call on my brother George W. Kellogg who is at the house of J.S. [John Sidney] Kellogg No. 49 North A Street & he will help you to get home." The letter reveals a highly personal world driven by intimate connections and family networks. Congressman Kellogg expected his brother, a clerk in the Pension Office, to reconnect Cowlam with his friends and family. The letter never reached him, unfortunately. It remains in Cowlam's pardon file in the National Archives.[51]

In some ways Lincoln's pardon of Cowlam was typical. Here was a youthful offender who had admitted his guilt and had already served more than three years of a lengthy prison sentence. His application came equipped with letters of support from several prominent politicians, along with numerous friends and supporters. The misfortunes that had befallen his family made his case a compelling one, and the plight of his orphaned sisters must have weighed heavily on the president's mind. Claims of his failing health, and the toll that further incarceration would take, only added to the list of reasons for clemency. Cowlam's case fit the mold of Lincoln's expectations for compassion and mercy. At the same time, the case was exceptional for the role that the secession crisis played in rushing his application to the president's desk. The imminency of secession compelled Lincoln to act despite the multitude of other demands vying for his attention. Lincoln needed the backing of every Republican in Congress, and Michigan offered a solid base of support. Secession made Cowlam's claims of failing health impossible to verify, and the rapid pace with which the case was elevated to Lincoln's attention permitted him to overlook factors that would have sunk the case in normal times. Secession also offered an opportunity for Lincoln to assert presidential authority at a time when national sovereignty had been questioned. The pardon created a constitutional conundrum for the governor of Virginia. By drafting the order weeks after the state had seceded from the Union, Lincoln probed the limits of Confederate nationhood.

TWO

SPY

> What are you? What am I? Nobody knows who anybody is. The data which life furnishes, toward forming a true estimate of any being, are as insufficient to that end as in geometry one side given would be to determine the triangle.
> —HERMAN MELVILLE, *The Confidence Man: His Masquerade* (1857)

Four years after receiving his pardon from Abraham Lincoln, Cowlam resurfaced to offer testimony to the detectives investigating Lincoln's assassination. In April 1865 he traveled from Detroit to Washington, D.C., with a sealed letter from Lieutenant Colonel Bennett Hoskin Hill, commander of the military district of Michigan, addressed to Provost Marshal General James B. Fry. The letter explained that Cowlam had information regarding Lincoln's assassination and the Confederate Secret Service Bureau in Richmond, and suggested that he might be useful to the investigation. Rather than delivering the letter to Fry as instructed, Cowlam approached Lieutenant Colonel John A. Foster, a judge advocate investigating Lincoln's assassination, and presented the letter to him. Perhaps impressed with his credentials or won over by his guile, Foster employed Cowlam as a detective on the case after reading the letter and returning it to him.[1]

In his meeting with the detectives Cowlam carefully concealed any indication that he had been previously incarcerated. Instead, he described himself as a twenty-seven-year-old clerk from Wayne County, Michigan, who "was at Richmond when the war broke out, having been there since 1857. Was unemployed at that time." Cowlam explained that he had been conscripted into the Confederate army on the first of September 1863 and received a detail as a quartermaster's sergeant. He did not remain in Richmond for long, however. After forging the signature of Thomas G. Hunt, the major commanding the

Department of Mobile, he stated that he received a transfer order to join that department on December 27. He boasted that he "never reported, but instead went to Mobile and engaged in speculation in brandy, bacon and whiskey." He remained in Mobile through the Battle of Mobile Bay, in August 1864, after which he explained that he returned to Richmond, where he reconnected with old friends who permitted him to observe agents of the Confederate Secret Service. Eavesdropping on these conversations granted him privileged access to the inner workings of Confederate intelligence operations, and the loose talk he purported to overhear pointed to a wider conspiracy surrounding the assassination.[2]

His story seemed plausible. Here was a northerner forced into the Confederate service who had done everything in his power to avoid aiding the enemy. He had taken the initiative and infiltrated the Confederate Secret Service, and relayed this information to the Union army at the first available opportunity. His arrival must have been a pleasant surprise for the detectives in the initial days after the assassination. Although the story he told offered an outline of his wartime activities, it only divulged part of how he spent the war. Filling in the gaps in Cowlam's narrative reveals how his postwar accounts selectively chronicled his wartime exploits and how difficult those claims could be to authenticate. It would have been impossible for the detectives to corroborate Cowlam's whereabouts. Between the Confederacy's haphazard record keeping and the smoldering ruins of Richmond, the Confederacy was like a black box. The aftermath of the war presented an opportunity for Cowlam to repackage his identity. He presented himself as a loyal northerner who spent the war spying for the Union, a position that he would maintain for the rest of his life despite several glaring holes in his account.

RECALLED TO LIFE

In late August 1863 Cowlam was still confined in the state penitentiary in Richmond. He had been in prison for more than six years but was determined to secure a pardon that would grant his release. Wade Keyes, the Confederate acting attorney general, reported to Jefferson Davis that Cowlam's application for clemency included a petition "signed by the Jurors who found the verdict of guilty, by all the members of the Bar of Norfolk, and by many others of the most prominent Citizens of Norfolk and Portsmouth." Seeming always to ingratiate himself with prominent and influential persons around him, the application also included letters of recommendation from the judge who had sentenced him and the U.S. attorney who had prosecuted him. That Cowlam's application contained the missing petition alluded to in his application to Lincoln suggests that these letters had been returned to him after Virginia seceded from the Union. Cowlam claimed that President James Buchanan had promised to grant his request before leaving office, but neglected to do so with his attention focused on the impending dissolution of the Union. Acting Attorney General Keyes also noted that Cowlam "has many brave and worthy relatives in the Confederacy, and that some lie buried amongst the gallant dead on memorable fields." Keyes closed by noting the "the touching appeal of his maternal Aunt," whose "devotion and sacrifices to the South" included the loss of her property along with her "'three gallant sons, her only children'— one in a soldier's grave at Shiloh, and one upon the Rappahannock, and the other 'a maimed and helpless creature,' and, yet, the mother mourning that she has not another son to give to Southern independence."[3]

Unfortunately, the dramatic letter from Cowlam's "maternal aunt" has not survived. A careful search of his family genealogy has not located any relatives on his mother's side who could fit this description. Given that his mother was an emigrant from Scotland who had closer ties to Canada than to the Confederacy, it seems unlikely that the family would have produced a relation with such ardent support for the Confederate cause. The only relative of his actually fighting in the war was his younger brother, George B. Cowlam, who had left his position as a telegraph operator and enlisted in the 11th New York Infantry, known as Ellsworth's Zouaves, in New York City. The letter from his "maternal aunt" may have been a forgery crafted by Charles, or the product of his collusion with an outside party. The description of the letter certainly sounds like something he would have written.

Jefferson Davis drafted Cowlam's pardon on August 28, 1863, "in consideration of his youth, when the crime was committed, of his unusual promise, his talents, and amiable qualities, and his exemplary character, previous to that time." Davis also cited the temptations that led him to commit the crime, the length of his sentence, his good conduct while imprisoned, his "impaired health," and the "gallantry of his kinsmen, and the promise which it gives, in connection with his early character and subsequent good conduct, that his future life will be honorable and useful."[4]

That Davis would give Cowlam a pardon is striking. The Constitution of the Confederate States of America granted the president the power to issue pardons only "for offenses against the Confederate States."[5] A pardon offered for a crime committed against the United States would appear to be outside the scope of his authority. Granting the pardon might suggest that Davis held an expansive view of executive power. At the same time, the pardon calls into question the Confederacy's declared commitment to strict constitutionalism. Given that the pardon clauses in both the Confederate and U.S. Constitutions are identical in their word choice, scholars of Confederate constitutionalism have shown little interest in investigating this power.[6]

Davis and Lincoln often employed similar justifications when invoking the pardon power. Although Davis granted far fewer pardons than Lincoln, he exhibited a similar sympathy for young offenders, soldiers who had served honorably, and those condemned to death for momentary lapses in judgment. Of the twenty-one pardons recorded in his pardon book, seven cite the prisoner's youth and three note the offender's military service. In six cases Davis commuted death sentences for prisoners convicted of counterfeiting Confederate treasury notes, a crime treated more harshly under the Confederate government than under federal law. Davis and Lincoln also shared sympathy for pardon applicants convicted of mail robbery. Average sentences were harsher under federal law in this case, and prisoners convicted of mail robbery before secession would have served more than half of their sentences by the time the war drew to a close. Davis gave preference to applicants who had sacrificed for the Confederate cause or expressed willingness to serve as the supply of fresh recruits drew thin.[7]

A review of Davis's pardon book reveals three additional instances of pardons granted for crimes committed against the United States among the twenty-one pardons issued between December 1862 and December 1864. All four cases involved individuals convicted of stealing from the U.S. mails. Mail robbery was a frequent occurrence in the nineteenth century, when Americans were accustomed to sending large amounts of money through the post.[8] Isaac Aten received a pardon from Davis on May 11, 1863, for his 1857 conviction in Pontotoc, Mississippi. As in the case of Cowlam, Davis cited Aten's youth and also noted that, at the time of the crime, Aten was "ignorant and unlettered." Davis issued two more pardons on June 23, 1864, to Martin V. Brantley and Morgan Mosely, whose cases each originated in Georgia in 1860. Brantley had purloined money while working as a temporary route agent on the Southwestern Railroad and as a clerk in the Macon post office. Mosely had stolen the contents of two letters while working as a post rider between Ridgeville and Hinesville. At the time of his arrest, Mosely "succeeded in eating $30 of the money" in an effort to destroy the evidence. Here again Davis cited the prisoners' youth and inexperience, but also emphasized their eagerness to serve the Confederate cause. Davis noted that Brantley's "family is patriotic," and he observed that Mosely expressed a "strong desire to redeem his character by service in the field."[9]

The case of Martin V. Brantley presents an interesting example of Confederate constitutionalism. Almost immediately after Georgia seceded from the Union, Brantley filed a writ of habeas corpus in Milledgeville for his release. He had been sentenced only two months before, on November 13, 1860, to ten years in prison for mail robbery. Brantley's attorney, Colonel Osborne Augustus Lochrane, argued that the ordinance of secession had dissolved the state's connection with the government of the United States, making his detention unconstitutional and illegal. Lincoln's power to pardon criminals in Georgia had ceased with the act of secession, he noted, leaving Brantley without any recourse for clemency. In seceding from the Union, the state of Georgia had taken possession of federal prisoners much in the same way as it had seized control of federal armories, forts, and post offices. The act of secession transferred custody of Brantley from the federal government to state authorities, which possessed no statutes against mail robbery. To pass such a law now that the state had seceded would be *ex post facto*. Georgia could have continued to hold Brantley, acting as an agent of the federal government, Lochrane mused, but "in assuming to be the principal, she annulled the contract by which she held them as agent." The state argued that the ordinance of secession endowed the governor of Georgia with presidential authority, including the power to issue pardons. The secessionist constitution that would soon follow granted the governor the power to "grant pardons, or to remit any part of a sentence, in all cases after conviction, except for treason or murder, in which cases he may respite the execution." Lochrane emphasized that "we have no power to punish crimes committed against a Foreign Nation, or in violation of its laws."[10]

In denying Brantley's motion, Judge Iverson L. Harris noted that the petitioner had been convicted by a Georgia jury in proceedings that were both legal and constitutional at the time. The law violated had been assented to by a Congress that included representatives from Georgia, and the federal judge that sentenced him had been confirmed with the advice and consent of Georgia senators. Moreover, Harris noted that in addition to the ordinance of secession, the convention had adopted another ordinance that ratified and declared valid all previous judgments of the courts of the United States.[11] In closing, the judge described the state's arrangement with the federal courts as that of a contractor for the U.S. government. The state had agreed to feed, house, and clothe Brantley until such time as he had been "pardoned by the President of the United States, or performed the sentence of his conviction, or is transferred elsewhere by the authority of the general government." Only Lincoln could pardon Brantley, the Confederate court ruled, even though Georgia had left the Union.[12]

The *New York Times* noted that the ruling on Brantley's petition raised a "rather embarrassing question." If successful, the petition threatened to release all "mail robbers, counterfeiters of coin, pirates, land-warrant forgers, *et id genus omne* [and all of that kind]." By citing the contributions of the Georgia legislators and jury in Brantley's conviction, the ruling seemed to question the legitimacy of secession. After all, Georgia legislators had also participated in the drafting of the U.S. Constitution. If secessionists felt obligated to follow federal law and keep Brantley imprisoned because their representatives had consented to the adoption of those statutes, why would they not feel a similar duty to follow the Constitution? The article concluded by remarking that it "would have been much more dignified for Judge Harris to have boldly assumed the responsibility of revolutionary periods, and stated in so many words that expediency, and expediency alone, demanded the continuance in operation of Brantley's sentence."[13]

Added to the constitutional ambiguity that federal prisoners confronted after secession were the wartime disruptions that affected prison life. Before the war the inmates at the Virginia State Penitentiary labored in in-house manufacturing enterprises, producing leather goods, blacksmithing, and working as wheelwrights, carpenters, and hand-loom weavers. Convicts also performed the cooking, cleaning, and gardening within the prison. In July 1861 a fire destroyed the blacksmith shop and the weaving department. The shortage of raw materials limited the operation of the other enterprises, and many inmates remained locked down in their cells for months at a time. The constant threat of military action around Richmond only added to the sense of uncertainty inside the prison walls. As Union general George B. McClellan's Peninsula Campaign advanced on Richmond in the spring of 1862, Confederate authorities crafted evacuation plans in the event that the penitentiary would fall under Union control. In May 1862 Judge Halyburton, who had sentenced Cowlam in 1857 and now served on the Confederate District Court, ordered the federal prisoners in the state penitentiary be removed to the Pittsylvania County jail on the North Carolina border. Before the court could make the necessary preparations for the move, however, the Union advance toward Richmond ground to a halt and the directive was not carried out.[14]

Cowlam received his pardon from Davis at a time when overcrowding at the penitentiary had reached its peak. The prison began housing Union prisoners of war almost as soon as the war began. When prisoner exchanges ceased in the summer of 1863, Confederate authorities found themselves overwhelmed with the number of Union soldiers arriving in Richmond daily. Governor John Letcher had informed Robert E. Lee earlier that year that it was "entirely impossible to receive" additional prisoners into the penitentiary. Letcher noted that the present session of the state court included more than forty felony indictments, "most of whom will in all probability be convicted." "To make room for these, I will have to pardon some now in prison" Letcher stressed. To relieve the pressure, Letcher resorted to pardoning a larger number of inmates than ever before, releasing as many as half of the inmates each year.[15]

The circumstances with which Cowlam joined the Confederate service are unclear. In his interview with the detectives investigating the Lincoln assassination, he described being forced into the Confederate service on September 1, 1863, a date that aligns with the pardon he received from Davis. The pardon made no mention of enlistment as a condition of his release, and unfortunately no service record survives to offer additional detail. He was likely conscripted immediately after his release. The Confederacy already had conscription acts in place that mandated military service for white men between the ages of eighteen and thirty-five. At the same time, the Quartermaster's Department seems an odd choice of detail for a convicted thief. The unusual assignment might be explained by a proposal suggested by Milledge Bonham, the governor of South Carolina, two weeks before Cowlam's release. Bonham recommended conscripting commissary and quartermasters' clerks into military units and replacing them with those who were unfit for military service. The Confederate War Department reviewed the proposal favorably, and the Bureau of Conscription issued a circular to this effect on August 13.[16] The implementation of this order would have created vacancies in these departments. As a convict in poor health with strong ties to the Union, Cowlam would have made an unreliable soldier and constant flight risk. Perhaps Confederate authorities believed that stationing him in the Quartermaster's Department in Richmond, where he would have been closely monitored, would be safer than sending him to the front lines, where he could easily escape.

After nearly four months in the Quartermaster's Department, Cowlam told the detectives investigating the Lincoln assassination, he forged paperwork transferring himself to Mobile. Although we have only Cowlam's assurances that he traveled there, the details of his narrative suggest a familiarity with the city. He described his connections with several leading merchants, including John Scott, who served as one of two chief agents of the Produce Loan Bureau for the state of Alabama. The Produce Loan Bureau was an agency established early in the war that allowed farmers to purchase Confederate bonds with cotton, tobacco, or other produce. Bureau agents would then sell the produce to fund the Confederate war effort. Cowlam insisted that "I had no military business, and did not pretend to be in the service at Mobile. My business was this: I used to go up to Montgomery or up the Alabama River." His brief involvement with the Quartermaster's Department would have given him experience in purchasing supplies from local merchants, and Cowlam likely leveraged this knowledge to present himself as a wartime entrepreneur.

If he wished to become a speculator, it is understandable that would want to transfer to Mobile. By 1864 the city was the last remaining port available to Confederate blockade runners in the Gulf of Mexico. There he could have profited handsomely from selling provisions and speculating in commodities, although it is unclear how he would have obtained the capital needed to enter the business. He told the investigators that he remained there through the Battle of Mobile Bay, noting that he was "rather expecting that Admiral Farugut [sic] would come to the city." Cowlam left on August 18, nearly two weeks after the naval battle but in the midst of a siege raging over one of the forts guarding the entrance to the bay.[17] He claimed that he left the city "on account of my health" and went to Mississippi. In both of his pardon applications he had played up his weak constitution and possible consumption, but the timing and circumstances of his departure suggest that the exodus may have been for nontherapeutic reasons. Given that Lincoln had already pardoned him more than three years before, one would think that the arrival of the Union army would be a welcome sight. He could have crossed the Union lines and rejoined his friends and family in Michigan. At the same time, Cowlam might have wondered how he would be received as a Confederate speculator. Acting on an unfounded sense of caution, or for reasons unknown, Cowlam sidestepped the opportunity to make his way north.

Cowlam described returning to Mobile on September 5, but he stayed for only one day before making his way to Richmond, noting that he "came up on cars," hitching rides on freight trains until he reached the city around October 1. Soon after arriving, he "went to the provost Marshall and got a furlough, having made my own papers. Had gotten some blanks in North Carolina, which were blank soldiers' furloughs." His interest in obtaining a furlough seems superfluous for someone who had already deserted the Confederate army, but the furlough papers may have given him a good cover story that would have allowed him to travel freely without having to worry about being conscripted again. In Richmond he maintained that he spent his time in the vicinity of that city and Petersburg "doing nothing especially important, more than speculating a little as opportunity offered in conjunction with others." By the fall of 1864 Richmond was quickly becoming a city of strangers. Housing and food were in short supply. A sense of lawlessness pervaded. The power wielded by Confederate officials within the city induced some of them to profit from their positions by issuing passes or selling passports.[18]

Cowlam claimed to have already been acquainted with the editors of the Richmond newspapers, including the *Enquirer, Southern Punch,* and the *Daily Examiner*. He soon reconnected with Lieutenant Colonel John L. Milton, who remembered him from Mobile. The two men had shared a room for two weeks at the Battle House Hotel. With their friendship renewed in Richmond, Milton invited Cowlam to meet him "a few doors below" the Spotswood Hotel. The Spotswood had served as a temporary residence for Jefferson Davis before he moved to the White House of the Confederacy, and a nearby meeting place would have offered ample opportunities to overhear Confederate operatives. Cowlam met Milton frequently in the evenings, and the two men often went for long walks. Through Milton and another acquaintance, a clerk named Johnson, Cowlam would "see various members of the rebel detective force of the Secret Service coming to the office upon business." The Peninsula House in Richmond served as a meeting place, and Cowlam claimed he visited the house often, where he "heard frequent suggestions of plots by which the President might be murdered."[19]

Loose talk of assassination was everywhere to be found. Cowlam stressed that "all classes of people talked of it; many favored it; many decided it as a thing too insane to be seriously spoken of, while some, and these men who by position and character exercised influence, spoke of it as an act which could not fail to [illegible] to the benefit of the South by reason of the changes it would of necessity bring in the administration of public affairs." Although few men would declare their intentions to kill Lincoln themselves, such talk was generally regarded as praiseworthy. Cowlam remembered overhearing a conversation between two Confederate detectives, Washington and Thomas Goodrich of Baltimore, in which Washington exclaimed, "We will never get peace till we kill that God dammed son of a bitch." On another occasion he heard a Confederate detective remark shortly before the election of 1864 that Lincoln's reelection "must be prevented or the Confederacy's gone up." Cowlam noted that the Richmond newspapers abounded with fantasies of the president's murder. Some braggarts boasted that it would be easy to shoot Lincoln from a rooftop with an air gun or rifle as he made his way down Pennsylvania Avenue on Inauguration Day. Others celebrated historical assassins, such as Charlotte Corday, William Tell, John Felton, "as examples wherein by one bold stroke of a brave man a suffering nation had been redeemed from tyranny."[20]

Cowlam's testimony suggests that talk of Lincoln's assassination had been less prevalent in Mobile, noting that "it died away in the Journals until August 1864." But the successes of Sherman's campaign in Georgia reignited calls for the president's murder. He recalled an editorial published in the *Richmond*

Examiner and written either by John M. Daniel or Edward A. Pollard that appealed to loyal men of the South to kill Lincoln and Seward to deliver "their country from the power of a despotic tyrant." Once again Cowlam heard the word *assassination* on the lips of everyone. He pointed to speeches by prominent politicians that alluded to or encouraged such an event. Cowlam noted, "I am firm in my belief based upon personal knowledge of and intercourse with Southerners during this war that in the inmost heart of seven tenths of them this day exultation reigns supreme at the assassination of President Lincoln which would have been increased tenfold by the murder of Mr. Seward."[21]

Cowlam believed that the conspiracies against Lincoln and his cabinet were only one part of a larger plot to overthrow the state governments in Illinois and several other states. He suggested that the Knights of the Golden Circle had operated secretly under the control and orders of the Confederate government. The Knights were a decentralized secret organization whose members shared ambitions for a proslavery empire in Latin America and sought to undermine the Union war effort in the North. David Keehn, who has written the definitive history of the Knights, quotes Cowlam as an example of the "surprising number" of witnesses who referenced the secret society in their testimony to the Lincoln assassination investigators. By 1865 the general public would have been well aware of the Knights' activities. Newspaper articles brimmed with conspiracies that blamed the secret society for everything from the seizure of federal military installations to the New York draft riots. Claims made about the Knights are often quite difficult to verify. Keehn notes that many contemporary exposés "made a variety of sensational yet plausible claims." Yet the Knights also exerted considerable influence within the Confederacy, and their support for secession in the border states may have tipped the balance in favor of disunion. Cowlam's claims of prior knowledge of the Knights' activities would have boosted his credibility in the eyes of the Lincoln assassination detectives.[22]

At the Peninsula House in Richmond, Cowlam claimed to have overheard discussions regarding Confederate Secret Service operations in Canada. Confederates carried out the St. Albans Raid, robbing banks in Vermont before fleeing across the border into Canada in October 1864, shortly after Cowlam returned to Richmond.[23] Cowlam noted that he "never heard beforehand a town designated, but heard of the movements to be made." Before he left

Richmond he also claimed to have met John Taylor Wood, Jefferson Davis's nephew and aide-de-camp who had served as the commanding officer of the Confederate blockade runner CSS *Tallahassee*. By the time Cowlam sat down to debrief the detectives investigating the Lincoln assassination in the spring of 1865, the St. Albans Raid and the exploits of the CSS *Tallahassee* would have been covered extensively in the popular press. The whereabouts of the *Tallahassee*'s commander would have been a tantalizing detail, as Wood accompanied Jefferson Davis in his escape from Richmond. Davis and Wood were already in Charlotte, North Carolina, with the Union army in pursuit of them. It seems likely that Cowlam had read about these events in the newspaper, and attempted to pass off this information as the results of his own sleuthing.[24]

Cowlam's career as a wartime speculator and conspiracy eyewitness was short lived. His account of his adventures in the Confederacy omitted the fact that he had been arrested on December 22, 1864, by Captain Samuel McCubbin's detectives for theft and impersonating a Confederate captain, having stolen a commission from a Captain Hubert in September. Cowlam would spend Christmas 1864 behind bars in Castle Thunder, the notorious prison in the heart of Richmond. Castle Thunder opened in August 1862 and consisted of three brick buildings facing Cary Street and occupying the northern half of the square between 18th and 19th Streets. The buildings had previously served as tobacco warehouses and a small factory before being commandeered by the Confederate government. A large wall enclosed a courtyard between the three buildings that prisoners used for exercise and for the latrines. Cowlam likely would have been housed on the third floor, which contained two rooms, the larger one for Union prisoners of war and the smaller one for Confederate soldiers awaiting court martial.[25]

Cowlam arrived at Castle Thunder at a time when Confederate prison conditions had deteriorated to their lowest point. The commandant of the prison, George Alexander, had previously faced an investigation by the Confederate Congress into the mistreatment of prisoners under his care. Inmates were frequently subjected to physical punishment if they refused to follow the prison rules or attempted to escape. Deserters often received fifty or one hundred lashes upon arrival. The combination of gas lighting, unsanitary conditions, and poor air circulation left a foul stench that permeated the interior. Rations were meager. One inmate reported that meat allowances consisted primarily of horse and mule, and noted ominously that the portions were more generous after large cavalry battles. Whereas the state penitentiary housed common criminals, Castle Thunder's inmates were a mixed lot. Alongside prisoners of war, the residents of Castle Thunder included convicted felons, Union spies, Confederate deserters, political prisoners, and those suspected of disloyalty. One historian of the prison has argued that "it probably housed more desperate and dangerous prisoners than any other prison in the South."[26]

Commissioner Johnson H. Sands investigated the case against Cowlam while he remained confined in Castle Thunder. The docket describes him as a "detailed conscript," meaning that he had been conscripted into the Confederate service and assigned to a clerical position. Although detailed conscripts held ranks on equal footing with soldiers in the regular army, their units were composed of men deemed unsuitable for combat due to age or infirmity. This detail confirms that Sands was aware of Cowlam's assignment in the Quartermaster's Department.[27] The evidence against him included the forged papers found in his possession, a statement from William Summerville, and a letter and descriptive list from William H. Fry, the captain commanding the Camp of Instruction. The Camp of Instruction, often called Camp Lee or Camp Winder, was a central processing point for new recruits and those awaiting their return to their unit. It was located one mile west of the city, on the site of the Richmond fairgrounds. On December 31, Commissioner Sands recommended that Cowlam "be sent to the Camp of Instruction, at Richmond, for assignment, pursuant to the within written request of Captain Fry."[28]

Sending Cowlam to the Camp of Instruction "for assignment" suggests that Captain Fry did not intend for him to return to his position in the Quartermaster's Department. With Union forces closing on Richmond and the supply of new recruits drawing thin, Fry probably intended for Cowlam to receive a new assignment that would prepare him for combat. However, Cowlam deserted and left the city before that opportunity could materialize. He left Richmond on February 14 and crossed the Union lines at Norfolk a week later, on February 21. Among those arriving with him at Norfolk were five freedmen and their families, along with fifteen Confederate deserters and refugees. The provost marshal detailed the African American men to the Quartermaster's Department. Each of the rebel deserters and refugees received instructions to take an oath of allegiance and were detained awaiting further orders.[29]

In his interview with the Lincoln assassination detectives, Cowlam spun his return home into a story about a secret mission on behalf of the Confederate Secret Service. Before making his way north he described an interview with a mysterious "Mrs. M.A. Sands" of Nashville, Tennessee.[30] Ever the chameleon, Cowlam presented an imaginative new alias, explaining that

> I told her I was travelling under an assumed name; that I was a Major in the CSA; that I was by birth a Mississippian; that my name was Hamilton; that I had been a Cortisan Ranger or Guerrilla and that I had been North upon secret service business before; that my mission was one of extreme and vital importance; that I had sewed up in my clothing papers of great importance for parties in Canada; that I should not stop until I reached Canada; that I should return via Nashville & would probably be accompanied by several very distinguished men.

Cowlam alleged that Sands promised him all possible aid and told him that she "had plenty of friends in Nashville who could secure me safe and unimpeded transit through the military lines of the US Army." The pair also discussed financial support for the mission, and Sands assured Cowlam of "her willingness & ability to furnish any amount I might need; gave me for a keepsake a five dollar gold piece which she said she had carried for several years; also a meerschaum cigar holder which she had bought intending to send it to her husband in the south." To disguise their communication, should any prove necessary while Cowlam journeyed to the North, Sands instructed him to address his letters to "Mrs. E.A.J. Clark" of Nashville. Rather than signing his name to the correspondence, Sands directed him to use a wax seal that he owned with the image of a cornucopia at the center and the words "God gives us" circling it so that the design read "God gives us plenty." Sands begged Cowlam to state her sentiments to Jefferson Davis and his secretary of state, Judah P. Benjamin, when he returned south, as she believed her intentions had been misrepresented.

Cowlam claimed that he wrote her one letter from Plainwell, Michigan, approximately fifteen miles north of Kalamazoo, dated "in the woods of Michigan" in March 1865.[31] When that letter went unanswered he sent a telegram from Detroit, which received a letter in reply from "Mrs. E.A.J.

Clark." Cowlam presented the reply to the detectives, along with a list of names that Sands had given him whom she knew to be true friends of the South, emphasizing that the handwriting proved Sands's authorship. Cowlam had previously presented this list to Lieutenant Colonel Bennett Hoskin Hill, the commander of the Military District of Michigan, on March 21. The list of names included Morton J. Lawrence, S. L. Crampton, Abe. Fulkerson, Chesney W. Anderson, Marcus Lemington, Chauncey Barksdale, Martin Kicheloe alias Kennedy, Lewis Mosby, and [illegible] Imboden.[32] After Lincoln's assassination the scrap of paper took on new meaning, as it suggested a larger conspiracy and lent credibility to his claim of having infiltrated the Confederate Secret Service. Unknown to the detectives was the fact that Cowlam's younger sister, Elizabeth, lived in Plainwell, and that he began his journey from Norfolk, not Nashville. Although his movements in Michigan appeared to be part of a clandestine plan, he was simply traveling home.[33]

It is remarkable that Cowlam responded so swiftly to the news of Lincoln's assassination. In little more than twenty-four hours after the president's death, Cowlam had convinced the commander of the Military District of Michigan of the relevance of the information he possessed and begun his journey to Washington by rail. He acted decisively amid a swirl of rumors and false reports circulating across the country.[34] In the immediate aftermath of the assassination Secretary of War Edwin M. Stanton had appointed three army officers, Lieutenant Colonel John A. Foster, Colonel Henry H. Wells, and Colonel Henry Steel Olcott, to coordinate the investigation and gather evidence. As soon as Cowlam arrived in Washington on April 18, he secured a meeting with Lieutenant Colonel Foster, who promptly offered him a position as a detective under Colonel Olcott's supervision. From the receipts that Cowlam submitted for reimbursement it appears that his remuneration was not negotiated in advance. Lieutenant Colonel Foster instructed Timothy Ingraham, the provost marshal general of the Defenses of the Potomac, in early May to "please arrange the rate of compensation as your own men are generally paid remembering that one week board has already been paid by you." Cowlam ultimately received a total of $155.55 in compensation for sixteen days in attendance and service before the special commission investigating Lincoln's murder. Throughout his employment he received a per diem of $3.00, along with reimbursement for receipts submitted for stationery, messages, laundry, and one breakfast. He also received compensation for a return ticket from Washington to Detroit, for ten days of car fare, three days of board, two days of meals, plus $7.50 for "expenses incurred in obtaining information."[35] Ever the opportunist, Cowlam neglected to mention that the commander of the Military District of Michigan had already given him $30 to cover his return train fare.[36]

Upon his arrival in Washington, Cowlam checked into the National Hotel on April 18, and remained there until May 1. The hotel was located at the corner of 6th Street and Pennsylvania Avenue, and was a common haunt for Confederate sympathizers. John Wilkes Booth had been a frequent guest, and he had returned to the hotel as recently as April 8. One historian describes this part of the city, now occupied by Federal Triangle, as "then thirteen blocks of vice, a dense warren of low saloons, boisterous brothels, and hideouts for pimps, thieves, and pickpockets."[37] While working as a detective investigating the Lincoln assassination Cowlam posed as a Confederate sympathizer to procure information from several prostitutes. He reported his findings in a memo dated April 26, stating that a woman brought in for questioning the previous day was "not probably the one referred to" by another informant. The woman's name was Lizzie Murtry, and she had been living in room fifteen at the National for some time. Murtry was celebrated among the residents for having attempted to spit on Lincoln's head as the president gave a speech in front of the hotel one month before his murder. Cowlam reported that the wife of the proprietor, Mrs. Benson, "gave all the girls orders yesterday that if any officer came inquiring for any one they were not to give him any information as to the names of parties in the house unless the officer brought the full name. They were not to pay any attention to him." He claimed that all of the women expected to be arrested at any moment. After an hour-long conversation with another resident of the hotel, Kate Cannon, Cowlam had "become perfectly satisfied that from Mrs. Benson down to Kate Cannon (with two exceptions) all the whites male & female are Secesh."[38]

When Provost Marshal General Fry discovered that Cowlam had arrived in Washington without notifying him, he sent for and conducted an interview with him. Fry was outraged to learn that Cowlam had arrived more than a week earlier and, "through misapprehension or advice," had gone to see Foster instead of him. Foster had taken Cowlam's sealed letter from the commander of the Military District of Michigan, broken it open, and read it even though it was addressed to Fry, and subsequently hired Cowlam as a detective. When Fry demanded that Cowlam present the letter to him, Cowlam first consulted with Foster, who instructed him not to deliver it. Foster then took possession of the letter and "made other disposition of it," according to Fry. Fry sent Foster an angry missive chastising him for opening the letter and preventing him from meeting with Cowlam. Although he expressed hope that Cowlam had contributed to the investigation, he indicated that he had "reason to doubt his present usefulness."[39]

On April 29, Secretary of War Stanton placed the investigation under the supervision of Special Judge Advocate Henry L. Burnett with instructions to assist Judge Advocate General Joseph Holt in preparing the government's case against the conspirators. Cowlam's memos were among those papers deemed relevant enough to be turned over to Burnett when he took over the investigation.[40] Upon assuming the office, Burnett requested that each judge advocate write to him summarizing the relevant evidence collected. Cowlam's supervisor, Colonel Olcott, responded on May 17 to point out that a cipher alphabet found among John Wilkes Booth's possessions was identical to one recovered from Judah P. Benjamin's office, and that Cowlam "can swear positively to this being the cipher used by the Rebel Secret Service Bureau and can furnish the key." The Confederate Secret Service often used an alphabetical cipher, known as a Vigenère Square, that consisted of the letters of the alphabet arranged in a grid of twenty-six rows and columns so that the letters were shifted by one letter between each line. The pattern allowed the writer to encrypt a message using a keyword known to the recipient. Although the German military officer Friedrich Kasiski had recently published a method for decrypting Vigenère ciphers, it is unlikely that Cowlam would have been familiar with this technique, and he would have required the keyword to decode it.[41]

In recounting his whereabouts during the war, Cowlam presented a riveting adventure story to the detectives investigating the Lincoln assassination when he arrived in Washington in April 1865. Cowlam's claim to have infiltrated the Confederate Secret Service would have sounded credible. One historian of the Confederate Secret Service notes that intelligence gathering in the South was haphazard and that operatives often acted with "more enthusiasm than finesse."[42] At the same time, his arrest and imprisonment in

Castle Thunder cast doubts on his account of how he spent the war. All of his anecdotes relating to Lincoln's murder come from either newspaper articles or detectives. It seems more plausible that Cowlam eavesdropped on these conversations during his arrest or imprisonment, rather than at the Peninsula House, where he claimed to overhear Confederate operatives plotting. That Confederate authorities identified him as a "detailed conscript" suggests that he maintained some connection that identified him as having worked in the Quartermaster's Department.

Cowlam's sensational narrative has sometimes been employed to support conspiracy theories surrounding Lincoln's assassination.[43] His reports pointed to a wider plot involving the Confederate Secret Service and the Knights of the Golden Circle. His statements presented Secretary of State William H. Seward as the primary target of the assassins, noting that "Seward was the main object of their hatred, not Abraham Lincoln, because he was the head and brains of this Govt., by a great many people South." The colorful accounts of Cowlam's investigations at the National Hotel, his cloak-and-dagger interview with Mrs. M. A. Sands, and the list of names that he shared with the detectives offer captivating testimony then and now. Cowlam parlayed his bombast into a real job as a detective investigating the president's murder. He would latch onto these tales of spy craft for the rest of his life, insisting always that his time in the South was all an elaborate ruse to undermine the Confederate Secret Service. He would also channel his experiences as an investigator into a postwar career as a detective.

The end of the war brought with it a string of marriages for the Cowlam family. The marriage records give an indication of the pace of Charles's transience. His younger sister Elizabeth was the first to tie the knot. She married Edwin Woodhams, an emigrant from England and a blacksmith who had recently mustered out of the Union army, on August 30, 1865, in Plainwell, Michigan. Charles attended the wedding as a witness, giving his name as "Charley Cowlam of Racine, Wisconsin."[44] When Charles wed Mary Ives in Detroit six months later, on February 19, 1866, the marriage record described him as "of Chicago."[45] By the time his younger brother, George, married Mary McGregory in Detroit on October 18 of that year, Charles had already relocated to Milwaukee.[46]

THREE
DETECTIVE

Was the man a trickster, it must be more for the love than the lucre.
—HERMAN MELVILLE, *The Confidence Man: His Masquerade* (1857)

In 1868, newspapers across the country reported that hundreds of circulars signed "Cowlan Brothers, Post Office Box 637, Washington D.C." had been mailed to businesses in several major cities offering to advertise commercial and political interests for less than the cost of placing advertisements in the local columns of the same newspapers. The brothers proposed to operate by inserting a paragraph in the correspondence section of local newspapers across the country that would appear "exactly like any other item of news in the letter." The product or service would be mentioned in the heading of the article, and again in a subheading to attract attention, "thus giving it, in every respect, the appearance of an item of current *news,* of sufficient importance to justify the correspondent in making mention of it. Being devoid of every semblance of an advertisement, or 'puff,' it would be read as *news,* and carry weight with it." By placing the article in the correspondence column, the advertisement would attract greater attention than if it were placed in its customary location in the classified section.[1]

In some respects, the company was a pioneer. The brothers recognized that the distinction between advertisement and news was fickle. They proposed to publish a nineteenth-century version of an advertorial or sponsored content. Contemporaries sometimes called them "reading notices."[2] An article written by a correspondent could easily include a succinct testimonial for a product or service interspersed within a bit of local news. The big city papers of the emerging independent press, including the *New York Times,* quickly caught on to the brothers' scheme, however, and several of them published scathing reviews explaining that the brothers were unknown to the leading newspaper men of the city, which said all that was needed about the connections they boasted.[3]

The Cowlan Brothers advertisements circulated during a period of transformation in the news industry. Newspapers in major metropolitan areas had grown into major enterprises. The largest among these organizations routinely employed more than a hundred editors, reporters, and correspondents. Journalism was only beginning to develop as a profession, and the rules of objectivity, independence, and commitment to sources were not yet formalized. In the antebellum period newspapers were often party organs, serving as the mouthpiece of a particular candidate and broadcasting their opinions. Many reporters continued to cultivate close relationships with politicians in the postwar years. Politicians commonly offered patronage positions to members of the press who provided friendly coverage for the candidate. The familiarity that these relationships fostered led some in the press corps to enter into the world of politics and engage in intrigues of their own. One contemporary described how these "Bohemians" preferred to wait for the occasional opportunity to make an outsized profit rather than receiving a steady paycheck as a journalist. Newspapermen in the nineteenth century made ideal political informants and lobbyists. Committee clerks and telegraph operators had special advantages in their ability to leak privileged correspondence. The press connections Cowlam cultivated granted him access to privileged information that he could exploit for personal purposes. By alluding to his connections and access to privileged sources, he was advertising the veracity of his information. Having worked as a detective on the Lincoln assassination, Cowlam spent the next several years attempting to secure a position as a detective for the Canadian, American, and British governments.[4]

CANADA

"Which way is safest to go now?" the older man inquired of his younger associate. At the train depot in Kalamazoo, Michigan, Cowlam overheard two men talking in the waiting room shortly after their arrival on the 4:30 p.m. express train on April 9, 1868. The older man appeared to be in his mid-forties, and Cowlam reported that he was "very slim very stooping" and "looks like a school master" in his black clothes and flannel shirt with a paper collar. He also wore a heavy-looking seal ring on the little finger of his right hand. The younger one looked to be in his mid-thirties and went by the names "King" and "John" and dressed shabbily in brownish clothes. He suggested traveling via the Michigan Southern Railroad, adding, "I know this section well." "There is a terrible uproar over this thing," the older man continued. "It was too publicly done," the younger man agreed. The elder man reasoned that "D'Arcy McGee deserved public death and got his deservings." After making this remark the two men stood up, looked around, and walked closer to the stand. Cowlam tried to continue eavesdropping on their conversation but could only make out disjointed sentences. He followed the two men until they parted down the south road.

Cowlam returned to the depot that evening, where he observed the two men again but could not hear their conversation. The next afternoon he saw the older man return with two new characters. The older of the two went by "Mack" and appeared to be in his mid-forties. He was cleanshaven but slightly pitted from smallpox, standing around five foot nine with a heavy build, and wore gray clothes with a brownish overcoat and cape. The younger man went by "Doc" and looked to be about thirty years old with dark hair and eyes. He had a prominent thin nose and lips, and a "fuller mustache—dark with—dyed I think—look of a New York Irishman." He dressed in black clothes with a gold chain, fur boots, and a soft, black hat. Although he struggled to make out their conversation, Cowlam heard "enough to satisfy me that they were concerned also in murder of McGee, and that they have gone to Cincinnati." One of the men remarked that this was "but beginning of the reign of terror which would commence in Canada." He followed them to the depot for the Grand Rapids & Indiana Railroad and hastily penned a memo to the Canadian prime minister, John A. Macdonald, relating the encounters.[5]

Thomas D'Arcy McGee was born in Ireland but immigrated to the United States in his youth after participating in a failed effort to secure Irish independence in 1848. He later moved to Canada, where he is best remembered in Canadian history as the Father of the Confederation, the agreement that united the Canadian provinces in 1867. McGee's support for Canadian nationalism drew the ire of the Irish nationalists, however, particularly among a group known as the Fenian Brotherhood. The Fenians were committed to the idea of achieving Irish independence through revolutionary means. In North America the group organized a series of armed incursions in Canada with the goal of convincing the British government to grant self-government to Ireland. Successive raids in 1866, 1870, and 1871 failed to produce the desired result.[6] McGee was shot in the back of the head on April 7, 1868, as he entered his boarding house after walking home from a late-night parliamentary debate in Ottawa. Canadian authorities arrested Patrick James Whelan, an Irish tailor and Fenian sympathizer, the next day and later convicted him of the crime, but historians have debated the extent of his participation. Whelan confessed shortly before his execution to having been present on the night of the murder but denied pulling the trigger, but much of the evidence presented at his trial was circumstantial and raised significant questions regarding his involvement.[7]

Prime Minister Macdonald shared Cowlam's intelligence with Gilbert McMicken, the head of the secret police in Canada West and later commissioner of the Dominion Police.[8] From his headquarters in Windsor, across the border from Detroit, McMicken oversaw a rudimentary organization that he had built from the ground up to monitor Fenian activities in Canada. McGee's assassination produced a flurry of dispatches from informants like Cowlam who claimed to possess pertinent information. Separating fact from fiction proved a constant challenge. The foremost historian of the Canadian secret police has noted that in the early days "there was no shortage of con men who would say anything that sounded plausible in return for cash." The problem was especially acute when dealing with informants in the United States, as Canadian authorities struggled to verify information across the border independently.[9]

Even though Canadian authorities had arrested McGee's assassin on the same day that Cowlam first observed the two men at the train station, McMicken found Cowlam's intelligence so promising that he and another detective traveled from Windsor to Kalamazoo the next day to meet with him in person. The trio remained in Kalamazoo for the next two days, presumably probing Cowlam's knowledge of the Fenian organization, and perhaps searching for the mysterious Irishmen at the local train stations.[10] That McMicken would travel to meet Cowlam a week after a suspect had been apprehended is a testament to the confidence placed in Cowlam's information. Canadian intelligence officials felt certain that Whelan had not acted alone, and they believed McGee's assassination was the product of a widespread conspiracy. Macdonald also apparently shared Cowlam's letter with other members of the Canadian government, including Hewitt Bernard, the prime minister's brother-in-law, private secretary, and deputy minister of justice, who led the investigation into McGee's death.[11]

A month later, on May 26, Cowlam informed McMicken from Chicago that "since I had the pleasure of meeting you at Kalamazoo I have not heard *from* you, but have heard *of* you in various ways." Cowlam revealed that he had discovered "through my press privileges" that on McMicken's trip to Kalamazoo he was "not only known but well watched from the time you left the wharf at Detroit till you got to Kal[amazoo]." He had talked with one of the men who followed McMicken. The man's name was Ross and he was from Ireland, having served in the British service and been stationed for many years in Canada. Cowlam described him as "sort of aide de camp to Gen. O'Neill." John O'Neill had commanded a detachment of Fenians during the invasion of Canada, and had recently become president of the Fenian Brotherhood.[12] Cowlam added that in the weeks since their meeting he found that one of the men he had surveilled previously in Kalamazoo was now in Chicago, "and, as I expected, hand & glove with Scanlan." Michael Scanlan was an Irish nationalist poet who immigrated to the United States and strongly supported the Fenian raid in 1866. By including references to prominent Fenians like Scanlan and O'Neill, Cowlam hoped to convince McMicken of the merits of his intelligence.

Cowlam informed McMicken of the names of two men who acted as receivers for the Fenian organization, relaying information under various aliases, in Guelph and Windsor, Ontario. He also described a man named Grey or Graves from Ottawa who had been traveling around Chicago, Indianapolis, Cincinnati, Louisville, and Nashville raising money and enlisting men to secure the release of Whelan. In an effort to infiltrate the group, Cowlam explained that he "gave $1.00 toward the enterprise and if you ever get the roll of subscriptions you will find my signature as bold as anyone's." Cowlam claimed to have met Graves twice, and he described him as "a smart, intelligent well posted man but with a singularly humbly know nothing look about him." He suspected that Graves was now in Canada, as he had ventured east several days before. It is not clear whether Cowlam was aware that the Canadian government had already arrested several suspected Fenians in Guelph earlier that month.[13]

Cowlam believed that he was in a position "to learn something important before long." He mentioned that all of the messages heading to Canada were now transmitted in cipher. Cowlam had no doubt informed McMicken of his experiences observing the Confederate Secret Service. He believed he could decrypt these messages, explaining that he had a starting point to work with, and he volunteered that he would inform McMicken immediately if his efforts were successful. A historian of the Canadian secret police finds that the Fenians wrote coded telegrams by substituting letters, a method that was "ridiculously easy to break" compared to the sophisticated ciphers employed by actual intelligence officers. Cowlam emphasized that "I can further assure you that the most voluminous kind of reports reach F[enian]. Hdquers *daily* from Canada, every thing said and done is sent." Cowlam suggested that if McMicken expected to be in Windsor for some time, he might travel there to meet him, as he planned to return to Kalamazoo the following day. He closed the letter on a serious note, remarking, "Be on your guard, you have awakened the deadly hostility of every Fenian by your late exertions and your name is ready in their mouths."[14]

Four days later, after arriving in Kalamazoo and finding no reply from McMicken, Cowlam penned another letter. This time he listed the names of twelve suspected Fenians in Hamilton, Ottawa, Toronto, Quebec, and Kingston. He could not determine whether these names were real or aliases, only that they were regular correspondents with Fenian headquarters. In a bit of dramatic flair Cowlam closed by writing, "I shall not sign this—you will know who writes it and where to address & sign as you did to me on your arrival."[15]

Two weeks later Cowlam wrote again from Kalamazoo to alert McMicken that the Fenians had been shipping weapons to Canada in preparation for another raid. He described a shipment of over thirteen hundred Henry rifles, six hundred or more Henry carbines, and a large number of revolvers sent to Port Huron, Michigan, located along the Canadian border at the southern end of Lake Huron. Cowlam described how Colonel James F. Cosgrove, of the 14th Regiment of the Irish Republican Army, "are or will be within 24 hours *en route* for the border on an exploring expedition." Cowlam also claimed to have decoded part of the key to the cipher he referred to in an earlier letter. The cipher contained a message from General O'Neill, transmitted from Detroit to Indianapolis, and concerning the movement of gunboats along the Detroit River. Cowlam described the message as otherwise unimportant aside from demonstrating that he might be able to decipher future correspondence.

Cowlam's dispatches increasingly sounded the alarm of an imminent invasion. He observed that an immense number of circulars, numbering perhaps thirty thousand or more, were already spreading across the Dominion in support of the Fenian cause. He described how Patrick Murphy, considered by many to be the best pilot on the Great Lakes and stationed aboard the USS *Michigan*, was a "rank Fenian," noting that "it is said that he would ground the steamer before she should interfere again." If Murphy was a Fenian, he held his cards close. Murphy was serving aboard the *Michigan* two years earlier when it intercepted and captured Fenians crossing the Niagara River during the June 1866 raid. Cowlam added that two prominent Fenians had received instructions to make a "tour of inspection" to expose vulnerabilities in Canadian defenses. He concluded, "From movements in this state and at Chicago I feel certain that an attack not only from the Vermont but from the Michigan border."[16]

By the early summer Cowlam seemed irritated that McMicken had ignored his reports since their last meeting. In an effort to restore McMicken's attention he complained that he was overwhelmed with the vast quantity of relevant intelligence regularly crossing his desk. He emphasized that "not a day passes but some point or other reaches me which, having no certain means of transmission to you, I scarcely notice. Besides, I have not been solicited to furnish you what information I may come across and it appears to me that I may possibly be annoying you with a great many matters you care little about." Cowlam proposed to enlighten McMicken on the source of his information. He had neglected to mention it during their meeting in Kalamazoo, but now he was willing to reveal his source in the hopes of being restored to favor. As he explained, "You may be somewhat surprised to find out *how* I became possessed of so much of other peoples business, people too who are using very strenuous exertions to keep their business within proper bounds. I am a newspaper man—have a longer correspondence with newspapers than anyone in the United States, make up more telegraphic news and mail correspondence daily from Chicago & Washington through my employees than any other person does in a month, and consequently am inside the ring upon everything which is done whether it obtained publicly or not." Cowlam added that his brother, George, was his agent in Washington, having learned to operate a telegraph from Henry Izard, the late superintendent of the Montreal Telegraph Company and former superintendent of the Provincial Telegraph Company. He thought it was probable that McMicken knew Izard, and he described the recently deceased superintendent as his cousin.[17] Charles enclosed copies of his circulars to give McMicken an indication of the business he operated with George. The circulars he enclosed were almost certainly from Cowlan Brothers, which would soon receive unflattering coverage in the press. He added, "*Should I wish to know* the telegraph has no scents [secrets] from me as I can read it as far as I can hear it sound."

Cowlam highlighted his sympathy with Canada, explaining that he had contacted McMicken initially out of kindness and "for the good of your people." He noted that he had been elected an honorary member of the St. George's Society of Chicago, a charitable organization for the benefit of Englishmen in distress, during the first Fenian raid in 1866 while he was working as an editor for the *Evening Post*. Cowlam added that the Chicago chapter had contributed George R. Kingsmill, who served as lieutenant of the Chicago Company of volunteers who aided Canadian defenses. He closed the letter by repeating his suspicions that McMicken was being watched, and indicated that he sent his message by express as he did not trust the mail to be delivered unopened.[18]

In late August Cowlam sent a telegram from Washington to report that the largest firearms dealer in the United States, Schuyler, Hartley and Graham, had telegraphed Alexander B. Dyer, the chief of ordinance for the U.S. Army. The manufacturers requested to purchase two thousand precision rifles from the federal government, to which Dyer consented. Cowlam contended that the rifles were being purchased secretly for the Fenian organization. Again he bemoaned the lack of correspondence since their meeting in Kalamazoo and closed by noting, "Can give you many things from here if proper arrangements are made." He requested that McMicken write to him at the same address in Washington, D.C., that appeared on the Cowlan Brothers circulars.[19]

DETECTIVE

Cowlam continued to send letters to McMicken that the latter forwarded to Macdonald through the summer of 1868. Yet Cowlam never received the offer of employment that he desperately craved, and Cowlam's repeated protestations suggest that McMicken never replied to his letters after their initial meeting in April. The apparent lack of reciprocity in their correspondence raises the question of whether McMicken continued to view Cowlam as a reliable source. That the invasion that Cowlam signaled the alarm about never happened casts doubt on his reports. It is not clear if Cowlam believed them to be genuine, or if he was simply blowing smoke in the hopes that his energies might lead to a paid position. Some of his descriptions sound overly stereotypical, and almost cartoonish, but the details he provided remained convincing. Clearly McMicken continued to find the letters credible enough to forward them to the prime minister, along with a substantial volume of correspondence from other informants. McMicken may have simply been inundated by the reports he already received from other sources concerning Fenian activities, or he may have shifted his attention to the east when the threats Cowlam described along the Michigan border and Lake Erie failed to materialize.

INTERNAL REVENUE

Stymied in his efforts to secure a position with the Canadian government, Cowlam parlayed his detective experience on the Lincoln assassination to secure a position with the federal government. From October 19, 1868, until February 28, 1870, he worked on a contract basis as a revenue detective for the Internal Revenue Secret Service in a district covering Georgia and Florida. The Internal Revenue Service possessed a Secret Service of its own, leading many of Cowlam's friends and acquaintances to believe, mistakenly, that he was or had been an agent of the U.S. Secret Service.[20] The confusion proved to be a useful pretense for upselling his influence and authority. An article written several years later summarized Cowlam's time in Savannah by observing that the "indignation was so intense against him that had he been caught at the time no doubt he would have been lynched."[21]

While employed there, Cowlam uncovered a whiskey smuggling ring in Savannah. He presented evidence of the ring to U.S. Attorney Henry S. Fitch in February 1869 before sharing his report with Commissioner of Internal Revenue Edward A. Rollins. In his letter to Rollins, Cowlam described how "this smuggling is conducted in an apparently legitimate way, papers are properly made out, every thing on the surface is square and honest and business like, but underneath all is fraud." Through the use of fraudulent certificates, members of the whiskey ring had evaded taxes on imported spirits. Cowlam noted in his report that he could not account for how he had obtained his information, but explained that "the ones who are to work out this matter for the Government must be allowed some scope in personalities."[22]

A week later Cowlam realized that the scandal extended further, implicating the U.S. marshal, William G. Dickson, and U.S. Attorney Fitch, with whom he had entrusted his initial reports. Cowlam alerted Commissioner Rollins that Dickson had absconded with public money under his care totaling "$18,000 to $25,000 that I am certain of, though it might go much higher."[23] Dickson had left Savannah on March 2 to travel to Macon to sell property seized by the government, and from there proceeded to Atlanta. Cowlam believed that Dickson intended to return secretly to Savannah to leave for the Florida coast, and from there to flee to Cuba. Dickson had recently received $13,000 in proceeds from the sale of the brig *George,* and several thousand more from the sale of another vessel, yet Cowlam noted that Dickson had not remitted "one dollar of public or private monies since his appointment." Cowlam added that Dickson had in his possession "a large number of executions and has, probably, collected the greater portion of monies due on them." The total amount of these executions, Cowlam speculated, might reach $75,000 to $100,000. The assessor of internal revenue in Savannah, Lloyd D. Waddell, had also fled the city around the same time that Dickson left. Given the extensive corruption Cowlam had identified, he emphasized that "I dare not go to any official of the United States Government in this City for aid."[24]

The following month investigators opened a package that had been deposited by Dickson at a bank in Savannah, believing that it might contain the proceeds of the sale of one of the vessels. Instead the package contained a sum of counterfeit treasury notes. A grand jury convened in the U.S. District Court in Savannah indicted Dickson, Fitch, and Waddell, along with Albert S. Bigelow, Alexander H. Robinson, Samuel Page Edmunds, Monroe J.

Alder, and William J. Williams. The members of the ring had conspired to receive and sell five hundred barrels of whiskey with a value of $40,000 without paying the internal revenue tax. The indictment withheld the names from the press until May. By the time of the indictment several of the men had already fled to New York or were believed to have left the country, and several of the others fled the state after posting bond. Ultimately the U.S. attorney on the case declined to move forward with the indictment, given the difficulty of producing witnesses or defendants.[25]

In July 1869 Cowlam worked on a case involving Henry McNeal Turner, an African American minister, politician, and postmaster in Macon, Georgia. Turner had maintained an affair with Marian Harris, a mixed-race prostitute who was in possession of several hundred dollars of stolen currency. Harris had received the notes at Turner's home in Philadelphia from James H. A. Schurman, an African American messenger working in the Treasury Department. Schurman had stolen $12,000 worth of unsigned banknotes issued on the First National Bank of Jersey City, New Jersey, and offered some of the currency to Harris on the condition that she give him $60 for every $100 that she passed into circulation. Because the signatures applied to the notes were spurious and the notes were stolen before they could be issued to the public, the government considered them to be counterfeit. After Harris was arrested in Atlanta for passing some of the banknotes, she initially implicated Turner, but changed her story numerous times. Cowlam investigated Harris's claims and testified for the defense that Turner had no prior knowledge of the counterfeit money in Harris's possession. Cowlam's testimony assisted in Turner's release and the dismissal of the charges against him.[26]

Cowlam's supervisor was Włodzimierz Krzyżanowski, an emigrant from Poland who became a brigadier general in the Union army. He accepted a position as supervisor of internal revenue for the District of Georgia and Florida on May 26, 1869. Krzyżanowski used Macon as his headquarters but also maintained regional offices in Jacksonville, Fernandina, Atlanta, Augusta, and Savannah. Upon assuming the office, Krzyżanowski prioritized the detection of illegal distillery operations in the district. In one five-month span Krzyżanowski's agents led raids on over eighty illegal distilleries and discovered eighty-five illegal stills. The men seized or destroyed 122,260 gallons of beer and mash, 1,794 gallons of wine, 700 gallons of peach and apple brandy, and 390 gallons of corn whiskey. Cowlam participated in the whiskey raids in Heard and Carroll Counties in January 1870, leading to the capture of more than a dozen stills, valued at $3,500. On one of the raids Cowlam narrowly escaped death after a suspected still operator shot at him and the bullet passed through his hat. This near-death experience made the national news.[27] Although the detectives displayed great zeal in apprehending illegal distillers, recordkeeping at the Savannah branch was haphazard. When citizens paid taxes or fines, clerks added a check mark next to the citizen's name without recording any indication of the amount paid. In October 1871 Krzyżanowski was indicted for fraud in Savannah. An internal investigation in the Treasury Department later acquitted him, but he was removed from his position as supervisor in early November.[28]

Despite Cowlam's apparently praiseworthy efforts, his tenure in the Internal Revenue Service was not without allegations of impropriety. Once established in the role, he developed a penchant for extortion and bribery. The *Savannah Daily Advertiser* later recounted that Cowlam's "manner of doing business with his, and the Government's victims was pretty generally known" among those involved in the liquor trade. Cowlam "was of a speculative turn of mind, and esteemed the companionship of dollars and cents of more value than all the world besides. Nothing could wean him from his pursuit of lucre, and his ambition was to make what he could by any means possible." When Dickson disappeared, Cowlam offered to locate the missing marshal if Dickson's creditors would only pay him $500 toward the expenses he would incur in tracking the fugitive. His "gift of gab" smoothed over the gentlemen's hesitation. Cowlam looked the part. The men could see that Cowlam "was a Government agent, was smart, had plenty of cheek—yes, square yards of it, forsooth—and it was reasonable to suppose that he had a grain of honesty to make the composition palatable." Yet "who has seen Cowlam or Dickson since?" the article continued, "Anybody?" The article also noted that, while in Georgia, Cowlam had written "long letters to Northern and Western papers detailing terrible KuKlux outrages upon government officers, his own conscience at the time telling him that he, above all others, deserved a halter."[29]

Cowlam was also implicated in extorting the Savannah merchant John Nicholas Muller, which the *Savannah Morning News* described as a case "equal in blackness and rascality to any thing else of which the heart of a villain is capable." Muller stood accused of several violations of the revenue laws, but the U.S. attorney had dismissed all of the charges except one count of operating as a rectifier without having paid the special tax. Rectified spirits are highly concentrated liquors, often distilled from wine, that can be used in flavored cocktails. Muller had reused revenue stamps on barrels of alcohol after emptying their contents, mixed spirits and repackaged the contents without submitting them for inspection, and concealed these transactions by failing to record them in his books. The list of property seized from Muller's storefront reveals all of the ingredients needed to manufacture rectified spirits. The confiscated goods included an eighty-gallon pipe (a large barrel) containing cherries and bitters, along with numerous barrels of gin, whiskey, brandy, and other liquors. The value of the contraband totaled $14,886.74 according to the court inventory. To collect his property, Muller needed only to submit a bond equal to the value of the items seized.[30]

After the property had been confiscated, however, Cowlam approached Muller with an offer of assistance. Cowlam explained that he was a special assistant assessor under General Krzyżanowski, and that together with Major John H. Gould, the collector of internal revenue, the case was in their hands.[31] If Muller would only pay him $1,000, he could make the case disappear. Cowlam would present Muller with a clean receipt from Gould and Krzyżanowski that would release his property. Muller would be responsible only for the court costs, which he would have to settle anyway. If Muller did not agree to the *quid pro quo,* Cowlam explained, his business would remain closed for another four or five months while awaiting trial. The *Savannah Morning News* reported that Muller unfortunately "consulted his wife instead of his lawyer," and he agreed to pay Cowlam rather than risk shuttering his business. Muller had only $500 at the time, and Cowlam agreed to accept this amount on the condition that Muller pay the remaining balance when the detective returned from Florida. When Cowlam returned a few days later without a receipt, he explained that Krzyżanowski was in Macon but that he could obtain signatures from him and Gould as soon as Muller paid him the balance. Although Muller did not have the other $500, Cowlam "magnanimously" agreed to accept $250 more to produce the receipt. By this time, however, Muller had explained the situation to his friends, who cautioned him of the illegitimacy of Cowlam's proposal, and he refused to pay anything more. When this evidence came to light at Muller's hearing, the jury acquitted him on the grounds that Cowlam had acted with impropriety.[32]

Shortly after his contract expired with the Internal Revenue Service at the end of February 1870, Cowlam moved in with his brother, George, in Washington, D.C. The brothers lived at 800 F Street NW in a four-story Italianate building, across the street from the present location of the National Portrait Gallery. The household included Charles's and George's wives, George's infant son, and two African American domestic servants, Frances Smith, age twenty-two, and "Brown Brown," age twelve, both of Maryland. George worked as a clerk at the Capitol, while Charles listed his occupation as "in Treasury." Each of the brothers reported $300 of personal property.[33]

IRELAND

With his schemes in Savannah exposed, Cowlam sailed from New York to Liverpool via Queenstown aboard the Inman Royal Mail steamer *City of Brooklyn* on November 26, 1870. Cowlam's passport application describes him as thirty-three years old and standing five feet, ten inches tall, with an oval face and round chin. He had an aquiline nose, brown hair, gray eyes, and a light complexion. During his time in London, Cowlam lived at 12 Redcliffe Gardens, in a recently constructed row house southwest of the city center.[34]

Cowlam could not have picked a better time to visit the United Kingdom. His former patron, Francis W. Kellogg, was traveling there at the same time, having arrived in the spring of 1871. On August 12, 1871, Kellogg sent a letter to Spencer Compton Cavendish, the Marquess of Hartington, who served as Prime Minister William Gladstone's chief secretary for Ireland. Kellogg had spent the past three months traveling in Ireland for health and pleasure. He had witnessed a riot in Dublin several days before that had prompted him to contact Lord Hartington with a proposal. The riot began when more than three thousand demonstrators assembled in Phoenix Park near the Wellington Monument to demand the release of several Fenian prisoners. When the police intervened and gave orders to disperse, violent clashes ensued that left dozens injured. The riot coincided with a visit from the Prince of Wales, who cut short his trip in response to the demonstration.[35] Kellogg could not help noting the comparisons between the British presence in Ireland and his experiences with southern Reconstruction.[36] He noted, "With an experience gained during our Civil War and the years of violence and lawlessness which have followed it in some of our Southern states, I was not altogether unprepared for many things which came to my knowledge during my stay in Ireland, but the feeling of bitterness which culminates in midnight murder, arson, outrage, and riot is quite as terrible as any it has been my lot to know of, even in our worst days." Equally remarkable to Kellogg was the small proportion of these outrages that resulted in arrests or convictions. Where many observers might have attributed this outcome to ineffective policing, Kellogg proposed another explanation. Despite "all the exertions an earnest and uniformly intelligent magistracy and police could make, their hands were tied by the fact, that they themselves and their agents were so well known." Anyone who dared to offer information to the British authorities risked assassination. "Every well disposed Irishman is watched, every Englishman an object of suspicion at least, while an American can go at will throughout the country," Kellogg emphasized. By posing as a curious tourist, an American could travel unmolested without the hint of suspicion, eavesdropping on local gossip and relaying information better than the "most astute local detective or the cleverest English 'special'" could ever hope to discover.[37]

Through his public service Kellogg had experienced the Civil War and southern Reconstruction. Early in the war Kellogg helped to organize three cavalry regiments, and served as colonel of the 3rd Michigan Cavalry, an honorary rank he maintained while holding his congressional seat. With a prominent forehead and a considerable chin-curtain beard, Kellogg bore some resemblance to Lincoln's secretary of war, Edwin Stanton. One colonel who had served in the Michigan cavalry mused in his memoirs that the similar appearances of Kellogg and Stanton may have contributed to their strong friendship. After the war, President Andrew Johnson appointed Kellogg as collector of internal revenue for the Southern District of Alabama in 1866. Kellogg resigned his position in 1868 when the residents of Mobile returned him to the House of Representatives to serve the remainder of a partial term.[38]

Kellogg had just the man in mind to carry out his proposal. He informed Lord Hartington that "there is at present in England a gentleman who was during the Civil War in the United States, the Chief of the Secret Service of the United States within the Confederate lines. During the entire war he was within the limits of the Confederacy gaining information for the use of the Federal Armies." He recounted how, after the war, Cowlam completed a "very difficult and dangerous service" for the Treasury Department, "having for his district the states of Georgia, Florida and Alabama, where he remained some two or three years resigning a year since, after under going an experience quite as trying as during the war but bringing all matters put in to his hands to a successful issue." Kellogg indicated that General Robert C. Schenck, currently serving as minister to Great Britain, was intimately aware of Cowlam's character and could vouch for him if necessary. He explained that Cowlam was currently employed by a New York banking firm, traveling the United Kingdom for health and pleasure, and Kellogg believed that he was currently visiting some of his relatives in Lincolnshire, the place of his father's birth. To smooth over his recommendation, Kellogg suggested that Cowlam was already contemplating a trip to Ireland with his wife. He noted that Cowlam had been a journalist for many years "with an experience in unearthing crimes of a political nature of a very high order." Kellogg closed the letter by noting that "having known this gentleman from boyhood I can guarantee his honor to the fullest extent that any success may attend his exertions." The congressman instructed Hartington to write to him at his forwarding address, courtesy of Bowles Brothers and Co., at 449 Strand.[39]

Lord Hartington was not unfamiliar with American affairs. He had completed a six-month journey across the United States in the midst of the Civil War, from August 1862 to February 1863. While Hartington spent most of his time in the Northeast and Midwest, he made a side trip to Richmond despite failing to obtain a pass to cross Confederate lines. In the course of his travels he met both Abraham Lincoln and Jefferson Davis. Although Hartington was only a few years older than Cowlam, their personalities could not have been more different. While Cowlam was enterprising and extroverted, Hartington was often brusque, boring, and cheerless. At the same time he was sensible and practical in his thinking, disdaining the pretentions of his class. Hartington was heir to one of the largest estates in the United Kingdom. The family possessed nearly two hundred thousand acres in England and Ireland, whose rents produced a substantial annual income. He remained financially dependent on his father for much of his life. He did not inherit the dukedom until he was fifty-eight, and did not marry until he was fifty-nine. Hartington preferred to spend his time at home surrounded by family. When offered the position as chief secretary for Ireland he nearly declined, and only accepted on the condition that he remain in London rather than relocate to Dublin.[40]

Studies of British policing emphasize the inadequacy of English detectives in investigating politically motivated attacks in Ireland. The detectives at the London Metropolitan Police were too few in number and insufficiently trained in the art of espionage to infiltrate Fenian networks. Domestic surveillance also threatened to undermine the prevailing sentiments of a liberal nation-state. Instead, English authorities relied primarily on the web of spies and informants developed at the Irish intelligence bureau at Dublin Castle. Cowlam arrived in the United Kingdom at a time when Fenian organizing was on the decline. The most active period of Fenian agitation was between 1865 and 1870. Patrick Quinlivan and Paul Rose note that "by 1872 the heat had largely gone out of the movement." Yet the prospect of a Fenian resurgence remained an ever-present threat in the mind of the British officials. In a letter to Hartington written several months before Kellogg's proposal, the lord lieutenant of Ireland emphasized that "even now when Fenianism is much less formidable, it seems to be of great importance to keep an eye on it."[41] It would have been difficult for British authorities to fully grasp these trends at the time, however. The threat of Fenianism appeared to loom large. Support for the Home Government Association, founded in May 1870 with the goal of achieving self-government in Ireland, only increased after Parliament disestablished the Church of Ireland the following year. As approval for home rule intensified, British officials responded by suspending habeas corpus in Ireland in June 1871.[42] From the perspective of British authorities, the movement for home rule appeared as Fenianism in disguise, indistinguishable from earlier forms of Irish nationalism.[43]

Lord Hartington replied to Kellogg requesting that he provide additional information about himself, as General Schenck was traveling in continental Europe. Kellogg answered that he intended to leave for the continent himself, but recommended that Hartington to speak with Henry Wilson, a senator from Massachusetts and future vice president, or Nathaniel P. Banks, a congressman from Massachusetts, both of whom were visiting London. Kellogg enclosed Cowlam's card and mentioned that he would arrive in the city by August 24. He added that he would send a letter to Cowlam to make him aware of his proposal.[44]

In explaining the situation to Cowlam, Kellogg highlighted the connections between Cowlam's experiences in the South during the Civil War and Reconstruction and the events currently taking place in Ireland. "It will not be difficult for you to conceive how readily when reflecting upon the many recent acts of assassination and outrage in Ireland, especially those of a political nature," Kellogg elucidated, "I thought of similar ones in the detection of which you had borne so prominent a part and especially in the investigation of the assassination of President Lincoln." Kellogg explained that "your report to Sec. Stanton previous to the murder and the foresight displayed in it have all recurred to me." It is not clear what report of Cowlam's Kellogg had in mind. No report from Cowlam to Stanton survives, and Kellogg seems to have believed Cowlam's tall tales about his time in the South. Kellogg also hinted that Cowlam had been the first to suggest that the investigations in Ireland would be more successful if conducted "by those who were not known wherever they appeared as agents of the government." It is clear from Kellogg's letter to Cowlam that the two had remained in touch in the decade since Cowlam's pardon from Lincoln in 1861.[45]

After waiting a week to hear from Hartington, Cowlam sent a letter to the chief secretary introducing himself. He emphasized his credentials as a detective, volunteering "that after the assassination of Hon. D'Arcy McGee, at Ottawa Canada, I tried to assist the Hon. the Governor General of the Dominion, and the stipendiary magistrate who specially investigated the affair—Mr. Gilbert McMicken, of Windsor C.W. and, though my efforts were fruitless they were acknowledged by Sir. John Young as valuable." In his usual fashion, Cowlam added a bit of mystery by suggesting that their correspondence might be monitored. To keep their communications secret, he insisted on enclosing a self-addressed envelope for Hartington's reply.[46]

In the meantime, Lord Hartington sent inquires to Robert Schenck concerning Kellogg's and Cowlam's respectability and character. Schenck replied that he knew Cowlam but not very intimately. He believed Cowlam was a newspaper correspondent, and that he had held a clerkship with a committee of Congress. He described Cowlam as a "shrewd, intelligent young man, capable, I should think, for apt & efficient service in any business matter." Schenck sent a second letter two days later indicating that he had additional information on Cowlam that he wished to express verbally and confidentially with Hartington. Schenck later explained that Cowlam had approached him requesting a letter of recommendation for the purposes of seeking employment "either in the Irish Office, or in the Emigration Department, especially with respect to Florida." Schenck also recalled that it was Charles's brother, George, who had held the committee clerkship, and he wished to clarify that while both brothers possessed the character he had described in his earlier letter, and both brothers had connections in Washington, only George had worked previously for General Benjamin F. Butler. By November 16, Cowlam still had not received an interview. Kellogg and Wilson had returned to the United States in September after receiving no word from the Marquess.[47]

At the same time that Cowlam was soliciting letters of recommendation for a position with Hartington, a series of advertisements appeared in newspapers across the United Kingdom soliciting relief for the victims of the 1871 Chicago fire. The advertisements introduced the philanthropist organizing the relief effort as "Charles Cowlam, Esq. of Sherwin & Co., Bankers, New York, and who formerly held important positions at the Chicago press... and now acting in London as Commissioner of Emigration." Some of the articles began with a telegram from L. C. Monroe dated October 10 that read "the best of the city is in ashes, from Chicago Avenue to Van Buren Street. Fire not yet subdued. Burned from lake to river, north side; nearly same south side; west side not so much. Over 150,000 people houseless, penniless, and naked. Help us." In one Irish newspaper Cowlam pleaded for support for Americans "who did not forget their obligations to Ireland when she was in sore distress."[48] In another advertisement Cowlam claimed to have made arrangement with three steamship lines to forward clothing and packages to the survivors. While Cowlam asked that packages be forwarded to the respective steamship lines, he added that "contributions in money—large or small—can be sent to me at my office" at No. 2 Lower James Street, or care of Bowles Brothers and Co., at 449 Strand.[49] A Lancaster paper described Cowlam's title as "Deputy Commissioner of Emigration For Florida."[50] In the following weeks Cowlam wrote to the newspapers to acknowledge receipt of donations totaling several pounds along with assorted packages of clothing.[51]

Cowlam's seemingly selfless act of philanthropy may have boosted his credibility and elevated his stature with Hartington, but it is not clear if any of the money or parcels of clothing ever made their way to their intended recipients. The "L. C. Monroe" whose telegram surveyed the damage from the fire was Elisha Lyman Cole Monroe, Charles's brother-in-law who had married his older sister, Sarah. Although Charles would later use stationery from the Florida Office of the Commissioner of Land and Immigration, a predecessor of the Commissioner of Agriculture that encouraged economic development and sought to attract settlers to that state, the records of the commission make no mention of him having ever been an employee. His encouragement that readers send money directly to his forwarding address with Bowles Brothers sounds suspicious, given his criminal history.

On December 2, Cowlam wrote again to Lord Hartington. This time he enclosed a letter from Edward A. Rollins, the former commissioner of internal revenue whom Cowlam had served under during his time with the Treasury Department. Rollins had handed the message to Cowlam two years before, and written it days before he left office. The letter described Cowlam as "the ablest and most valuable assistant I had in a field where the corruption among officials and the terrorism exercised by rebels over all government officers had been too powerful to be overcome until you went South." Rollins wished that he could reward Cowlam's service with "an appointment to one of the highest offices within my gift" and suggested that "if you should reconsider the determination expressed when last I saw you to go into the banking business and conclude to continue in the government service I shall be glad to exert any influence I may have in advancing your interests in any direction." He praised Cowlam for exposing and breaking up the whiskey ring, emphasizing that the Treasury Department had brought in $12 million more than it had in any previous year thanks to honest men like Cowlam who brought corruption to light.[52]

By early January 1872, Lord Hartington decided to retain Cowlam as a detective. Cowlam set to work immediately, and even traveled to Dublin before working out the details of his assignment. Perhaps influenced by Cowlam's earlier claims that their correspondence was susceptible to being intercepted, Hartington concluded "that upon consideration it is thought that there should be some objections to keeping up a direct correspondence," and proposed that Cowlam relay his reports through Lieutenant Colonel Edmund Henderson, commissioner of the London Metropolitan Police.[53]

By the end of the month the details of Cowlam's employment had been settled. However, a dispute soon arose over his remuneration. Henry Atwell Lake, the commissioner of the Dublin Metropolitan Police, informed Hartington that "he tells me you promised him 30/ per diem, personal allowance. I understood your lordship to say 20/ & told him so, but he said I was wrong." Cowlam had also presented a bill for reimbursement for his living expenses at the Gresham Hotel that month, and explained that £20 per month for living expenses would be typical moving forward. He also insisted that his traveling expenses should be reimbursed at actual cost each month. Cowlam forwarded an itemized account for the current month, seeking reimbursement for the £70 6/ of expenses associated with the work he had already completed. The compensation that Cowlam insisted upon for his first month of work was more than three times his monthly income while working as a detective in the Internal Revenue Service. Lake concluded the letter by remarking, "he is an expensive gentleman & I only hope we may get some value for the money."[54]

Four days later Lake informed Hartington that he had paid Cowlam for the current month's expenses but cautioned him that "your Lordship considered his terms very high and that under such circumstances it was not likely that the arrangement would be of any long continuance." After some discussion Cowlam agreed that he would only receive the "subsistence" money of £20 per month "while actually employed on special duty," and that when not on assignment he would only receive his normal per diem. Lake was unable to convince Cowlam to implement these changes retroactively to lower his expenses for January, and reported that "he seemed to insinuate that it was not *his* fault having to remain here, as he received no specific instructions."[55]

Hartington's relationship with Cowlam seemed only to deteriorate with each passing letter. On February 18, Atwell Lake reported that "I saw C. today & put your questions to him verbally. I made him write the answers in my presence." In response to Hartington's inquiry into the true intentions of home rule advocates, Cowlam explained that home rule supporters were earnest in their desire to separate from England and were not simply promoting home rule as a way of achieving personal ends as he had believed originally. He clarified that there was strong overlap between supporters of home rule and those who considered themselves Fenians. Cowlam found that support for home rule was widespread among the various classes in Ireland, from the peasantry and small tradesmen to the higher ranks of magistrates, whose support offered moral and official encouragement to the movement. In response to a question about the Ballot Act, which introduced the secret ballot in British elections later that year, Cowlam offered a quotation that he attributed to the Irish nationalist Alexander Martin Sullivan, remarking, "we will sweep Ireland from end to end for Home Rule and what is to follow so soon as we get the ballot." The Ballot Act would prove to be consequential in Ireland, as it allowed voters to participate in elections without being observed by landlords or employers for the first time.[56]

By the time that Cowlam arrived in Ireland, resistance to British authority had made it impossible for prosecutors to secure convictions. Witnesses routinely refused to cooperate with detectives, and jurors sometimes acquitted defendants with Irish nationalist sympathies. In one case, Hugh Fay stood trial three times in County Cavan for the murder of Mary Lynch. In each trial the jury failed to reach a verdict despite the testimony of a neighbor who claimed to have witnessed the murder and evidence that the belt used to strangle the victim had been presented to the accused as a gift. Atwell Lake believed that Fenians on the jury had prevented their fellow jurors from reaching a guilty verdict. He suggested that the petty sessions clerk, John McCabe, held Fenian sympathies, and insinuated that McCabe permitted the Fenian jurors to serve with full knowledge of the likely influence on the outcome. In describing local officials' indifference in applying the law, Lake concluded that "some no doubt neglect their duty from fear, others are too much occupied by other offices."[57]

Cowlam traveled extensively across Ireland by rail, carriage, and saddle horse. His receipts submitted for reimbursement reveal that he often made multiple journeys within the same week, and sometimes slept in a different town every night. He spent most of January and February in County Kerry, in the southwestern part of the island, but he returned each month to convey his reports in person in Dublin. His time in County Kerry coincided with a by-election where the home rule candidates emerged victorious.[58] In April he conducted investigations around Galway, a port city on the western coast. Many of Cowlam's trips appear aimless. Shortly before he returned to the

United States, Cowlam explained that his recent trip to Tullamore, on the outskirts of Dublin, had been motivated by the murder of a landlord, Harriet O'Neill. O'Neill had been shot in the heart by an unknown assailant in the doorway of her home after she had delivered several eviction notices earlier that day. Cowlam noted that "upon my arrival at Tullamore I found a great number of detectives & c. searching about, and, as my power under such circumstances seemed unclear I returned to town." The *Guardian* noted that more than fifty detectives were actively working on the case.[59] It is not clear what Cowlam hoped to accomplish by traveling to the scene of a murder, only to leave moments after arriving. The hurried pace of his movements suggest that he lacked direction or awareness of his responsibilities.

By early March the permanent undersecretary at the Irish Home Office, Thomas Henry Burke, began to raise suspicions regarding the usefulness of Cowlam's efforts. Burke informed Hartington that "the convening of the Fenian Convention in May was published in the American and national journals. It is easy to infer from this that Irish Delegates would be sent." Cowlam seemed to be parroting news to London that he had gleaned from Irish newspapers. He had also focused his attention on William Henry O'Sullivan, where Burke noted that the "Sullivans are not and never were Fenians & the Fenians not only dislike them but are personally hostile to Wm Sullivan." Cowlam's previous letters exposed his unawareness of the major Fenian publications, and Burke opined that "if he cannot give us more information about them than he is giving, I should be disposed after a further fair trial to get rid of him."[60] In a subsequent message written three weeks later Burke explained his reluctance to inform Samuel Lee Anderson, who worked in the intelligence bureau in Dublin Castle gathering information on the Fenian threat in Ireland, of Cowlam's efforts, noting, "I shall not mention anything to Anderson about C. for the present—but in the event of his obtaining good information, shall avail myself of your permission." Burke added, "I do not think we shall find C. of much use."[61] Years later Burke would become a victim of assassination, along with Lord Hartington's younger brother, Lord Frederick Cavendish. Both men were stabbed repeatedly with surgical knives as they walked through Dublin's Phoenix Park in May 1882.

Cowlam spent much of May in Dublin. His investigations appeared to have stalled, and he claimed only one day of per diem while on assignment.

Despite his slackening workload, however, Cowlam attempted to obtain reimbursement for copies of documents sent to him by his brother in New York, totaling $385. Cowlam explained that "my brother acting on my urgent request that he should obtain some information of the doings of the Fenian Assembly seems to have excited himself somewhat, and, as he says, the expenditure of $385.00 only represents the money part of the cost." After reading through some of the circulars, Cowlam believed that they contained information of some importance, and offered to follow up on the matter when he returned to the United States on June 6. He explained that since "George has a foothold with some one there I feel sure we shall succeed in obtaining such information as will be of importance to the Govt." In parting, Cowlam thanked Hartington for the "very kind and considerate manner in which you have been pleased to express yourself regarding my efforts, and only regretting that I have not been of more service—although I have done what little I could find to do as well as I was able."[62] Atwell Lake sent Cowlam his final paycheck drawn on the Bank of Ireland and informed him "that the extra charge made in your account cannot be entertained by the authorities."[63]

Without inside information from George intercepted from the telegraph wires, Charles possessed no special advantages in his detective work. His efforts at cloak-and-dagger gave him a mysterious quality that bolstered his claims to expertise and made his stories more convincing. Government officials in three countries were captivated by Cowlam's charm, connections, and sense of urgency. His efforts to secure a position with the Canadian government failed when Fenian threats in the Midwest failed to materialize. As a revenue detective for the Internal Revenue Service he seemed to make an earnest effort at an honest living for a time, exposing frauds among federal officials before committing some of his own on the side. In the United Kingdom Cowlam seemed to float aimlessly without a clear sense of purpose or direction. Clearly unqualified and without any privileged information to sustain him, his employment there was short-lived.

Carte de visite of an unidentified man, matching descriptions of
Charles Cowlam, and found alongside photographs of his first wife, Mary Ives
Cowlam, and her family. Courtesy of the Charles Family Photographs,
South Caroliniana Library, University of South Carolina.

Elizabeth Cowlam Woodhams, Charles's younger sister, with her son, Edward LeGrand Woodhams. Courtesy of Susan A. Gehrman.

The Virginia State Penitentiary as it appeared in April 1865. Cowlam spent nearly six years in prison there between 1857 and 1863. Courtesy of the Library of Congress Prints and Photographs Division.

Castle Thunder, the notorious Richmond prison where Cowlam spent Christmas 1864. Courtesy of the Library of Congress Prints and Photographs Division.

Francis W. Kellogg, the Michigan congressman who lobbied for Cowlam's pardon and recommended his employment as a detective in Ireland. Courtesy of the Brady-Handy Photograph Collection, Library of Congress Prints and Photographs Division.

Spencer Compton Cavendish, the Marquess of Hartington and later 8th Duke of Devonshire. Lord Hartington hired Cowlam as a detective while serving as chief secretary for Ireland. Author's collection.

Harrison Reed, the governor of Florida who recruited Cowlam's help in his scheme to remove federal officeholders and swing the election for the Democrats. Courtesy of the Wisconsin Historical Society.

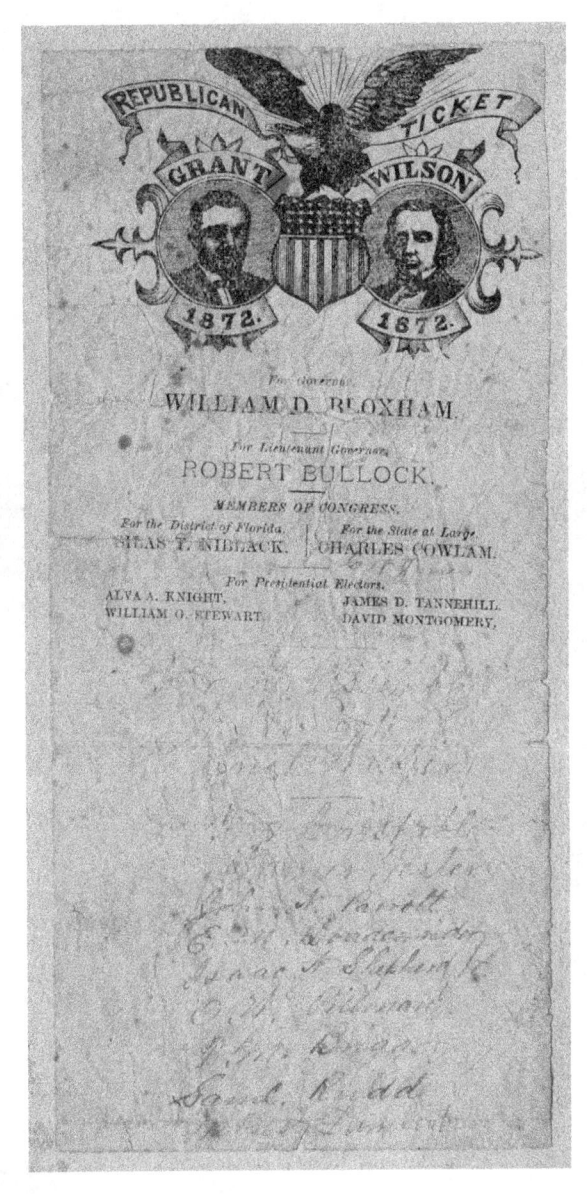

Florida Republican ticket, 1872. The broadside combines the Republican nominees for president and vice president along with the Democratic candidates for state and congressional offices. Cowlam's name appears crossed out, with C[harles] W. Jones written underneath. Courtesy of the State Library and Archives of Florida.

Ira Shafer, the pugnacious attorney who exposed Cowlam's frauds in New York. Reprinted from David McAdam et al., eds., *History of the Bench and Bar of New York* (New York: New York History Company, 1897), 2:355.

Mary Ives Cowlam, Charles's first wife, who filed suit against him for bigamy. Courtesy of the Charles Family Photographs, South Caroliniana Library, University of South Carolina.

"Old Soldiers at Dinner" in the Central Branch soldiers' home in Dayton, Ohio. At forty-eight years old, and claiming to be a forty-one-year-old colonel, Cowlam would have appeared to be one of the youngest inmates in the home. Author's collection.

FOUR
CANDIDATE

> Money, you think, is the sole motive to pains and hazard, deception and devilry, in this world. How much money did the devil make by gulling Eve?
> —HERMAN MELVILLE, *The Confidence Man: His Masquerade* (1857)

In late 1871 the Republican governor of Florida, Harrison Reed, was concerned about his political future. Reed was a small man with a slight build. He sported a bushy chin-strap beard that, when coupled with his prominent forehead, thin lips, and the small, round eyeglasses he wore, gave him a look that contemporaries sometimes described as resembling an owl. His demeanor was calm and business-like, perhaps as a consequence of his New England origins or his years as a journalist and small business owner in Wisconsin. As governor he presided over one of the stormiest periods of the state's history. Whereas Republicans had united behind him in 1868 as a compromise candidate, Reed's tenure as governor had courted controversy and fueled opposition from seemingly every corner. The coalition of freedmen, carpetbaggers, conservatives, and southern Unionists that elevated him into the governor's office proved a difficult alliance to maintain. While Black voters had provided the strongest base of support in his election, the governor often paid lip service to Black leaders, appointing carpetbaggers and former Confederates to fill the state's offices and vetoing much of the civil rights legislation that crossed his desk. He had already been threatened with impeachment three times, including one state Senate trial that resulted in a conviction vacated by the state supreme court, and he would soon face a fourth effort to remove him from office. He lamented that he had faced three years of intense opposition where he had hoped to govern with bipartisan cooperation. Having lost the confidence of his party, Reed seemed destined to serve out his term as a lame-duck governor in the coming year.[1]

In soliciting feedback on his political prospects, Reed contacted Edward Carrington Cabell, a Wall Street attorney and former Whig politician who supported the Democrats from afar, having long since retired from Florida politics. Cabell described the future of the Democratic Party in bleak terms. The party's repeated failure to win local elections had left a general impression that future electoral success was impracticable without "compromise or combination with a portion of the Republican party." At the same time, he emphasized that "the people of most of the Southern States are more interested in the control of their local governments than in the success of the national party to which they may belong." He felt certain that the southern Democrats would happily join with conservative Republicans to form a combination "by which the Federal Offices may be filled by the latter & the State Govts. given to the former." Cabell suggested that Reed might find common ground with his opponents in the Democratic Party without sacrificing his principles. He noted that Florida Republicans were divided in the choice of Senator Thomas W. Osborn's successor, and that some within his party wished that Reed might be elected to fill his seat in the U.S. Senate. The source of Reed's opposition, Cabell insisted, came from the tough choices and alliances he had made, and Reed himself had explained in his earlier letter that many of those decisions had been made in conflict with his own thinking. Reed clearly felt thwarted by his own party, and Cabell added, "Some of those democrats now appreciate the situation." He signaled that the leading Democrats could be trusted to send Reed to the Senate if he would "only take active & efficient measures to prevent the perpetuation of frauds at the next popular election, which will ensure a really fair election & returns, and give a faithful expression of the pride of the people, by which they believe they will secure a majority of votes for their candidates for *state offices*." Cabell closed the letter by noting that he could not be a party to such an understanding, as he was no longer a Floridian, but he advised Reed that he maintained regular communications with many old friends in that state who could procure such an agreement.[2]

In calling for a faithful expression of popular rule in Florida, Cabell had in mind only the state's white electorate. The only way that Democratic candidates could fill the ranks of state offices would be if the state's Black voters were unable to cast their ballots freely. The frauds he alluded to are evocative of similar statements, made frequently by southern Democrats, concerning the suitability of African American voters. Many Democrats believed that Black men were unfit for the polling booth, and were convinced that Republicans manipulated gullible freedmen into voting for their party to remain in power.[3] Cabell's recommendations to Reed foreshadowed events that would materialize in the coming year. Having lost the support of his party, Reed set in motion a plan to remove his political opponents from office, dismantle the institutions that protected Black voters, and secretly swing the state elections for the Democrats with a promise that a Democratic majority in the state legislature would send him to the U.S. Senate. Cowlam would act as Reed's right-hand man in carrying out the plan, operating in the shadows at first before making a grand entrance in the months before the election. Cowlam participated in these intrigues in three acts. First, in the removal of federal officeholders to weaken the governor's opposition and sever the flow of local information to Washington. Second, by presenting himself as a candidate for office on an unsanctioned fusion ticket designed to trick unsuspecting voters into casting their ballots for Democratic state nominees. And finally, Cowlam helped Reed remove Republican county commissioners and replace them with Democrats in a last-ditch effort to steal the election.

Although historians of Florida politics have chronicled many of the carpetbagger intrigues surrounding the 1872 election, Cowlam's involvement has always been treated as a footnote to the campaign. Reed's decision to recommend his appointment as a U.S. marshal seems like a bizarre decision made by a lame-duck governor who had lost the support of his party and appeared determined to sabotage its prospects by appointing a politically unconnected recent arrival. In truth, Reed's appointment was cunningly calculated as part of a larger strategy to swing the state elections for the Democrats in exchange for sending him to the U.S. Senate. Though his actions appeared unbalanced in the lead-up to the election, the governor was simply tilting the scales for his rivals to deliver on a bargain he negotiated months before. Cowlam's involvement in Reed's schemes produced a peculiar partnership. Before becoming governor, Reed had served previously as a special agent for the Post Office Department. His duties would have included investigating crimes against the post office. It is remarkable to think that a former special agent had teamed up with a convicted mail robber. Cowlam had likely arrived in Florida in June 1872, after returning from the United Kingdom. It is not clear how Reed and Cowlam first became acquainted, but it is likely that the pair met while Cowlam worked as a detective for the Internal Revenue Service, as his district encompassed Georgia and Florida.[4]

PRELIMINARY MANEUVERS

The 1872 election exposed fissures in the Republican Party. Even before the Republicans could nominate Grant for reelection, a faction calling themselves the Liberal Republicans held a separate convention in Cincinnati and nominated Horace Greeley, the editor and founder of the *New York Tribune,* for president. When the Democrats organized their convention later that summer, they coalesced behind Greeley in the hopes that a combined ticket might prevail. The Liberal Republicans sought an alliance with southern Democrats that would offer home rule and amnesty to former Confederates, in exchange for promises that the latter would uphold the Reconstruction amendments to the Constitution. The platform rested on the belief that northern carpetbaggers had encouraged corruption and lawlessness, and the expectation that self-government would curtail Reconstruction's excesses if only the "best men" of the South could be restored to political favor. Effectively, the Liberal Republicans proposed an end of federal oversight if white southerners would promise to respect some African American rights. Black voters saw clearly that such a compromise would mean the end of Reconstruction. The lone Black member of Florida's Republican State Executive Committee, Jacob D. Enos, considered the prospect of African Americans voting for Greeley as "simply rediculous [sic] to even *think* about."[5]

Within the Republican Party, the state's federal officeholders were the most vocal opponents of Governor Reed's administration. Although these officials always denied that they represented an organized faction, observers frequently described them as members of the "Ring." Many considered Senator Osborn to be the unofficial leader of the group. Whereas Reed claimed to represent a broad coalition, and adopted a halfhearted endorsement of Reconstruction in his strained effort to please all sides, the Ring represented the radical wing of the Republican Party and was composed primarily of carpetbaggers. Reed declared war on the Ring almost as soon as he took office. One of Reed's first acts as governor was to purge the state legislature of officeholders who held joint appointments, declaring that all seats occupied by those holding another state or federal office simultaneously would be considered vacant. Reed's shakeup in the state legislature threatened the future of Osborn's position in the Senate, as Osborn had been elected before Reed's political maneuvering. As long as Reed remained at the helm, Osborn's tenure seemed uncertain. In anticipation of the 1872 election, Reed's opponents launched a renewed effort to impeach and remove him from office. The state House of Representatives impeached him unanimously on February 10 on sixteen counts, including embezzlement, bribery, and corruption.[6]

Reed's enemies did not actually need to remove him from office to restrain his influence. The state's constitution prescribed that "any officer when impeached by the assembly shall be deemed under arrest and shall be disqualified from performing any duties of his office until acquittal by the Senate." This clause created an interesting loophole, whereby the legislature could impeach Reed and postpone convening a Senate trial indefinitely, having already achieved their object of removing him from office. The 1872 impeachment trial was complicated, however, by the fact that a Democrat had a claim to the lieutenant governorship. Although Republican Samuel T. Day was the presumptive winner in 1870, Democrat William D. Bloxham had challenged the legitimacy of the results before the state supreme court, and the outcome was still pending at the time of Reed's second impeachment trial. If Bloxham's claim was upheld, Reed's removal could result in a Democratic governor who would disrupt the balance of power. Republicans in the state Senate elected to tread carefully, as the party held a slim majority of only one vote. Rather than take the risk of pursuing the case against Reed, the impeachment managers adjourned with no indication of when the proceedings might resume. Reed interpreted the legislature's adjournment as an acquittal, and waited until the lieutenant governor had left the capital, whereupon he returned to his former offices and proclaimed himself governor. Reed then appealed to the state supreme court to issue an opinion clarifying his status. The Reed-appointed court sided with the governor, ruling that his subordinate had merely been carrying out his duties in his absence.[7]

Once acquitted, Reed found himself in a unique position to undermine the state's electoral integrity. The Florida state constitution granted the governor extraordinary powers over the state's officeholders. The governor had the power to appoint and remove county commissioners, whose duties included organizing voting precincts and appointing election supervisors. Local officials that canvassed at the county level, including sheriffs, clerks of the court, and justices of the peace, also served at the governor's behest. In Governor Reed's hands, these officeholders served as political machinery that could undermine the Republican Party's efforts. One federal official in Florida emphasized that many of these officeholders held their positions as interim appointments. They were "creatures of his appointment—and his *will.*"[8]

By the spring and early summer, rumors circulated that Reed was marshalling his appointment powers to gradually replace Republican county election supervisors with Democrats. One county clerk doubted the prudence of Reed's strategy, proposing that if Reed truly wished to defeat the Ring, he should appoint moderate Republicans rather than untrustworthy Democrats who might double-cross the governor and bring down the Republican Party.[9] Reed announced his plan publicly in early July in an address he gave in Gainesville, where he proposed that while the majority of the county commissioners should hail from the Republican ranks, he believed that two-fifths of them should in fairness represent "the conservative element."[10]

Reed believed that the state's federal officeholders had conspired against him during his impeachment inquiry, and the governor now hatched a conspiracy of his own. He petitioned President Ulysses S. Grant to remove the "thieves and villains" who had led the charge against him.[11] This was not the first time that Reed had attempted to remove the state's federal officeholders. Reed had written to Grant two years earlier to accuse federal officeholders of colluding with the Democrats in an effort to impeach him. Although Grant took no action on Reed's demands in 1870, the aftermath of the second impeachment trial gave Reed additional leverage that he lacked in his earlier bout with the federal officeholders.[12]

On July 6, Reed wrote to Grant requesting the removal of William J. Purman as assessor of internal revenue and recommending John Tyler Jr. as his replacement. In addition to his position in the Treasury Department, Purman served as chairman of the Republican State Executive Committee, whose members aligned themselves with the state's federal officeholders. Reed told

Grant that "Purman is a dishonest, treacherous disorganizer, and sustains position here only through the office he holds at your hands."[13] Simon B. Conover, the state treasurer and a Reed supporter, added that members of the Ring now sought to "throw distracting influences into the State nominating convention of the 7th August, and are using their official patronage to that end, in which, if they succeed, the Party will be defeated in the fall election and the State be lost to your Excellency."[14] Grant consented to Reed's recommendation, and replaced Purman with Tyler on July 24. Members of the Ring worried that other removals might soon follow.[15]

Tyler was the second-oldest son of the tenth president of the United States. For much of his life he practiced law and held various odd jobs, but often lost them due to his lifelong struggle with alcoholism. In his early career he served as a captain in the Mexican-American War, and worked as his father's private secretary until he was fired for "general inefficiency." During the Civil War he served briefly as the Confederate assistant secretary of war and as an officer in the Confederate army. When the war ended he became a Republican and fervent supporter of Grant. Having arrived in Florida within the year, Tyler established himself as the editor of the *Tallahassee Sentinel* and aligned himself with the Reed wing of the Republican Party. He corresponded regularly with Reed and Cowlam regarding their movements in "the political game."[16]

In anticipation of the Republican state nominating convention on August 7, the party's leaders wondered whether Reed would do his part to maintain party unity and support the nominees for state office. The governor had not yet declared his intentions, although everyone knew that Reed stood no chance of being renominated. Reed's newest appointee, John Tyler Jr., had also refused to endorse any candidates, declaring that he would wait until after the Democratic convention met on August 14 to announce his decision. Senator Osborn wrote to William E. Chandler, the secretary of the Republican National Committee, to inform him that all of the state's Republicans had united and agreed to work together, with the exception of Reed, who remained "the only dissenter & is very obstinate and is stumping the state against every body & both parties." If Reed and his supporters persisted, their actions threatened to fracture the Republican Party and make "each man a candidate for governor who has one county back of him & from that hope he can win on a general demoralization of the con[vention]." Osborn described Tyler as "a new comer & most desperate drunkard, disorganizer & vicious man" and claimed that Tyler had threatened to remove every Grant officeholder in the state "if matters do not go to suit him" at the Republican convention, adding that "judging from his own absurd and idiotic appt. it looks as though it might be true." Even the recently removed Purman suggested that a prominent federal appointment might placate Reed and bring him back into the fold, insisting that the "the next Administration can certainly find some nooks in which to stow Harrison Reed 'during good behavior.'"[17]

The delegates at the Republican state nominating convention met in the Hall of Representatives in the state capitol and initially gravitated toward the state's surveyor general, Marcellus L. Stearns, for governor in an informal ballot and on the first formal ballot. Stearns, who had lost an arm at the Battle of Winchester, surprised everyone by withdrawing his name from consideration at the last moment in favor of Ossian Bingley Hart, who received the second highest number of votes. Hart was a southern Unionist on the state supreme court.[18] The convention then unanimously nominated Stearns for lieutenant governor and Josiah T. Walls for Congress. Walls was the first African American congressman elected from Florida. The census of 1870 had awarded Florida a second congressional seat, and an informal ballot revealed strong support for Robert Meacham, the African American superintendent of common schools for Jefferson County. After several competitors withdrew their names, the delegates who had supported other candidates rallied behind William J. Purman, who Grant had recently removed as assessor of internal revenue. On the second day of the convention Governor Reed gave a "short but excellent speech and was loudly applauded at its close." The delegates then adopted a resolution expressing their unwavering confidence in Reed's character and pledged "to stand by him in the future as long as he stands by the principles of the party."[19]

Cowlam wrote to Tyler on August 22, informing him that the Liberal Republicans in Florida were planning to make their own state ticket rather than align themselves with the Democrats. If they did so, Cowlam believed that the Republicans would win handily. The Democrats had nominated a slate of candidates that Senator Osborn described as a "straight-out radical rebel ticket," and Cowlam believed that Liberal Republicans could never stomach combining with them unless the ticket were altered, noting that "Daily scores of letters come from all over the State begging that something be done to change the complexion of the Dem. State Ticket so more good Republicans can see a way to aid in the defeat of this Ring without sacrificing all party feeling principle and spirit."[20]

Making the Democratic ticket palatable for the Liberal Republicans would require substantial effort. One concern that impeded their collaboration was Silas L. Niblack's effort to contest Josiah T. Walls's seat in the House of Representatives that had been ongoing since the election of 1870. Walls was not affiliated with the Ring and had expressed willingness to compromise with Reed, and his removal would have been very unpopular among Republicans. Cowlam suggested, "If Niblack has the foolish idea that Congress can work a reversal of its act sustaining Walls he must be soft in the head—such arrant nonsense is no excuse at all. Well, Jones is not so afflicted; is he? Guess not." Niblack and Charles W. Jones were the Democratic nominees for Congress in 1872. Cowlam noted that Reed had suggested that the sheriff of Tallahassee, Alvin B. Munger, might be able to mediate the situation and "may be able to do some little good in the matter." Cowlam closed his letter ominously, noting that "you will find very shortly that other influences will be brought to bear on them to bring them where we want them."[21]

Cowlam's solution soon became evident when he made clear his intentions to run for Congress. On August 23 Cowlam met with Wilkinson Call, a Jacksonville attorney, who conducted a lengthy interview to discuss the prospect of a fusion ticket. Call often had a manner of speaking that one contemporary described as floating "amid the ethereal realms of astounding rhetoric, soaring aloft into the ambiguous glossary, so incomprehensive to the illiterate portion of his hearers," but he seemed caught off guard by the proposal.[22] Bloxham had written to Call before their meeting but had only hinted at the plan Cowlam had prepared. Cowlam told Tyler that Call seemed to favor the idea, but "desired to know if anything but the nomination to Congress would do me—I told him there was nothing else. I have views which I can only carry out by going to Congress and will accept nothing else." In a postscript Cowlam added "as to my being acceptable to the Liberal Republicans you can say that I am. I have seen the leading men—or my friends have, and they are anxious that some northern man be put on the ticket—they want only the man who can carry strength enough to make the ticket win. Put your best zeal out on this General and we will win."[23]

Governor Reed expressed reservations about Cowlam's strategy. In two letters to Tyler he described the plan underway to create a third ticket and ventured, "I doubt if the C[owlam]. project can be carried. I have no fear of C[owlam]. playing false, but see that it would hardly be possible to induce the Bourbons to accept him." The Bourbons represented the conservative wing of the Democratic Party, who would have been less inclined to compromise with Reed Republicans. In the same breath Reed exclaimed that he had been offered $25,000 to resign, but stated, "I cannot consider as matters now stand." Reed ventured that "the situation can be adjusted either with or without Colam [sic]," and he described his plan to push the Democrats to meet them halfway and accept Halstead H. Hoeg for lieutenant governor and Jonathan Clarkson Gibbs for Congress. The governor even considered the possibility of Tyler as a candidate, reasoning, "If the conservatives will take you it will be satisfactory to me, but I fear it would baracade [sic] you with Genl Grant & will also weaken me in that division." In encouraging Tyler to keep this information confidential, he added, "Colam is a little to [sic] open & 'brash,'" and he expressed amusement that Cowlam had "telegraphed a canard for effect yesterday. I doubt the policy, but let it serve." Reed concluded the letter "burn this."[24]

On August 26, Cowlam was still waiting to hear news of his nomination. He described a meeting taking place that afternoon between Bloxham and Samuel T. Day that he believed would produce an agreement between the Reed Republicans and the Democrats. By this time the state supreme court had upheld Bloxham's claim, and this meeting between Reed's current and former lieutenant governors from opposing parties was a curious sight. The only point in which all parties "seem to hang fine on is whether—in event of their doing what we desire—R[eed]. will do his part." He told Tyler that he expected to learn whether his congressional aspirations would be sanctioned once the meeting concluded, emphasizing, "we must work them straight through until they decide finally—if against us, then I'll bring up my reserve and flank the whole line. I can do it and *will* do it." Cowlam enclosed an outline of the arrangement the parties agreed to on a separate page, explaining how Bloxham would prepare the names of two men he desired appointed in each county, along with one Republican who would work with the conservatives to secure a majority on each board of county commissioners. The same formula repeated in the case of the inspectors of elections, which would consist of one Republican, one conservative, and one Republican "who will act with the Conservatives—thus keeping a majority of men favorable to Conservative interests in charge of the Polls. This will utterly nullify the presence of Inspectors sent by the 'Ring' under the direction of [U.S. Marshal Sherman] Conant." It is remarkable that Cowlam would so brazenly outline the process by which Reed planned to undermine the election and circumvent the U.S. marshal. Cowlam suggested that the list of names should be put forward immediately and the appointments introduced gradually so as not to attract attention, adding that the "Governor will appoint every man desired by B[loxham]. in the manner aforesaid."[25]

Cowlam's intrigues soon attracted the attention of the Ring. Senator Osborn wrote to Chandler, the secretary of the Republican National Committee, on August 27 to inform him of a recent arrival in Florida politics. Osborn noted that "there is a man here by the name of Chas. Cowlam whom I understand is in the secrete [*sic*] service of the Govt. This is all well enough but he is meddling in the political affairs of the state in such a manner as to be very injurious to us. The details it is not necessary to state but his action so far is pernicious." Osborn continued, "If the man is here as a political looker on then I have no objection but would only say he is more fool than detective." He asked Chandler to look into the matter and "if he is not sent here for purely political have him ordered from the state at once." Osborn mentioned that Cowlam had not yet spoken with any member of the State Executive Committee about the campaign, so he could not report what Cowlam's intentions or plans were, but that he had already presented himself as "a go between for the sore heads & democrats." Chandler docketed the back of the letter with the summary "has the nightmare in regard to a 'Times' reporter," suggesting that Chandler believed that Cowlam was merely a journalist.[26]

Although Reed had brokered an understanding with the Democrats, the alliance proved to be frustrating for both parties. Neither Lieutenant Governor Bloxham nor Governor Reed could openly advocate for one another's interests, lest their adversaries discover their collaboration. On September 3, Reed reported to Tyler, "It will never do for B[loxham]. to take open ground for [Charles H.] Pearce unless he wishes him defeated, nor will it do for us to take the position you indicate at least for the present."[27] Pearce was a bishop in the African Methodist Episcopal Church and a state Senate candidate who had aligned himself with Reed. In subsequent letters Reed mentioned that the "conduct of the conservatives renders our situation difficult. I must either act as a Republican or resign."[28] He compared his situation as analogous to navigating between Scylla and Charybdis, a reference to two sea monsters Odysseus encountered in the *Odyssey*, and added, "There is no faith either in the Conservatives, *or* the 'ring,' & we must work independently of either as far as possible." Reed encouraged Tyler to request a leave of absence in preparation for a possible trip to Washington to plead their case. He mentioned that "Colam [*sic*] had an interview with [U.S. Marshal Sherman] Conant yesterday & he seems disposed to strike hard if possible, which is doubtful."[29]

On September 13, Tyler wrote to James M. Ray, the third deputy commissioner of internal revenue, with a proposal of a Grant reform ticket. He enclosed two letters from Reed to the Republican State Executive Committee, along with newspaper clippings that illuminated the state of Florida politics. While it seemed clear to many in Florida that Greeley would lose the national election based on the outcome of the recent state elections in Maine, he noted that many voters "feel they have no alternative other than to sustain the candidates selected for them already, rather than support those odious men forced through fraud in the Convention upon the Republican banner." A reform ticket would combine national support for Grant with a compromise slate of state candidates. The ticket "would be sustained by all the dissatisfied and all the disaffected on every side, as well as by all those who are doubting which side to take," including "All the Reed, Pearce, Gibbs, & Bradwell men, all the African Methodist Church People, all the Southern loyalists . . . together with many of the old line whigs, and not a few doubting Democrats in the opposition."[30] Here Tyler sought official authorization from Republicans in Washington to proceed with the fusion ticket that Reed and the Democrats had envisioned. News of Tyler's proposal made its way to Chandler at the Republican National Committee and had its intended effect. Chandler sent a telegram to Reed immediately, requesting that he apprise him of the situation in Florida, and inviting him to come north to speak on southern issues.[31]

U.S. MARSHAL

Reed informed Tyler on September 18 that he had dispatched Cowlam to New York on a secret mission to meet with Chandler, adding, "but of course the public must understand he goes to Key West."[32] At the same time Reed sent a letter to Chandler explaining that he had sent Cowlam north to update him on the recent developments in Florida. "If you can give us Mr. Cowlam for U.S. Marshal & F.B. Basnett," Reed proposed, "I can secure this state to Genl Grant without question & a Legislature which will send a good Republican to the Senate."[33] Reed added a postscript to the margin of the page, indicating, "if this can be done I can speak in New York or elsewhere & fully refute the calumnies of Greeley & Brown." Here Reed offered his assurances that he would fall in line and support the Republican platform if Grant would make the appointments he recommended.[34] After meeting with Cowlam in New York, Chandler wrote letters to the president and the attorney general supporting Cowlam's appointment as U.S. marshal and requesting that each of them meet with Cowlam personally. Chandler explained to Grant that "from my knowledge of affairs in Florida I am confident Govr Reeds recommendation should be carried out . . . Mr. Cowlam is personally known to me as an energetic and capable person who will make an officer of unusual ability." In his letter to the attorney general, Chandler described Cowlam as "the accredited representative of Governor Reed" and added, "I am sure the Governor is entitled to consideration from the administration and I think his recommendations should be carried out."[35]

Cowlam sent a telegram to Chandler on September 25 informing him that the attorney general was ready to issue the commissions as soon as the president would send him a telegram ordering U.S. Attorney Horatio Bisbee's and U.S. Marshal Sherman Conant's removal. He asked Chandler to send word to Grant and instructed him to notify him at Massachusetts Congressman Benjamin Butler's office in Washington so that he could leave that evening and return to Florida.[36] The next day Cowlam sent a telegram from Butler's office. He was still waiting for the attorney general to issue the order, and indicated his intention to leave the city before the president returned to Washington. He requested that Chandler contact General Ely S. Parker and to apprise him when the order was issued.[37] Grant returned to Washington on September 27, and the following day Cowlam wrote to Chandler informing him that, after meeting personally with Grant, Parker, and Acting Attorney General Clement Hugh Hill, he had at last received their approval.[38] On September 28, Ulysses S. Grant appointed Cowlam to serve as U.S. marshal for the Northern District of Florida.[39]

The biographer Ron Chernow notes that "the mystery of Grant's presidency is how this upright man tolerated some of the arrant rascals collected around him." Grant had a trusting nature and a sense of discernment that often failed him. To insulate his decisions from political influence, Grant sometimes made appointments without consulting party bosses or members of Congress. By sidestepping the traditional appointment conduits, Grant believed that he would make more objective decisions based on merit. Yet isolating himself from these partisan channels made the president oblivious to the local knowledge they offered, and susceptible to intriguers like Cowlam with thin connections and a patina of respectability. Chernow adds that the "con artist and the scoundrel always found a ready target in U.S. Grant."[40]

News of Bisbee's and Conant's removal unleashed a deluge of controversy in Florida. A Democratic newspaper speculated that "Grant must have been decidedly drunk" when he made the decision to remove Conant and Bisbee.[41] It seemed as though every Republican in the state wrote to Grant to protest their removal. Much of the criticism centered on Conant's and Bisbee's effectiveness, and Cowlam's and Basnett's inexperience. One Republican emphasized that Cowlam "is scarcely known in Florida, is a non-resident of the state, has rendered no service toward Reconstruction there, and his appointment will be unsatisfactory and detrimental in many regards."[42] Others criticized the president's decision to swap officers weeks before an important election without consulting anyone in their camp. A Republican in the U.S. attorney's office in Jacksonville, described the removals as "a sad mistake." "We have too many bad men in office, to be willing to have an honest one removed as long as he is willing to stay in," he emphasized.[43] Edward M. Cheney, the newly elected chairman of the Republican State Executive Committee of Florida, wrote to Chandler at the Republican National Committee on October 3, emphasizing that Conant had been "an efficient officer and constant terror to the Ku Klux and other evil doers." Bisbee had performed his duties promptly and "is more hated by the elements than any other man in the state." Cheney could not understand why the two officials had been removed, and suggested that this attack on party unity would cost the Republican Party thousands of votes in November.[44]

Alva A. Knight, one of Grant's presidential electors and judge of the Fourth Judicial Circuit Court of Florida, stressed that Conant and Bisbee were indispensable in safeguarding Reconstruction. He described his return home after a successful canvass in west Florida to draw attention to the sacrifices that he and other Republicans had made, and to highlight the unfinished work in the South. In Milton, in Santa Rosa County, white southerners shot at the canvassers, seriously wounding three of them. Knight underscored that the "spirit of opposition is not extinct." He had returned to Jacksonville via Macon and Columbus in time to witness the state elections in Georgia. All of the men he encountered at the train stations were Democrats, and they assumed Knight was one of theirs. From engaging them in conversation he quickly learned that the whites had all conspired to prevent African Americans from voting. Some of the men in Macon "boasted of the success in causing a riot & rejoiced in the number of 'niggers' killed and wounded." Judge Knight warned that with Conant and Bisbee removed, the "rebels" would have nothing to fear in repeating the same outrages in Florida. The only power that white southerners respected, Knight argued, were the federal courts. As marshal and attorney Conant and Bisbee had prosecuted cases against the Ku Klux Klan. Without them in office, the Republicans could lose their slim majorities in the state and Reconstruction could fail.[45]

By October 4 Cowlam had arrived in Savannah, and news of his appointment spread quickly to his former associates in that city. Walter M. Walsh, a local druggist and physician, heard Cowlam boasting of his appointment and immediately telegraphed the attorney general to inform him of Cowlam's earlier blackmailing of John N. Muller. Telegrams flooded in from the Treasury Department and soon made their way to the attorney general. Even Muller's attorney wrote to furnish details from the case. Special Agent Moses H. Hale telegraphed his superiors, "I do not hesitate, on my own knowledge, to pronounce [Cowlam] a fraud. The evidence of his blackmailing the late John N Muller of this City was developed in a trial in this city in the United States District Court; he is well known here and his appointment to those who know him is a great surprise. Unless these appointments are stopped at once Florida will go Democratic." Special Agent Charles S. Park recalled a conversation he had a day or two before in the portico of the Savannah Customs House, in which "Cowlam said that he was interested in these southern states until the 5th of next November at sundown and no longer, and after that he didn't care who had his place."[46] Cowlam's bragging makes clear that he recognized how his position as marshal could be used to influence the November elections.

In a matter of days Republicans in Florida had pieced together a rough outline of Reed's conspiracy, and rumors circulated about Cowlam's involvement and his past. Some of the gossip was muddled, but it is clear that someone had discovered his criminal history. Senator Osborn alerted the attorney general that Cowlam had "served two years in Jackson Mich[igan] penitentiary."[47] Osborn's former secretary, Morris H. Alberger, noted, "I have heard it publicly stated on the Street that Mr. C[owlam] is debarred by law from holding any office of profit or trust in the U.S."[48] Florida state legislator William K. Cessna accused Governor Reed of having bribed state senators to vote against his impeachment in 1870. He described Tyler, Gibbs, Adams, and the state supreme court's chief justice, Edwin M. Randall, as his accomplices in this latest act of subterfuge, but he reserved his harshest criticism for Tyler, who he portrayed as "a notorious 'drunken sot'—who has been picked upon the streets of Tallahassee and dumped into a wheelbarrow and wheeled like so much litter to his office and dumped out." Cessna emphasized that "Conant with the Marshalship is to the Republicans of Florida what Genls Sherman and Sheridan were to you in the armies of the Tennessee and the Valley of Virginia."[49]

Others in Florida had a clearer understanding of the nature of Reed's and Cowlam's intrigues. One Republican told Grant that the entire scheme had been concocted by Reed "through his tool Tyler, and one or two others" to elect the Democratic ticket and return Reed to the Senate. He added that he regarded Reed as dishonest to his core, noting, "I told that man before he was Governor, I, would not believe him under Oath, and although I have met him almost daily, I never recognized him, I not only regard him in the highest degree untruthful, but *as dishonest* as *a man can be.*"[50] State Executive Committee chairman Edward Cheney explained in a follow-up letter that he was flabbergasted by the nominations. He now suspected that Chandler had known about the appointments before they were issued, and could not believe what he was hearing from Washington. Cheney indicated that he had reason to believe that Governor Reed had contacted "certain leading democrats" and negotiated a deal whereby he would secure the removal of Conant and Bisbee in exchange for the Democrats supporting Reed for the U.S. Senate. He emphasized, "I know that Reed is working solely to secure his election to the Senate and he recently stated that he meant to go there even if he had to elect Bloxham . . . to do it." Cheney explained that the Republican Party's electoral success in the state was totally reliant on the African American vote, noting, "we never expected to and we cannot in any way gain many votes from the opposition. . . . All we wanted was to pull our full colored vote which would have given us a majority." Without Conant and Bisbee projecting the power of the federal courts, Black voter turnout could not be counted upon. Cheney described Cowlam as "formerly a detective in the Rev. service" who had "come here some months ago and spent all his time . . . in consultation with Gov Reed and the leading democrats, and at the time, in connection with Gov Reed endeavored to induce the democrats to put his (Cowlam) name on the democratic ticket as a candidate of Congress."[51]

Judge Knight threatened to resign as an elector for Grant unless the administration reversed its course and restored Conant and Bisbee to favor. He described Basnett as "a young man some twenty-three or four years of age connected with all the leading Rebels in this county." Knight pointed out that Basnett had entered into a law partnership with Wilkinson Call, who headed the electoral ticket for Greeley. Several weeks previously Knight had asked Basnett to become a member of the Grant and Wilson Club in Jacksonville, but Basnett declined, stating that joining the organization might damage his reputation in the city. To refute the charge that Knight and his associates were carpetbaggers, the judge noted that while he had lived in Florida for eleven years, Basnett had arrived the year before and Cowlam had shown up the previous month. Knight emphasized that the removal of Republican officeholders had already demoralized the party. A canvass event the previous day proved a total failure after the candidates were all too discouraged to attend. Knight noted that "our vote is worth but little in the Electoral College, we would gladly cost it for the administration if the administration will let us but I fear we shall now have to pack up, leave the state & let the Greeley ticket have its own way."[52]

On October 9 the recently removed Bisbee suggested that the only reason that the state convention had endorsed Reed was to prevent his manipulation of the county election commissioners. Bisbee added, "Reed has asserted that he would use his power, to elect Bloxham, if it was necessary to *serve him a Senatorship*" and "the democratic leaders know that if we are out, their rank and file will not hesitate to use violence at the pools [sic] & drive republicans away—just as it has recently been done in Ga." Their removal made clear to him that "Grant does *not understand* the situation & has *been deceived* grossly." He clarified that Cowlam "is a stranger here, but we know enough of him to know that he is utterly unworthy." The shake-up in the Justice Department had even led him to question his faith in Osborn's leadership, remarking that "*Osborn is weaker here now than ever. Conant himself* has lost all *confidence in him as a political power.* I will not, I think, support him for reelection."[53]

Cowlam described the reaction in Florida very differently. In a statement endorsed by Reed and forwarded to Chandler, Cowlam noted that he had returned to Jacksonville on October 5 and "found, as I expected, a little local stir over the removals of Conant & Bisbee." Cowlam attributed the fuss to "one or two badly disappointed worn out politicians" who had opposed the Reed administration at every step. He noted that these men had been "writing and telegraphing to Washington all sorts of stuff greatly to the amusement of Gov. Reed and the real leaders and controllers of the Republican Party in this State." He assured Chandler that true Republicans considered the removals "as the best act done by President Grant for the good of this State and for the good of the party during the past four years," and added, "you need not heed the clamor of the disappointed and defeated rogues whose plans of rascality have been foiled by the timely interference of the President." Cowlam explained that he and Reed had been "working in perfect harmony" with state Republicans to carry the election for Grant, and underscored this by remarking, "We receive by daily mail hundreds of letters from the *working* Republicans of the State congratulating us on our success."[54]

To counterbalance the torrent of telegrams and letters calling for Basnett's and Cowlam's removal, friends of Reed took up their pens in support of the new appointments. John S. Adams, who served simultaneously as state commissioner of immigration and as the federal collector of customs, congratulated Grant on the removals. He cited Reed's endorsement by the Republican State Convention in August as evidence of the governor's popularity despite the several unsuccessful impeachment efforts initiated against him by his enemies. Although Adams acknowledged that the recent removals had jeopardized the state's Republican ticket, he argued that the governor's "friends look upon the changes made as practically endorsing him and will take hold with new zeal." Adams expressed hope that Osborn would soon be replaced in the Senate and accompanied by two new Republican congressmen.[55]

Cowlam wrote to Chandler on October 8 asking him to "keep Gen. Grant advised through Gen. [Horace] Porter of the tricks of this crowd of thieves." Their adversaries were "telegraphing in the names of all sorts of people all sorts of rubbish to Gen. Grant, don't let such trash influence him." By then Grant had already rescinded Basnett's nomination, and Cowlam pleaded, "if I am sustained it is all that is asked."[56] Cowlam also penned a letter to Reed the same day noting that Osborn's former secretary had raised the money for Congressman Walls to travel to Washington "to undo our work." He noted that Judge Knight would likely accompany Walls, and accused Knight of having been under indictment for mail robbery. Cowlam enclosed an example of messages being sent to Washington, and claimed that Knight had authored numerous telegrams and encouraged others to sign them to give the appearance of widespread support for Conant's and Bisbee's reinstatement.[57] Curiously, Cowlam also sent an appeal to the attorney general the same day requesting copies of federal laws pertaining to elections. In particular, Cowlam wished to know "information relative to the appointment of special deputy marshals to preserve order at the polls on election day, the matter having been brought to my notice by the Governor of this State."[58] The request looks suspicious in light of Cowlam's collaboration with Reed to replace local election supervisors with Democrats. It is telling that his first formal request was to solicit information that he could have used to interfere in the coming election.

Days after news of their removal reached them, Bisbee and Conant made appearances at the Grant and Wilson Club of Jacksonville. Both men pledged to continue their work to ensure the success of the Republican ticket, and their brief remarks received ample cheers from the audience. After one club member proposed to draft resolutions expressing the organization's disapproval of the removals, three men adjourned to write them, and upon their return the members adopted the resolutions unanimously. To carry the message to Grant, Congressman Walls left Jacksonville for Washington on October 7 and arrived on the morning of October 10. He met with Grant as soon as he arrived, and sent a telegram to Conant at 11 a.m. informing him that the removals had been reversed. In anticipation of Walls's return to Florida, Jacob D. Enos called for the principal African American Republicans to organize a reception for Walls at the Planter's Hotel. Walls returned a day earlier than expected, but on the evening of October 14 the hotel was decorated elegantly with flags, wreaths, flowers, and a life-size portrait of Walls above the mantlepiece. Flags of Ulysses S. Grant and Henry Wilson adorned the second story piazza. Waiters in white coats and aprons served the distinguished guests, which included nearly all of the state's prominent Republicans. The Union Brass Band surprised the attendees with a spontaneous rendition of "Hail to the Chief," and festivities continued into the early hours of the morning.[59]

While Walls was in Washington, Reed requested a meeting with the State Executive Committee to deliver an ultimatum. In the preceding week he had continued to give speeches denouncing members of the Ring, and he now believed he had sufficient leverage to pressure them into changing the party's nominees. With all of the committee members and state candidates assembled, Chairman Cheney recalled how Reed demanded that "unless all he wanted was conceded to him, he would resign as governor and leave the state in the hands of Bloxham." Before the meeting could conclude, a telegram from Walls arrived announcing Conant's and Bisbee's reinstatement. Upon hearing the news, Cheney described how Reed's demeanor changed noticeably, his confidence deflated. With the wind taken out of his sails, Reed now seemingly had no choice but to work with the Republicans.[60]

In all likelihood Cowlam never received his commission before Grant rescinded it. The chief clerk transmitted Basnett's commission to him on September 30, but Cowlam's commission was not ready at that time. On October 7 the acting attorney general instructed Basnett by telegram not to assume his duties as U.S. attorney until further notice, and Grant formally revoked Cowlam's and Basnett's appointments on October 10 and 11, respectively. His commission remains undelivered in the National Archives, with "Cancelled

Oct 10th 1872 By direction of the President" written across it by Grant's secretary, Horace Porter.[61]

Reed could not blame Grant for changing his mind, but insisted in a letter to Chandler that had the president remained committed to the initial appointments for two more days, then public outcry would have dissipated. He blamed the federal officeholders, especially Osborn, for waging a war against him and breaking the promises made to him at the state nominating convention. Reed requested that the Republican National Committee withhold further funds from the State Executive Committee until Reed could make an appeal to Grant and Chandler in person to explain himself. Reed closed the letter with a Cowlamesque postscript indicating that "no letter of mine is safe at our P.O. here or at Jacksonville, nor is any telegram sound."[62]

DESPERATION

With his appointment rescinded and Reed's influence crumbling, Cowlam decided to make a run for Congress on his own. Perhaps like Horace Greeley, Cowlam may have believed that his editorial prowess made him a natural power broker. To accomplish his aims, Cowlam appealed to a group of African American Republicans who were dissatisfied with the nomination of William J. Purman for Congress. At a meeting held on October 16 in Leon County, the county that included Tallahassee, a group of Republicans chaired by Jonathan Clarkson Gibbs, the first Black secretary of state of Florida, nominated Cowlam for Congress. John W. Wyatt, an African American signer of the 1868 state constitution, served as secretary. The convention unanimously adopted resolutions announcing that Purman had been proved "unworthy of the support and confidence of the Republican Party of Florida" and nominated in his place "Charles Cowlam Esq., of Duval County." Two days later Osborn reported to Chandler that "Cowlan [*sic*] announced himself day before yesterday as candidate for Congress. Will get four or five votes. Reed gave Cowlan a letter to Bloxam [*sic*] candidate for Govr. Democratic & pledged his influence to Bloxam but says he wishes to work in the dark as he can hurt the republicans more in that way than he could openly." Osborn added, "I assure you it has been a hard and expensive fight to fight both the Governor with his long patronage and the democratic party at the same time." A week later Osborn sent a telegram to Chandler warning him that Reed had sent an agent to Washington in yet another effort to remove the U.S. marshal. He pleaded with Chandler to "stop it, a change will ruin us."[63]

The opportunity for Cowlam's candidacy materialized out of Black Floridians' disenchantment with the Republican congressional nominee, William J. Purman. The source of this antagonism originated with Purman's persecution of Bishop Charles Pearce of the African Methodist Episcopal Church. Pearce was one of only three Black state senators elected after the 1868 constitution. Although he identified at first with the radical wing of the Republican Party, he opposed the earlier efforts to remove Reed from office. When Pearce challenged the Ring faction's candidates in the bitterly contested 1870 election, Purman and Florida's surveyor general, Marcellus L. Stearns, accused Pearce of attempting to bribe a fellow state senator. Pearce was convicted of bribery in Leon County after a short trial presided over by a former Confederate. The evidence of Pearce's guilt was very thin, and he received a suspended sentence while appealing the verdict. He would later receive a pardon from the state pardoning board. Although Pearce's support for Reed had waned, and he now aligned himself with the Osborn wing of the party, resentment against Purman remained.[64] At an August 7 meeting of the African Methodist Episcopal Church in Hamilton County, which met the same day as the Republican nominating convention, the Reverend Allen Jones rebuked Purman and Stearns for their participation in Pearce's conviction. The congregants demanded that Purman's name be removed from the ticket because he had "said that Bishop Pearce was the personification of Belzebub and the A.M.E Church an incarnation of the spirit of Satan and should be crushed out."[65]

Cowlam's decision to align with the A.M.E. Church presents another peculiar partnership. Whereas A.M.E congregants resented Purman and Stearns for railroading Bishop Pearce, Reed Republicans rallied against the politicians for leading the charge in Reed's recent impeachment proceedings. As the election approached, a number of rumors surrounding Purman's candidacy surfaced in the press. The *Tallahassee Weekly Floridian* reported that Purman, "who once declared that he had 'saved the State from being niggerized,' came to Florida in 1866, as poor as a church mouse and the very personification of a carpet-bagger." The article noted that Purman worked as an officer in the Freedmen's Bureau in Jackson County and "in that capacity swindled the

Freedmen out of fees for making contracts with planters." Others claimed that Purman had amassed a fortune of $30,000 in 7 percent bonds after speculating in state scrip and reinvesting the profits. Despite his wealth, rumor had it that he "has never paid even so much as a poll-tax," as the bonds he held were not taxable.[66]

In the week before election day, numerous newspaper articles pleaded with residents not to carry firearms to polling places, to "vote only one ballot," and to observe the proceedings, anticipating rampant fraud. The merchants in Live Oak mutually agreed to not sell any liquor on election day, and it was rumored that those in Tallahassee might follow suit.[67] Despite these precautions, Reed assured Grant on October 31 that no military presence would be warranted on election day. The only threats of violence or disorder, he explained, originated in one or two counties where Conant and his friends had aligned against the governor. Reed reiterated his call to remove the U.S. marshal, U.S. attorney, surveyor general, and collector of internal revenue. He requested that if the military were sent to Florida, that the soldiers should be "ordered to report or to act in Conjunction with the state officers in enforcing the laws," explaining that if "the military are placed at my disposal I can answer for the peace of the state & the election of the republican electors by five thousand majority." Placing the military under the control of state authorities could have only served one purpose in the days before the election. It was an audacious request to the former commanding general of the U.S. Army. Grant replied the following day in a tersely worded telegram, "Your dispatch of yesterday was received. It is of so remarkable a nature coming from the Executive of a state that I decline further answer."[68]

Amid the backdrop of Cowlam's appointment as U.S. marshal, Reed continued to remove county election supervisors. Reed had deposed William R. Random, one of the commissioners in the overwhelmingly African American Gadsden County, in September and replaced him with Robert F. Jones. When the Board of Commissioners proceeded to prepare for the election and appoint inspectors, it was clear that the commissioners had designed policies with the intention of giving the Democrats control of the polling places in that county. When Marcellus Stearns, the candidate for lieutenant governor, learned of this outrage in his home district, he met with Reed at the governor's Jacksonville home and left carrying a commission to restore Random to office. Stearns traveled across the state that night to the Gadsden County seat at Quincy to deliver the commission to Random personally. Several days later, Reed traveled to Quincy and removed Random from office a second time, claiming that he had been fraudulently reinstated. One concerned resident informed Florida's Secretary of State Gibbs that the county commissioners in Gadsden now numbered three Democrats to one Republican, explaining that Reed's latest appointee was "an out and out Democrat" and "his appointment throws us in the hands of the enemy!" The resident concluded the letter by stating, "I expect you to act in this case as an honest Republican, having the interests of the party at heart. Act as your judgment dictates, you will be held responsible." Another anxious local suggested that the Democrats intended to use their majority on the board to open additional polling places in the county, beyond the board's ability to monitor them, which would almost certainly lead to Republican defeat.[69]

A similar incident transpired in Jefferson County, on the other side of Tallahassee. Like nearby Gadsden County, the electorate in Jefferson County was more than 60 percent Black. In this case the Democratic county commissioners appealed to Reed to intervene in drawing up the election precincts. Reed requested that the county clerk and a Republican county commissioner meet him at the train depot in Monticello that evening. There Reed ordered the men to redraw the precinct boundaries to make them more favorable to the Democrats. The county commissioner protested that such a change would be illegal, as the law required twenty days' notice to inform the public. Reed explained that either the precincts would be moved or the commissioners would be removed and replaced with others who would follow his instructions. The next day the commissioners met and agreed to move five of the county's ten polling places.[70]

The day before the election, Judge Knight notified Chandler that in Leon County Republican election inspectors retained a majority in only one of the district's sixteen precincts. He stated further that in Gadsden County one of the polling places had been organized in a store owned by a Mr. Scott, a Democratic candidate for the state legislature. Knight emphasized that "many of the freedmen are indebted to him [ink on page] it is expected that many colored voters will be compelled to vote for Mr. Scott simply because he can be present & watch the proceedings and as many of them owe him, we fear the result."[71] Reed was replacing local election officials in the counties with the largest African American populations. Everything seemed to be going according to plan. Reed had assured Tyler in early September that "Every thing is *working well* & our colored votes can be secured in Jackson, Gadsden, Leon, Jefferson & Marion & the split in Alachua may be useful."[72]

Cowlam's nomination to the Republican ticket was short lived. His name appears on a surviving broadside with his name crossed out and "C[harles] W. Jones" written underneath. The advertisement is a curious artifact of the campaign, as it endorses the Republicans Ulysses S. Grant and Henry Wilson for president and vice president while listing the names of the Democrats running in the state and congressional elections. Cowlam received a total of ninety-two votes across the state. His strongest show of support was in Leon County, the county that includes Tallahassee, where he received sixty-four votes. He also received eight votes in Clay, Duval, and Marion Counties, two votes in Hamilton County, and one vote each in Gadsden and Walton Counties. The winner, Republican William J. Purman, received 17,537 votes, compared to 15,811 for Democrat Charles W. Jones.[73]

An initial count of the ballots revealed a substantial Republican majority. Nonetheless, the Democrats sought to overturn the election by challenging the result. Senator Osborn advised Chandler that Cowlam was working with the Democrats in this regard.[74] Recently reinstated U.S. Attorney Bisbee requested that the Justice Department send detectives to investigate instances of voter fraud in several counties.[75] Irregularities left the results up in the air for several weeks. As late as November 28, Democrat David Yulee believed that Bloxham had won the election.[76] John Tyler Jr. described the chaotic state of Florida politics after the election, observing that several Democrats and Republicans had traveled to Washington in the hopes of convincing the Grant administration to intervene. Tyler believed the Democrats were trying to "steal in at the back door of the Republican House, and to make their way by stealth into its most private and precious chambers." At the same time, "extreme Republicans" who had exceeded the limits of their patience were busy spreading alarm at the situation. Neither view, Tyler argued, merited serious consideration.[77]

Jonathan C. Greeley, who served simultaneously as assistant assessor of internal revenue and mayor of Jacksonville, reported that "the partizan [*sic*] feelings of the Board of State Canvassers" had left the election in doubt. Although the Republicans appeared to have carried the state, "the way is open for them to count Bloxham in." If the effort succeeded, Greeley noted, Bloxham might be able to "form the Cabinet, and perhaps get himself elected U.S. Senator, before he could be *ousted* by the Courts." Consequently, he found it "impossible to divine the result of the coming election of Senator." Greeley believed that Reed stood no chance of election, but thought that railroad promoter Milton Littlefield might be able to mobilize the money to bribe legislators, and if so, he would "stand the best chance of an Election among the Republicans—because it is generally believed that he would not scruple to use money in that direction." If the Democrats united behind Bloxham or another candidate, Greeley estimated that "they would only have to buy about 3 Republicans to give them the majority."[78]

By December it was clear that the Republicans in Florida had prevailed, securing four electoral votes for Grant and a sixteen hundred-vote majority in the congressional and gubernatorial elections. Reed left office quietly and retired to a farm he purchased outside of Jacksonville. He devoted his later life to journalistic pursuits and would later serve as postmaster of Tallahassee. The newly elected legislature selected Simon B. Conover, a Republican who had endorsed Bloxham in the recent election, as a compromise candidate to replace Osborn in the U.S. Senate. The election was a triumph for Ossian B. Hart and his followers, and the next two years witnessed the enactment of moderate civil rights legislation. At the same time, the 1872 election represented the twilight of Republican influence in the state. Hart's successor, Marcellus Stearns, would become the last Republican governor in Florida for the next ninety years.[79]

Cowlam arrived in Florida at a time when the state was bustling with newcomers and temporary visitors, nearly all of whom were from the North. The era represented the beginnings of a nascent tourism industry, and Cowlam's base of operations, Jacksonville, was a city of strangers. One contemporary estimated that fifteen thousand travelers visited Jacksonville in the first six months of 1872. The St. James Hotel alone recorded 3,842 guests between November 1 and May 10.[80] The number of tourists dwarfed the city's population by a factor of two to one. Amid this transient atmosphere it would have been easy for Cowlam to blend in and establish connections. The state's burgeoning population would have offered him the anonymity he needed to operate in the shadows, and the relative inexperience of the state's politicians would have given him all he needed to curry favor with those at the center of political influence. His adventures in Florida reveal just how easily northern carpetbaggers could acquire political power and patronage in the Reconstruction South. At the same time, Cowlam's escapades reveal the precarious nature of southern Reconstruction. His foray into politics rested on manipulating the state's African American vote and undermining the institutions that protected it. The removal of federal oversight would have meant the effective end of Reconstruction. It is equally remarkable that Republicans in Florida could piece together Reed's conspiracy and Cowlam's past in a matter of days despite the careful steps taken to conceal the efforts. In a sense, Cowlam's intrigues demonstrate how patronage politicians could respond quickly and verify information. Through their intermediaries in Washington, Republicans in Florida acted as a sounding board as they aggregated local knowledge and relayed this information to President Grant.

FIVE
SWINDLER

The cosmopolitan turned on his heel, leaving his companion at a loss to determine where exactly the fictitious character had been dropped, and the real one, if any, resumed.
—HERMAN MELVILLE, *The Confidence Man: His Masquerade* (1857)

In the summer and fall of 1874, a curious series of advertisements appeared in the *New York Herald*. The first notice cryptically invited "Miss Cowlam" to write to the paper "and she will hear something to her advantage." The message mentioned that she had lived at 380 3rd Avenue only six months before, in an area bordering the Rose Hill and Kips Bay neighborhoods, and flanked by Grammercy Park and Murray Hill, between 27th and 28th Streets. A second advertisement circulated later that summer, offering that any information on Charles Cowlam, who had left the city on April 15, would be "liberally rewarded." The notice described him as five feet, seven inches tall with a medium build, sandy complexion, and hazel eyes. He wore English side whiskers and a mustache but had recently shaved the side whiskers. Until a year and half before he had been a resident of Washington, D.C., and had formerly edited the *Scythe* out of the Bennett Building. A third announcement, syndicated in the Detroit and Washington papers, read simply "will the minister who married Charles Cowlam and Mary Ives, of Detroit, on the 19th of February, 1866, please communicate with Ira Shafer."[1]

In January 1874 Cowlam had married another woman in New York City. Ira Shafer, a respected New York attorney, represented the unnamed woman and began placing advertisements offering a reward of $2,000 for the delivery of Charles's "person, if alive, or the same amount for his body, if dead, with proofs of identity." The reward amount increased steadily, until Charles's brother, George, supplied information "that Charles died in a foreign land, and that his death was sufficiently painful in its 'surroundings to atone for whatever wrong he could have done anybody.'" Subsequent notices reprinted George's attestation, and added that "my client has reliable information that Charles is alive, and inasmuch as her former reward of $3,000 for proof of his death has failed to bring the necessary evidence (which could easily be furnished by George, as she supposes, if he writes the truth), I am now authorized to offer a reward of $3,500 for apprehension and conviction" for the crime of bigamy.[2]

New York was the ultimate stomping ground for a nineteenth-century charlatan. Cowlam profited from the anonymity that the city offered. Amid a population of roughly 1.5 million, he could just as easily blend in as disappear. Cowlam relocated to New York sometime in early 1873, shortly after his failed attempt to run for Congress in Florida. With his patron, Governor Harrison Reed, out of office, and his inclination for intrigue well known among Florida Republicans, Cowlam ventured to the Empire City in search of opportunity. There he leveraged his prior journalistic experience to publish a newspaper, the *Scythe*, and organize a secret society that he called the Order of the Patrons of Industry. The society played upon the reputation of the National Grange of the Order of Patrons of Husbandry, an association of farmers known colloquially as the Grange or Grangers, who had organized collectively to extract favorable rates from the railroads and established cooperatives to purchase farm implements directly from manufacturers at a discount. The Grangers believed that the nation's industrial base had monopolized to the detriment of the farmers.[3] Cowlam's newspaper and secret society sought to co-opt the same rhetoric popularized by the Grangers into an association of urban workingmen. As he fueled his journalistic ambitions by day, Cowlam spent his evenings mingling among New York's elite, searching for his next opportunity, and flirting with eligible bachelorettes. While his schemes depended on anonymity for success, Cowlam could not remain anonymous for long. He underestimated the capabilities of the emerging independent press and an uncompromising attorney, who would expose his escapades.[4]

THE *SCYTHE*

Cowlam published the *Scythe* out the third floor of the Bennett Building, a seven-story cast iron edifice in the financial district completed in May 1873 at the corner of Nassau and Fulton Streets. In those days the structure would have been among the tallest in the area, sharing the skyline with a growing crowd of recently constructed office buildings, and sporting a mansard roof before an expansion in the 1890s added three stories to its profile. The building also had a connection to the world of publishing. It was named for James Gordon Bennett Jr., the publisher of the *New York Herald* and son of the founding editor, who commissioned the building shortly after his father's death.[5] Unfortunately for Bennett, the project's completion coincided with the Panic of 1873, and the building struggled to attract tenants amid the depressed economic circumstances.

The Panic of 1873 was a global financial crisis that propelled the American economy into a deep depression. A postwar boom in railroad construction laid the groundwork for an asset bubble that popped when speculative investments failed to produce their anticipated returns. The first signs of trouble emerged in May when the Vienna Stock Exchange crashed, but the panic manifested in the United States only after the brokerage firm of Jay Cooke and Company shut the doors of its New York office in September. The Wall Street observer George Templeton Strong recorded in his diary that passersby mulled about aimlessly, complaining of the "d--d infernal swindlers and thieves" who had caused the crash. By the end of the year twenty-five railroads had defaulted on their obligations, and nearly half of the railroads in the country would eventually go into receivership before the panic subsided. The New York Association for Improving the Condition of the Poor supported 88,473 persons over the course of its 1873–1874 fiscal year, and it estimated that a quarter of the city's workforce was unemployed that winter as a consequence of the depression. The surge in unemployment held political ramifications, galvanizing the labor movement and dampening congressional support for southern Reconstruction. Farmers and workingmen blamed Congress for demonetizing the silver dollar earlier that year, which tightened the money supply, and Cowlam's *Scythe* reflected the temporary alignment of these interests in support of loose monetary policy and regulations to challenge monopolistic industrial organization.[6]

The first issue of the *Scythe* appeared on September 21, 1873, just three days after Jay Cooke and Company closed its doors. The paper's motto was "by industry we thrive."[7] Its masthead read "*The Scythe*, to mow down Monopoly and Extortion" and featured a circular saw surrounded by implements employed in the mechanical industries.[8] At first the paper positioned itself as a resolute advocate of the Granger movement, but after four or five weekly issues the articles began to recommend the creation of a new order of workingmen called the Order of the Patrons of Industry. The paper offered a reassuring message at a time when the panic had shaken Americans' faith in the financial system: that a union of interests between farmers and workingmen would challenge monopoly privilege and restore confidence in the free labor ideal. George Templeton Strong recorded in his diary that "faith in financial agents is gone. Every treasurer and cashier is 'suspect,' and no wonder after the recent epidemic of fraud." In planting the seeds of a fraud of his own, Cowlam's brotherhood of workingmen marketed itself as an honest corrective to the excesses of capitalism. It is a shame that no copies of the paper appear to have survived.[9]

One technique that Cowlam employed to promote the fledgling newspaper was to write descriptive articles, such as one describing a visit to the National Grange Headquarters in Washington, that he could place in Granger newspapers alongside a flattering endorsement of the *Scythe*. The approach was successful. Granger outlets eagerly reproduced Cowlam's flowery descriptions and complimentary prose, and the new order soon received favorable coverage in prominent Granger publications. Jonathan Periam's early history of the Granger movement, *The Groundswell: A History of the Origin, Aims, and Progress of the Farmers' Movement* (1874), even included a chapter on the promising prospects of the new order. Periam trumpeted the Patrons of Industry as the perfect complement to the Patrons of Husbandry, and proposed that "the united strength of these organizations will become a power for good absolutely irresistible."[10]

Another strategy that Cowlam employed to generate excitement about the secret society was to advertise its teeming membership rolls. By the end of October, the Patrons of Industry claimed to have initiated more than two hundred lodges across the country. By early December the organization purported to receive more than forty new applications each week, and to have established sixty-nine lodges in the largest cities, with a total membership of more than eight thousand. One article published in early January 1874 boasted that one thousand lodges would be organized in the vicinity of New York City by the early spring. Such assertions were flagrant exaggerations meant to parallel the exponential growth of the Granger movement. The Grangers opened more than three thousand local granges in the last three months of 1873. Whereas the Grangers were most popular in the rural Midwest, the urban Northeast remained a relatively untapped area susceptible to Cowlam's intrigues. It is not clear how many initiates Cowlam actually attracted. There is evidence of lodges having been established in Philadelphia, Chicago, Springfield, Massachusetts, Bronson and Fairfield, Michigan, and Bismark, Dakota Territory, along with a special deputy appointed for southern Michigan and northern Indiana. It is likely that the order never attracted more than a few hundred members.[11]

The Patrons of Industry marketed themselves as an auxiliary to the Patrons of Husbandry, meant to appeal to "blacksmiths, carpenters, masons, printers, machinists, shoe-makers, and tailors." The order admitted men and women into its ranks under a system of three degrees: apprentice, laborer, and journeyman for men, and apprentice, maiden, and matron for women. In encouraging workingmen to initiate their wives, daughters, and sisters, announcements insisted that "a pure, moral atmosphere must prevail." The different levels of membership imitated secret societies that Cowlam claimed familiarity with, such as the Knights of the Golden Circle. Prospective lodges paid a $16 charter fee, and the initiation fee was $2 for men and $1 dollar for women, with monthly dues of 10 cents each. Once initiated, patrons would learn a secret phrase that would allow them to communicate with fellow members, "so arranged that a word changed will confound a traitor thrust from our fellowship. There is absolutely no chance for treachery to escape our detective system." The elements of secrecy added a flair of mystery to the order, reminiscent of the freemasons and benevolent societies that became popular in the nineteenth century.[12]

The Patrons positioned themselves as a grassroots organization. Local members would closely and carefully review prospective applicants, and no candidate would be admitted unless they received almost unanimous approval of the local lodge. Three negative ballots would be sufficient for any lodge to reject a potential member. Leadership within the local lodges consisted of eight male and two female officers elected annually, with the presiding officer styled the Master Workman. Master Workmen and their wives who had taken the third-degree orders could claim membership in the state lodge, who in turn would elect the state officers and a Master Workman to represent their state in the national lodge. Advertisements announcing the new order variously claimed October 3 and 7 for the founding of the national lodge, and declared that twenty state lodges had already been formed.[13]

Although the order presented itself as a secret society, editorials advertising the organization described its rituals as simple and unassuming. The order's bylaws prohibited all discussion of religion or nationality, in the expectation that membership would transcend both. Like many secret societies of the era, the Patrons of Industry expressly forbade politicians and speculators from joining the ranks of brotherhood. The society claimed no political affiliation, although its circulars did occasionally borrow language from the Labor Reform Party, a short-lived political party that advocated for an eight-hour working day and monetary policy reform.[14] J. H. Brown, the secretary of the national lodge, emphasized that "there is danger of anarchy, famine, and even bread riots in this country, and we proclaim ourselves against all oppression, all outlawry, all conspiracy." Brown expressed his disappointment that millions of honest farmers had toiled for years to make "the western wilderness bud and blossom as the rose" only to find themselves deprived of the fruits of their labor by the same "merciless monopolists" who had denied eastern workingmen of their employment and threatened them with starvation. Despite the *Scythe*'s sometimes inflammatory rhetoric against capitalists and politicians who had reduced the masses to serfdom, the order presented itself as committed to the rule of law and devoted to enacting change through the ballot. Its constitution proposed to look within its ranks for political candidates who would purify the state and national legislatures, in the same way that the Grangers anticipated fielding third-party candidates from among their members. The Patrons also emphasized the social benefits of joining a society of workingmen, and purported to care for all sick and destitute members, a claim that was evocative of mutual aid organizations that proliferated in the nineteenth century.[15]

In addition to its social and political functions, the organization claimed to act as purchasing agent to rescue its members from the extortionate profits of middlemen and speculators. The Patrons claimed to have purchasing agreements in place to allow members to obtain supplies "for their larder, the wardrobe, the dining room, sitting room, or parlor, at reduced rates from those they are now compelled to pay." Promoters of the order proposed that mechanics and workingmen stood to benefit the most from such an arrangement, as workingmen had no choice but to purchase all they consume, whereas farmers could consume at least some of their produce. The order's constitution proposed that each local lodge would appoint a "General Purchasing Agent," who would have the authority to negotiate the sale of "all sorts of commodities" on behalf of his fellow patrons. The general purchasing agent would give bond for security, and would supply a price list to the Master Workmen of all local lodges, allowing members to purchase goods at no markup. The secretary of each local lodge would deposit all monies received each month into the "Fiscal Agency holding the funds for the National Lodge." The officers of each local lodge would receive no compensation for their efforts except reimbursement for actual expenses. Through such methods the Patrons claimed to have reduced the price of sewing machines by $20 or $30 exclusively for their members.[16]

The journal's authorship came under investigation by a New York reporter in January 1874, the same month that Cowlam married the unnamed uptown widow, after complaints from initiates stirred suspicions about the legitimacy of the operation. Marie Howland, of Hammonton, New Jersey, wrote to the editor of the *Daily Graphic,* inquiring if any information could be furnished on the secret society. Howland was a working-class feminist, Granger, and utopian socialist whose novel *Papa's Own Girl,* published later that year, explored themes of feminism, socialism, and free love.[17] A group of workingmen and women in Philadelphia, believing that they did not have sufficient members to obtain a charter under the Patrons of Husbandry, inquired about joining its lesser-known imitator. The workingmen and women submitted their

$16 to obtain a charter and were soon initiated into the mysteries of the order of Pioneer Lodge No. 474. No sooner had the lodge organized than a letter arrived from New York demanding additional money "for regalia, &c." Several of the new members wrote to J. H. Brown, the secretary of the organization, to press him for an explanation. The society listed a post office box for an address, and the letters in reply supplied only excuses for why the editor could not be found. Letters from Brown and another reply from "Hoyt, Assistant Secretary" were found to be "unmistakably in the same hand-writing." The Philadelphians sent a representative to New York to investigate, but could not locate Brown, any other employees, or any of the other 473 lodges that the society claimed. After failing to produce a new issue for two weeks, the December 20 issue of the *Scythe* made clear that the Philadelphia lodge would soon have its charter withdrawn for nonpayment, a threat that was soon carried out.[18]

A week later a reporter at the *Daily Graphic* published the results of his investigation. With a copy of the *Scythe* in hand, he traveled to the third floor of the Bennett Building on Nassau Street via the Anne Street elevator. At the end of a long corridor to the Fulton Street hallway the reporter discovered two doors opposite one another, the first marked "*The Scythe*—Editor's room," and the other, "*The Scythe*—Correspondence." Most of the other doors on the hall appeared unoccupied, placarded with signs indicating that they were available for rent. The door to the editor's room was locked, and with no answer he turned to the open door of the correspondence room, where he greeted a "tall, pleasant-voiced young man" who stood up from a table opposite the doorway and said his name was William E. Burlick. "Mr. Brown is out of town" Burlick rhymed, but "I expect him in every minute." The reporter took a seat and surveyed the room. Sitting near Burlick was "another young man with a handsome face and short, black moustache" smoking a corncob pipe and reading a newspaper. When the mustachioed man spoke up about a ball the previous evening, Burlick scolded him and "read something from a paper about the excellence of the lands in southern Georgia and northern Florida, and remarked in an agricultural manner that he knew every foot of that land, and it wasn't worth ten cents an acre for farming purposes." The reporter mentioned that a "colored boy" returned to the room a short time later, and the four men sat silently for the next hour while Burlick practiced his penmanship on waste paper.[19]

Burlick's extensive knowledge of southern Georgia and northern Florida made him a dead ringer for Cowlam. He had traversed those states regularly during his time with the Internal Revenue Service and as a congressional candidate, and it is unlikely that anyone else in his entourage would have possessed the requisite knowledge of both. While the *Daily Graphic* reporter did not realize it, he had been speaking to the editor of the *Scythe* the whole time.[20] After an hour of waiting, the reporter decided to inquire at the post office to see if the editor had any letters waiting for him. Upon finding four letters sitting in his P.O. box, he returned to the Bennett Building, only to be informed that he had just missed him. The editor had even left his overcoat hanging behind the door. Another long wait ensued until one o'clock, when all four men looked at their watches and one of them explained that at this point it was unlikely for the editor to return. The reporter wondered how the editor had managed to navigate Manhattan in January without an overcoat, and asked Burlick for the editor's name and home address. Burlick replied that his name was Cowlam, but that there was no point in trying to find him and no one could tell where he had gone.[21]

The reporter returned the next morning at 10:30 sharp. He greeted Burlick and asked if Cowlam had returned. "No; but I expect him every minute," Burlick replied. After half an hour of silence Burlick briefly attempted to make conversation about Matthew T. Brennan's imprisonment before taking up an almanac and reading it. Brennan was a sheriff with connections to Tammany Hall who had arrested Boss Tweed several months before, but found himself under arrest after he allowed a fellow Tammany associate to escape from his custody. Another half hour passed, and the reporter again pleaded with Burlick to tell him where Cowlam lived. "I don't know," Burlick declared, "exactly where he does live." Here he punctuated his words the way one does when they are trying to fill gaps in their story or provide cover for falsehoods. Burlick continued reading the almanac silently, apparently not reading the jokes at the bottom of each page, as the journalist commented that he never smiled. The retinue who had been there the previous day soon returned. The "colored boy" began drawing the outline of a house on blotting paper, while the handsome young man read a newspaper. Whenever footsteps were heard in the hallway Burlick would raise his head quickly to peek through a clear patch of ground glass set in the door that allowed him to identify those traveling past. Shortly after twelve a boy with a very red and white face arrived and exclaimed "he ain't a-coming down to-day." "How do you know?" asked the handsome young man, "have you been at the house?" Burlick appeared to cover up the child's indiscretion by sternly explaining that the boy did not know what he was talking about. The boy explained to the reporter that he had been only joking. This conversation may have been a ploy to convince the reporter to leave, or the slip of the tongue may have concealed some relevant clue that would have exposed the whole charade. By this time, nearly 1:00, the reporter realized that his chances of locating the editor were dwindling. As he turned to leave he mused, "I suppose while the paper is new you don't have a great deal of correspondence to attend to." Burlick replied, "no; we're not very busy just now."[22]

With J. H. Brown exposed as a myth, and the *Scythe* revealed to be a swindle, the favorable press coverage that the Patrons of Industry had heretofore received began to dry up. News of the *Daily Graphic*'s exposé trickled slowly across the country. Some of those who had been hoodwinked rebranded their lodges under new names. A group in Springfield, Massachusetts, restyled themselves the Sovereigns of Industry, and a lodge in Chicago renamed their organization the Order of the Advocates of Justice. These new societies drafted nearly identical constitutions and bylaws, initiated new temples and councils, and began placing advertisements in papers across the country that matched the language of the ones used by the Patrons of Industry. It is not clear if these later imitations continued the same ruse under a different guise, but in other respects the swindle did carry on. Before the scandal came to light, Cowlam had appointed special deputies to drum up support for new lodges in various regions. Some of these special deputies continued to lure unsuspecting workingmen into joining the secret society for several months after the organization had been exposed as a fraud.[23]

THE GAY DECEIVER

The Panic of 1873 not only united workingmen and women against the ravages of the depression, it also joined wealthy New Yorkers concerned about threats to the social order. Cowlam's earlier schemes had preyed upon the lower classes, but he now turned his attentions to the city's finer sort. This was the golden age of New York society, in which upper-class women might order forty gowns from Paris for the season. The balls and galas were so frequent that even in frigid January, Manhattanites might flock to six festivals in a span of ten days. In hobnobbing with the city's upper crust, Cowlam quickly became a "gay deceiver," a deceitful rake who leveraged the anonymity of the age to commit bigamy. The origins of the phrase date to the early eighteenth century, but it became a popular way of describing bigamist swindlers between 1870 and 1900. Newspaper stories of good-looking, respectable, and seemingly wealthy newcomers who courted and deserted their brides became more common in the Gilded Age. Such bigamists not only violated established social norms by desecrating the sanctity of marriage, but they also intruded on class sensibilities by trespassing their way into the inner circles of elite society. The fear of bigamists passing their way into the upper class even emerged as a popular theme in Victorian literature. At a time when only 31 percent of the city's economic elite were native New Yorkers, the feared intruder in their midst was a real danger.[24]

As the secret society swindle started to unravel, the New York attorney, Ira Shafer, began to piece together the details of Cowlam's life. Over the course of the summer and fall of 1874 he placed advertisements in the *New York Herald* seeking information. To describe Ira Shafer as pugnacious would be an understatement. After being admitted to the bar and serving as the Albany County district attorney and a state senator, he moved to Manhattan and established a lucrative law practice. He stood nearly six feet tall with a rotund figure, and in his later years he sported a bushy handlebar mustache. Shafer was fond of strong language, and his speeches and opening statements were filled with sarcasm and mocking derision. As a leader among the anti-Tammany Democrats in the 1870s, he sparred frequently with John Kelly after the latter attempted to rebuild the Tammany political machine. In court he would harangue witnesses relentlessly with thunderous interjections, his words often slurring together in excitement, shouting "ibe jeck" instead of "I object." When a witness crumbled under pressure, he would stand up and wave his arms for dramatic effect. One contemporary compared his mixture of sluggishness and rage to a "slumbering volcano." His irrepressible temper frequently got the best of him. He once threatened to shoot Joseph Pulitzer, the editor of the *New York World*, on sight for the unflattering press coverage he received during one of his trials. When asked whether he worried about being convicted of murder, he is said to have remarked that no man worth half a million dollars could ever be convicted of murder in New York.[25]

In December 1874, the *Detroit Free Press* ran an article that attempted to summarize Cowlam's life in an effort to locate him. Several crossheads appeared underneath the title, underscoring Cowlam's "Wild, Vagabondish, Reckless and Criminal Career" as a mail robber, penitentiary convict, revenue detective, Confederate agent, U.S. marshal, and candidate for Congress. After reprinting Shafer's advertisement that featured George's statement regarding Charles's death, the author attempted to relate "the history of an adventurer whose remarkable career—if it could be written up fully—would compare with ancient or modern romance," adding that "he has as many *aliases* as there are letters in the alphabet." The story related glimpses of Cowlam's early life in Battle Creek, and his association with a group of young thieves that called themselves the "Red Rangers," adding a claim that the group disbanded after their plot to blow up the Union Block, the meeting house of a local religious society, was discovered. The article attributed the boys' early criminality to reading dime novels featuring famous highwaymen, such as Jack Sheppard and Claude Duval. Residents of Battle Creek could not recall exactly when Cowlam left the town, but speculated that he had first "gone to Canada to escape the penalty of some violation of the law."[26]

At times the article seemed to confuse elements of Cowlam's chronology, and some of the anecdotes suggested that they had filtered their way to residents of Battle Creek secondhand. The exposé described his return to Battle Creek "after the lapse of a few years" as taking place shortly *before* his arrest for stealing from the mails, noting that he appeared "seemingly much improved in appearance and morals. He claimed to be in some business connected with the government. He had plenty of money, of which he was lavish, but old acquaintances were fearful that all was not right, and so it proved." The story makes sense only in the aftermath of his release from prison, after Cowlam returned to Michigan in 1865 claiming to have infiltrated the Confederate Secret Service and working to secure a position as a government detective. Those who had known him since childhood mused that he must have traveled to Europe as a Confederate agent after receiving his pardon from Jefferson Davis, and no one could remember his exact status in the Internal Revenue Service, recalling only that "he had a mysterious and reticent manner, and when he spoke of his authority he left so much to inference that every one supposed his power much greater than he told them." Memory of Cowlam's escapades in Florida were clearer. Those who knew him remembered his appointment and removal as marshal and his congressional candidacy. During the campaign he had "proclaimed boldly" of having served as a government detective during the war, and insinuated that he reported personally to General Grant, which the article described as a "complete *canard*." The article also claimed that Cowlam's congressional bid collapsed when detractors wrote letters to residents of Battle Creek, who produced the letter from the superintendent of the Virginia State Penitentiary revealing his criminal past. Ira Shafer likely wrote the exposé as a way of gaining attention for his client's case, and the story was carried in newspapers across the country.[27]

Subsequent articles added dubious accusations that presented Cowlam as the impenitent swindler. The *Cedar Rapids Republican* asserted that Cowlam cheated employees of the *Chicago Evening Post* out of $2,500 while working there as editor, and claimed that he supplemented his lucrative salary by "buying up bounties at a large discount, from soldiers in the late war who were entitled to a one hundred dollar bounty." Cowlam supposedly encouraged these "gentlemen to invest their money in his hands, giving his note as security, claiming that he had a particular friend in Washington who would shove the business through for him, on a certain per centage."[28] These reports also alleged that Cowlam had worked for the British banking house Bowles Brothers, which failed shortly after his arrival, after which he returned to work in the advertising department for a New York insurance company.[29] As in the original, the follow-up pieces offered several recollections that missed the mark. Cowlam had worked at the *Evening Post* sometime between 1866 and 1868, but it would not have been possible for him to have profited from soldiers' enlistment bounties after the Civil War had ended. Although Cowlam had given Bowles Brothers as his address during his time in the United Kingdom, the banking house also operated as a mail forwarding agent for Americans traveling in Europe. The correspondent may have misremembered Cowlam's association with Frank R. Sherwin and Co., the New York banking firm with which Cowlam claimed association, which also failed in 1873. Each of these accusations had a veneer of plausibility, but offered false memories of the particulars.[30]

Other newspapers soon furnished additional details on the bigamy scandal, reporting that Cowlam had presented himself in New York as "Charles Harry Cowland" and explaining that the "stylish and agreeable man of 35 years, formerly of Chicago," had first introduced himself to the fashionable society of the city in 1872. Cowlam had made regular trips to New York that year carrying messages between the governor of Florida and the secretary of the Republican National Committee. Presumably these visits offered him the opportunity to make himself known among the city's high society. One article noted that "his antecedents were not well known here, but he apparently had plenty of money, a pleasing address, and was evidently respectable, he was welcomed by the 'upper ten' families of Fifth and Madison Avenues." It was not long before Cowlam had been introduced to several marriageable young women, who described him as "an awful flirt." Invariably Cowlam was most attracted to women with considerable fortunes. The newspapers reported that "he claimed to have a snug fortune himself, and affirmed that he would marry no woman who had not a competency to match his." After a year of flirting he married a wealthy uptown widow, and shortly after the wedding he disappeared with roughly $100,000 of her money. The article explained that the unnamed woman had offered the $3,500 reward for information on Cowlam's whereabouts and was prepared to spend $50,000 "getting even" with him, an amount with a purchasing power of more than $1.3 million today.[31] He had been last heard from in Texas, the article claimed, and in addition to his two living wives, Cowlam had "deceived no less than half a dozen women, all of whom are well-to-do in the world. Some of the ladies are maidens, it is alleged, but the majority are rich widows." Cowlam had a "whole trunk full of letters from members of the fairer sex in various parts of the United States." His exploits were said to have extended from Maine to California, and from Canada to the Gulf of Mexico.[32]

It is an unfortunate artifact of history that none of the newspapers named any of the women that Charles defrauded. Identifying the victims of bigamy in the nineteenth century is incredibly challenging. Whether the women withheld their names out of shame or embarrassment, or newspaper conventions that rendered women's names invisible, is not clear. Revealing abandonment came with a reduction in social status and would have diminished their marriage prospects. The stigma of having been deceived undoubtably prevented others from coming forward. The task of finding nineteenth-century bigamists in the historical record is not much easier. Although their names might be known, these elusive figures often left a scanty paper trail. Bigamists rarely returned to the same church or minister, given the risks of exposing their previous marriages, and the use of aliases only compounds the difficulty of tracking them. That the newspapers reported Cowlam's name, without any reference to an alias, suggests that he used his real name while courting prospective brides in New York, yet a thorough search of the Manhattan marriage and divorce records has turned up nothing relating to Cowlam's escapades. New York did not require marriages to be registered with the city government at that time. Instead, marriages conducted privately at places of worship frequently went unreported.[33]

Lawrence Friedman argues that bigamy proliferated in the late nineteenth century because women did not possess the same degree of mobility as men, noting that "victimization by bigamists was part of a system of truncated mobility, and a reflex of their limited social role." In an earlier era, Americans would have viewed an outsider with suspicion. Family members would have independently confirmed the veracity of the stranger's claims. Bigamy was less frequent in centuries past, when arranged marriages cemented familial ties. By the end of the century, the limits of elite society were more well defined. The centralized authority of the Progressive Era made vital records easier to verify. In the transient Gilded Age, however, strangers were commonplace. Bigamists like Cowlam promised the potential for upward mobility, to start a new life, or to avoid all the perils that remaining unmarried entailed for women.[34]

Bigamy was primarily a working-class crime in the nineteenth century. When members of high society committed it, newspapers reported the scandalous details in sensational terms. It was less common for middle- and upper-class men to marry above their station. When they did so, they often used marriage as a pathway to elevate their status. When instances of bigamy were uncovered, it was far more likely for the second spouse to bring the case to the attention of the authorities.[35] The crime occurred with enough regularity that clerks at the Pension Bureau came up with a shorthand to identify claims disputed by two or more "contesting widows." Among the successful claims granted, the notation appears in just under 1 percent of all applications, compared to upward of 3 percent of unsuccessful cases. Few bigamists fit the stereotype of the confidence man supporting multiple households simultaneously in different towns. Instead, most bigamists used falsehoods to conceal past experiences with matrimony, using a manufactured story to make a fresh start in an era where divorce was difficult to obtain. In this sense historians of sexuality have treated bigamy as a form of "serial monogamy" or "fluid marriage." Cowlam's case is unusual in this regard. Rather than using bigamy as a means to start a new life, he used it as an instrument to cheat his victims and disappear.[36]

Cowlam never faced charges against him for bigamy. Instead he disappeared in the summer of 1874 and spent the next twelve years as a fugitive. Although his name and reputation were forever tarnished, he had little to fear from the courts. Bigamy was relatively difficult to prove in the nineteenth century, as many states required prosecutors to present both marriage certificates, along with testimony from ministers and witnesses, to argue their case successfully. Although no comprehensive statistics on bigamy exist for the United States, the marriage records from England from the second half of the nineteenth century offer some evidence of the infrequency of bigamy prosecutions. For divorce decrees granted in England on the grounds of bigamy, only one out of every eight cases resulted in a prosecution. Among those prosecuted for bigamy, however, nearly 80 percent of cases resulted in a conviction. Those cases involving fraud, or serial bigamists like Cowlam, typically received longer sentences than those who sought to escape a failed marriage by marrying a second time.[37]

If Cowlam had wanted to obtain a divorce from Mary Ives, he could have done so in states like Indiana, which emerged as a haven for out-of-state divorce seekers in the nineteenth century. Although New York possessed some of the most stringent marriage laws in the nation, with adultery providing the sole grounds for divorce, the states in the Midwest generally adopted a more liberal approach.[38] Cowlam's older sister, Sarah, who had petitioned on his behalf while he was incarcerated, would later request that the court grant her separate maintenance from her husband, Elisha L. C. Monroe, in Chicago in January 1875. The couple had married in April 1870 and separated on June 23, 1873, after Elisha remarked that morning "if you do not apply for a divorce I shall light out, and leave you to shift for yourself." Both spouses alleged that the other kept irregular evening hours, and Sarah asserted that Elisha was prone to drunkenness. Elisha complained that Sarah would often go months without speaking to him, and insisted on allowing a dog to sleep in their bed. Although the court would not grant alimony to Sarah without a divorce decree, she did separate from Elisha and lived much of the rest of her life with her youngest sister, Isabel, in Washington, D.C.[39]

Charles's first wife, Mary Ives Cowlam, was born on December 15, 1846, in Detroit. After their marriage in February 1866, the couple relocated to Chicago. Mary likely accompanied Charles to the South while he worked as a detective for the Internal Revenue Service and made his foray into Florida politics. A *carte de visite* of her survives among photographs of the Charles family in the University of South Carolina library. The image matches a description of her given when she applied for a passport of her own in 1890. At that time, she stood five feet, two inches tall, with a thin face, dark complexion, high forehead and large nose, gray eyes, and dark brown and gray hair. The couple lived together in Washington, D.C., with Charles's brother, George, at the time of the census of 1870, and Mary traveled with him to the United Kingdom. When the couple separated in New York in the spring of 1874, Mary returned to Detroit to live with her parents. She filed suit against Charles for bigamy in the Superior Court of Detroit on July 29, 1876. A brief mention in the *Detroit Free Press* stated that Charles was "not a resident of the state of Michigan, but as she is informed and believes, he is a resident of Japan." The Superior Court granted Mary Ives Cowlam a divorce decree later that year on the grounds of desertion.[40]

SIX
VETERAN

"There," he laughed, "you know now what sort of soldier I am."
—HERMAN MELVILLE, *The Confidence Man: His Masquerade* (1857)

On June 18, 1886, Vernon Seaman of 52 Broad Street, New York, sent a letter to the secretary of war, William C. Endicott, seeking information on behalf of his friend, Colonel Livingston Grahame, who needed to establish his service record to continue living in the Central Branch of the National Home for Disabled Volunteer Soldiers, in Dayton, Ohio. Seaman explained that his friend suffered from "paralysis of the brain" and could not recall his military exploits. Confirming his service record would prove challenging, he reasoned, as Grahame had served "in the Secret Service Department of the U.S. during the War, mostly in Virginia, but probably under an assumed name." He hoped that Secretary of War Endicott could give this matter his full attention, and emphasized "that he was a soldier & officer in the Service is without a doubt & his friends are very anxious to establish the fact for the reasons named."[1]

Seaman was a prosperous commission merchant involved in numerous mining interests. Although he was born in Westchester, New York, he migrated to California as a young man and spent five years living in Shanghai and Hong Kong. His connections in China allowed him to establish a mercantile firm in San Francisco, and he soon started a business that connected Chinese laborers with southern plantation owners eager to expand their workforce after emancipation. After moving to New York, he supported the anti-Tammany Democrats and opposed the Chinese Exclusion Act of 1882, which barred Asian immigration to the United States. Seaman was tall and heavyset, and some described him as possessing "aldermanic rotundity." He was always well dressed and wore side whiskers that complemented his full cheeks. Despite his wealth and connections, Seaman had a checkered past. He had been arrested several times, and had faced charges for both assault and battery and assault with a deadly weapon. In one instance Seaman drew his pistol and shot at a man who tapped him with his cane after an argument between their wives became heated on Kearny Street, in San Francisco. Although he always seemed to secure an acquittal, his regular court appearances suggest a certain brazenness about him, and he walked a fine line between respectability and criminality.[2]

Endicott would have been unaware of Seaman's past legal troubles, and he took the case seriously. He forwarded the letter to the Adjutant General's Office, the branch within the army that maintained a registry of military service records. The clerks in that office worked tirelessly but could find no history of Grahame's service. Docketing on the case file reveals the division of labor within the department and the number of hands that reports passed through in the course of an investigation. Max Bock and David E. Holmes quickly verified that Grahame had never been an officer in the regular army. William J. Armstrong confirmed that the name could not be found in the Miscellaneous Records Division. After two days of searching, the clerks began to acknowledge the futility of the inquiry. John Bingham scribbled that "without a date or something to start from it would be a very long, hard strong, search for us. The question as it is now, carries too much at least to think of having it made special." Referring the case for special investigation meant sending a special examiner to interview the parties involved and record their testimony in a narrative affidavit. The process was typically employed to investigate instances of suspected fraud, but could also produce additional evidence with which to further a search. The other clerks in the office agreed that a special investigation would likely prove fruitless. Benjamin Engel emphasized that "with only this I hardly think it would pay to make a search," and another clerk added that "if under an assumed name it will be difficult if not impossible to find him."[3]

The Adjutant General's Office referred the case to the quartermaster general, reasoning that if Grahame had been in the Secret Service, he probably would have been a civilian and likely paid by that department. The quartermaster general failed to produce any record of Grahame or any information on him, but raised the possibility that Grahame had been employed by

Lafayette C. Baker during the war. Baker was a detective and spy who casts a murky shadow over the history of Civil War espionage. While serving as provost marshal for Washington, D.C., he organized an agency under the War Department that he called the National Detective Police. The organization was tasked with rooting out Confederate subversives, and he participated as a detective in investigating the Lincoln assassination. Baker often referred to his wartime department as the Secret Service, and after the war penned a memoir, *History of the United States Secret Service,* rife with exaggerations and distortions.[4] It is not clear if the War Department clerks consulted Baker's case files on Confederate sympathizers in their search for Grahame, but if they did they would not have found his name. On July 24 the chief clerk of the War Department sent Vernon Seaman a succinct reply, informing him that the search had "failed to discover any military official bearing that name."[5]

The case remained filed away in the War Department until early September, when the commissioner of pensions, John C. Black, visited the soldiers' home in Dayton. General Marsena R. Patrick, the governor of the Central Branch, brought Grahame's case to the commissioner's attention, and he agreed to initiate a special investigation "without any formal application" on Grahame's behalf. With prominent officials supporting the inquiry, the story of an officer who could not remember where he had fought took on a romantic quality. The newspapers described Grahame as "a dementea ex-soldier, about forty years of age," with the letters "C.C." tattooed on his arm in India ink. By all indications Grahame appeared to be "the wreck of a highly cultivated man as well as of a gallant Union officer." The search led the special examiners to make inquiries from Canada to Guatemala, where Grahame claimed to have traveled some thirteen years before, after which he allegedly returned "suffering terribly from eczema and nervous prostration, resulting eventually in paralysis and insanity." The investigation proved to be "one of the most difficult and persistent searches it [the special examiners at the Pension Office] ever made," sustained "alternatively by the most striking coincidences and the most exasperating contradictions."[6]

Grahame told the examiners that his former name was Charles Cowlam. He explained that he had been born on May 1, 1845, in Saline, Michigan, a birthdate closer to his younger brother George's than his own, which made him appear nearly eight years younger. He claimed the Pennsylvania legislature had changed his name to Livingston Grahame on May 3, 1878, and that the state had given him an annuity of $1,500 per year. He also insisted that he had served four years as an officer in the Union army. The inconsistencies in Grahame's stories were abundant. The newspapers noted that at times he "represented that it was the legislature of New York which had changed his name, and sometimes that it was the legislature of Pennsylvania. Sometimes he said he served in the Fourth New York Cavalry and at other times that he served in the Twenty-first New York Infantry." The New York and Pennsylvania legislatures soon confirmed that they had neither changed Cowlam's name nor granted him an annuity. The Treasury Department unearthed records of his time working for the Secret Service of the Internal Revenue Service, but the War Department could find no record of him ever having been a Union soldier. On October 18 the War Department updated Grahame's case file, having solved the mystery of the bewildered colonel. Clerk George W. Salter appended a brief update, and recorded that "he is at present an imbecile, and nothing further can be obtained in his case."[7]

The English essayist Samuel Johnson once remarked that "patriotism is the last refuge of the scoundrel."[8] After years of grifting, and with his finances exhausted after a decade of living on the run under an assumed name, Cowlam hoped to capitalize on the sympathy that Americans felt for veterans of the Civil War. In clothing himself in the mantle of veteranhood, he sought to blend in one last time by demonstrating his respectability and loyalty to the Union cause. That Cowlam would pretend to be a Union veteran is not surprising. He would have been twenty-three years old when the Civil War began, exactly the median age for Union volunteers. An overwhelming proportion of his peers would have served in the war. Had he been a decade older or younger his failure to serve would not have been unusual. Men in their thirties frequently failed to qualify for service. He could have pleaded poor health, a business interest, or family concerns that kept him tied to the homefront. But among men his age his failure to serve would have set him apart. How he spent the war would have been one of the first questions a new acquaintance might ask him. The common bond of service, even if fictitious in his case, would have created a sense of trust and connected him to others his age. On the surface, Cowlam gave the impression that he was doing everything that a Union veteran was supposed to do to assimilate into civilian life.

Beneath the surface, however, his claims to Union veteranhood disguised his criminal history and offered cover for his swindles.[9]

Imposters claiming to be soldiers emerged almost as soon as the war began and continued long after hostilities concluded. Unlike the Confederacy, which attempted to mobilize nearly all southern white men, the Union homefront counted large numbers of able-bodied men who elected to remain at home rather than enlist. As the war grew more deadly, public opinion turned against those who exploited patriotic fervor for personal gain. Popular periodicals ridiculed these "shoulder straps," who masqueraded as soldiers while failing to do their duty. Officers on the home front who flaunted their uniforms while balking at any real service also became targets of the public's indignation. Historian J. Matthew Gallman notes that both sets of hypocrites became "the war's new breed of confidence men, now operating under the guise of the Union cause rather than the banner of individualism." Northerners did not so much object to those who chose to sit out the war, but directed their ire at those who exploited others' sacrifices for their own gain.[10]

The most lucrative opportunity for charlatans who claimed to be veterans was to obtain a pension from the federal government. To receive a pension before 1890, Union veterans needed to provide corroborating evidence of a service-related injury. The standards for evidence could be rigorous, and claimants needed to prove that their injuries originated during the war. One applicant went so far as to fabricate a diary from Andersonville prison to support his claim. As the war receded into the past, the proportion of veterans eligible to claim pension benefits expanded considerably, which created new opportunities for fraud. One common source of fraud among pension claims was the practice of unscrupulous pension agents embellishing or manufacturing details to bolster an otherwise legitimate application. This form of fraud has been documented more extensively in African American pension applications, where dishonest pension agents took liberties in manufacturing evidence, often without their client's knowledge or consent. Investigations of these cases reveal how race, gender, and class served as proxies for the perceived respectability of the applicant and the validity of their claims.[11]

Deceiving the Pension Bureau grew easier in the twentieth century, as the number of veterans who could discredit a pretender's story faded away and the desire to expend considerable resources to investigate and scrutinize claimants' stories waned. It became relatively easy for elderly and impoverished applicants to add a few years to their age and invent generic wartime stories that would be difficult for anyone at the pension office to verify. When the states of the former Confederacy began offering pensions to former Confederates, haphazard recordkeeping made it even easier for southern imposters to stake their claims. In some cases, wartime dissenters presented themselves as southern Unionists to the Southern Claims Commission to receive compensation from the federal government, but later changed their story to declare that they had been loyal Confederates all along to receive pensions offered by state governments. Many of those who claimed to be the last surviving Civil War veterans acquired their pensions fraudulently during the deepest years of the Great Depression. As the last generation of legitimate veterans died, their younger pretenders felt compelled to carry on their lies despite their growing notoriety.[12]

Cowlam arrived at the soldiers' home in Dayton at an opportune time. Although the Central Branch had opened nearly twenty years before, Congress initially restricted admission only to those who suffered from wartime injuries. By 1884, however, Congress had dramatically expanded the eligibility requirements to include those "disabled by age, disease, or otherwise, and by reason of such disability are incapable of earning a living." Whereas Cowlam would have needed to document a wartime injury to be eligible for a pension, the requirements for entry into the soldiers' home were much more relaxed. To gain admittance he needed only to establish that he was a Union veteran unable to support himself.

The Dayton facility was the largest of all of the homes in the system. The National Home's board of managers had selected Dayton due to its convenient access to rail transportation as well as its ability to draw Union veterans from the Midwest, border South, and western mid-Atlantic. The grounds and architecture resembled a small city that was part military installation and part utopian community. The campus included workshops that offered veterans the opportunity to work for wages, as well as ample entertainment to keep their minds occupied. The home followed a military structure, with new entrants issued blue uniforms and organized into companies of roughly one hundred men. The number of men living in the home fluctuated over the course of the year, but at any given time there would have been between four thousand and five thousand veterans in residence.[13]

In seeking to blend in among the aged and infirm veterans in the soldiers' home, Cowlam would have been very conspicuous. A high-ranking officer, such as a colonel, would have been a rare sight. Virtually all of the inmates came from the lower enlisted ranks. Roughly two-thirds of the men were foreign born, and most were unmarried farmers or laborers who could no longer care for themselves. By representing himself to be forty-one years old, he would have appeared to be among the youngest inmates in the home. In fancying himself a Union colonel, Charles may have been trying to imitate his brother, George, who had actually served four years for the Union. George had enlisted as a private in the 11th New York Infantry, but soon obtained a transfer to the U.S. Military Telegraph Corps due to his prior experience as a telegraph operator. In his later life newspaper articles often referred to George as Colonel Cowlam.[14]

Cowlam entertained the special examiners with extraordinary stories of his wartime exploits. All of them were either gross exaggerations or works of pure fantasy. He repeated his claim to have been in the Secret Service, and variously implied that he had been a spy working for General Benjamin Butler or General Marsena Patrick. Given that General Patrick was the governor of the soldiers' home, it seems odd to think that he would not have remembered Cowlam if this claim had any basis in fact. Although Charles's brother, George, cultivated a correspondence with Butler for several years after the war, no letters from Charles can be found among the general's papers. In telling these and other stories, Cowlam wished desperately to be perceived as respectable and loyal. His tenuous connections to prominent generals, bogus officer's rank, and questionable claims of wartime espionage offered evidence of his allegiance to the Union cause and gave the impression that he was an upstanding citizen. Cowlam presented his wartime incarceration not as punishments for a crime, but as sacrifices borne for the Union cause. His falsehoods reveal both his personal feelings toward his wartime experiences and the challenges of ascertaining claims of loyalty once the war ended.[15]

To embellish his claims of having been a Union spy, Cowlam asserted that his efforts landed him in Libby Prison in Richmond, where he was sentenced to be executed, but escaped before the sentence could be carried out. Libby Prison was located one block away from Castle Thunder, where he had spent Christmas 1864 after his arrest for stealing and for impersonating a Confederate captain. The prison almost exclusively housed captured Union officers and important political prisoners, but it also served as the central clearinghouse and processing point for all prisoners of war. Introducing Libby Prison would have made his story appear more credible, as the prison was well known for having sheltered Union prisoners of war. The account of his escape would have also seemed believable. A massive prison break from Libby took place in February 1864, and Cowlam almost certainly would have heard stories about it that he could have employed to make the tale seem more authentic.[16]

In the course of the War Department's investigation, his brother, George, wrote a letter to Pension Commissioner Black explaining that Charles was "caught in the south by the war" but made two attempts to escape to the North. The first effort was unsuccessful and led to his being sentenced to death as a Union spy. In his second attempt he spent two weeks in the Dismal Swamp, which contributed to the "permanent ruin of his health," before reaching the Union lines at Suffolk, Virginia. There he "was welcomed by Gen. Grant to whom he gave valuable information." Although it is possible that Cowlam relayed some information after crossing the Union lines in Norfolk, the material he provided was more likely mundane than critical. Grant's intelligence apparatus, the Bureau of Military Information, routinely collected information from freedpeople, deserters, and refugees. The information gathered from these sources could be problematic. It could be difficult for interrogators to separate gossip and rumors from fact, and to discern useful intelligence out of embellished narratives. Cowlam's account would have reflected all of these limitations. He would not have hesitated to ingratiate himself with his captors and demonstrate his commitment to the Union cause. In his typical dramatic style, he would have emphasized the urgency of the information. Whether he would have been taken seriously is a different matter.[17]

Clearly Cowlam had been practicing these stories for years, and his contributions seemed to grow with each retelling. In recounting his time as a government detective, he told investigators that he had "discovered a plot to assassinate President Lincoln" that Secretary of War Edwin M. Stanton and Secretary of State William H. Seward "refused to consider."[18] No longer a mere detective on the case, Cowlam placed himself at the center of the investigation, and echoed the claim he had repeated for years that he had sent a report to Stanton warning him of the president's impending murder. He may have crafted his wartime stories to deflect attention from his incarceration. Historian Angela Riotto notes that Civil War incarceration "denied thousands of men the opportunity to prove themselves as soldiers on the battlefield." Consequently, these prisoners and prisoners of war emerged from the conflict with an uncertain position in postwar society. In a sense, the world had passed them by. Prisoners of war often emphasized escape attempts in their narratives to demonstrate their bravery, manliness, and patriotism. Many of those who had been held captive in Civil War prisons emerged from the war with an insatiable need to make their stories known.[19]

The first piece of evidence that helped the investigators to situate Grahame's story came from Bunting Brothers, metal brokers of 116 William Street, New York, located one block away from the Bennett Building, where Cowlam had published the *Scythe* a decade earlier. The firm had informed the New York chief of police in June 1886 that they had hired a man named Livingston Grahame the previous year to go to Colorado to inspect mines for them, but they had received no letters from him in the past two months. The break in communication began shortly before Cowlam's admittance to the soldiers' home. One of the partners in the firm recalled meeting Grahame in Guatemala eleven years before, and he remembered hearing stories of his adventures in the Secret Service during the war, his arrest for having been a Union spy, his escape from Libby Prison before the sentence of death could be carried out, and how he had served under General Benjamin Butler.[20] The unnamed Bunting Brothers partner who recalled meeting Grahame in Guatemala was almost certainly Thomas Browne Bunting, who had been a Union captain during the Civil War and traveled to Guatemala in 1876, where the Guatemalan president made him a general. Bunting resigned from the Guatemalan army in 1883 and returned to the United States.[21]

Justo Rufino Barrios, who became the president of Guatemala in 1873, shaped this entire period of Central American history. Barrios was a general and liberal reformer with a complicated legacy of modernization. His tenure witnessed the introduction of the first railroads and telegraph lines, and oversaw the ratification of the country's first constitution. At the same time, Barrios was a brutal dictator who persecuted his political opponents. To counter the political influence of his conservative opposition, Barrios confiscated property owned by the Catholic Church and disbanded religious orders. He pursued a radical policy of land redistribution, which concentrated land ownership, and introduced a system of forced indigenous labor on coffee plantations. In the last year of his rule, Barrios unveiled a bold plan to consolidate all of the Central American countries under one government, reminiscent of the government in place in the region for the first two decades after independence from Spain. Barrios proclaimed himself President of Central America, but the neighboring states were not eager to join, and he led an ill-fated invasion of El Salvador that ended with his death on the battlefield in April 1885.[22]

It is not clear when Cowlam first traveled to Guatemala under his assumed name Livingston Grahame. The exact chronology for his activities after leaving New York in 1874 and arriving in Dayton in 1886 is uncertain. The only evidence of his travels in Central America appears in shipping news columns announcing his arrival. Grahame arrived in San Francisco on August 16, 1880, aboard the steamer *City of Panama,* which sailed from Panama City on July 31. Another voyage is documented in a Panamanian newspaper reporting his arrival in Panama City on July 4, 1885, aboard the steamer *Honduras,* which had sailed from Champerico, Guatemala. The short article mentions that Grahame had recently returned after inspecting the Loma Larga and Divisadero mining operations in El Salvador.[23]

Americans flocked to Guatemala after a gold discovery in 1877 in the Atlantic Coast state of Izabal that the press heralded as the new El Dorado. The president of Guatemala designated Thomas Browne Bunting as the authorized agent for the Guatemalan government, instructing him to travel to New York to commission a mining engineer to survey the deposits and form a company that would develop the gold fields. Cowlam may have seized the opportunity to enter the mining business. His younger brother, George, had worked as a clerk for the Committee on Mines and Mining in the House of Representatives from 1873 until 1874, which may have given Charles enough familiarity with the industry to convince others of his expertise.[24]

Cowlam invoked his Guatemalan credentials in the first of two letters he penned to the editor of the *Chicago Tribune* within two weeks of one another in December 1880 under his alias Livingston Grahame. The letter defended the reputation of Guatemala's President Barrios in response to an article reprinted from the *New York Times* that accused Barrios of publicly humiliating twelve women who had criticized the expulsion of Catholic priests from the country. Although the *Times* article did not identify the source of the information, Cowlam alleged that the story had come from Susana Alcantara, a correspondent based in Puerto Cabello, Venezuela, and the sister-in-law of a prominent diplomat in Guatemala. After identifying the source of the accusations, and commenting on the long distance that the rumors had traveled, Grahame described President Barrios as "the wisest and most liberal President which any of the Central or South American Republics have ever known." He compared Barrios to Benito Juarez, the liberal and much-beloved president of Mexico. Grahame stated that Barrios was neither a "despotic buffoon" nor a "cowardly tyrant," and claimed to have personally observed the president "under such conditions as prove him a gentleman of education, refinement, and humanity."[25]

In defending Barrios's reputation, Grahame compared the Guatemalan reforms to southern Reconstruction. He admitted that Barrios had shot many traitors and attempted revolutionaries, but he took this as an opportunity to criticize the leniency American presidents had extended toward former Confederates. Grahame argued that Latin American leaders had "shown more sense and nerve than have the Presidents of the United States of America; they not only make 'treason odious,' but they make it dangerous." Here he echoed the American president Andrew Johnson's words that "treason must be made odious and traitors punished." Whereas American presidents had dithered, Grahame contended that Barrios knew how to handle treason and had the results to show for it, citing Guatemalan progress in education, railroad and telegraph construction, and improvements in public safety, roads, and banking.[26]

Grahame sent a second letter to the *Chicago Tribune* a little more than a week later, expressing his support for an editorial that defended the abolitionist John Brown's memory. Brown was hanged for treason, murder, and insurrection in December 1859 for attempting to seize the armory at Harpers Ferry in an effort to incite a large-scale slave revolt. The editorial came after derogatory comments made by U.S. Senator George Graham Vest, of Missouri, who suggested that Brown was an "old scoundrel who deserved his fate." Grahame supported the *Tribune*'s defense of Brown, and related a personal connection that motivated him to write. He claimed to have been engaged in conversation with the governor of Virginia, Henry A. Wise, in the governor's office when the telegram announcing Brown's raid on Harpers Ferry arrived. Upon reading the telegram, the governor "leaned back in his chair, chewed nervously the quid of tobacco which seemed a part of himself, and, while the saliva trickled down the corners of his mouth and corrugated his shirt front," he handed the message to Grahame and said, "Read this—can you understand it?"[27]

The message, according to Grahame, described Brown's forces seizing control of the arsenal, rifle works, and bridge over the Potomac River with a force of around five hundred. The telegram purportedly presented Brown's forces as occupying Maryland Heights, and suggested that a contingent of Pennsylvania abolitionists was expected to arrive shortly from Chambersburg. Grahame described watching as the governor dispatched messages to Charles Town, Winchester, and Petersburg. As panicked telegrams continued to pour in all afternoon, Grahame recalled Governor Wise remarking, "Why, this John Brown is playing Coeur de Lion—he attacks the world single handed—he must be a lunatic, or braver than Caesar!"[28]

Where Cowlam could have conceivably met President Barrios of Guatemala, his fantastical recollections of John Brown's raid could not possibly have occurred. Cowlam was confined in the state penitentiary in Richmond in October 1859 when the raid took place, and there would have been no reason for him to have been chatting casually in the governor's office. While the initial reports of the raid did advance exaggerated estimates of the strength of Brown's forces, the details of Cowlam's story are both oddly specific and unreliable, as though he had consulted a history of the raid for a general timeline and inserted imagined details of his own. His retelling of the aftermath is equally dubious. He claimed to have accompanied Governor Wise to Harpers Ferry the following morning, and to have witnessed Brown's arrest, trial, and execution. Although the governor did travel to Harpers Ferry on the second day of the raid, he arrived after Brown had been captured, and the arrest, trial, and execution took place weeks apart. Cowlam professed to have watched Brown die on the scaffold, recalling that his eye "never blenched as he looked around upon the armed and unmoved throng, here and there a black face with pitying tears, but in the white faces only a mortal hatred; here and there one in whose heart lived the knowledge that John Brown died to make men free." Here Cowlam alluded to the song "John Brown's Body," popular among Union soldiers during the Civil War and later serving as the inspiration for the "Battle Hymn of the Republic," which contains the line "As He died to make men holy / Let us die to make men free."[29]

Cowlam also spent time in the Chicago area, and he may have written his letters to the *Chicago Tribune* while passing through. Residents of Elgin and Capron, Illinois, recalled Livingston Grahame as a traveling photographer whose photograph car passed through the area several years before his entry into the soldiers' home in Dayton. Both towns are located northwest of Chicago, about forty miles from Waukegan, where his father built the town's first steam-powered gristmill in his childhood. Grahame's business mostly consisted of tintypes, which maintained a novelty appeal even after *carte de visites* and cabinet cards had become more fashionable. Charles may have learned the fundamentals of photography from his youngest sister, Isabel, who worked as a photographer for the Treasury Department for forty-nine years and later exhibited her work in the Corcoran Gallery of Art with the Capital Camera Club.[30]

The residents of Elgin and Capron remembered Grahame as a world traveler who "has been at the bottom and top of the ladder of fame and wealth many times." He had apparently told the locals that he had spent several years in Europe as a correspondent for the *New York Herald,* and had traveled the globe so extensively that "the only country he has not seen being Africa." In retelling his travels in Central America, he explained that he was an "intimate friend" of President Barrios, and through his connections with General Bunting he was the possessor of "valuable mining stock and railway franchise." He remained in touch after leaving Capron and made two trips to Mexico and Central America to oversee work in the mines, to which he attributed the decline in his health. The Illinois residents proposed another explanation for Grahame's weak constitution, noting that "he was always an extremely temperate man, but an inveterate smoker, and this caused paralysis of the brain." In the last letter he sent to his correspondents in Illinois he noted his intention to travel to London to sell his mining stock and thereafter to return to Mexico, explaining, "one more trip down there and I will be beyond want the rest of my days." Grahame apparently never completed his intended journey, and he checked into the soldiers' home shortly thereafter.[31]

Others recalled Grahame's literary talents. His friends in Elgin and Capron attributed the drama *Black Diamonds* to him, along with "the salient points of the comedy of 'Cheek,' with which Roland Reed has scored much success." Roland Reed was a popular nineteenth-century stage actor, famous for his role in the comedy *Cheek*. Both productions are easily attributable to other authors, but Grahame may have adapted or revived them for local audiences while drafting other performances of his own. The story of *Black Diamonds* features a mining engineer among the main characters, and Cowlam may have tailored the role based on his own experiences. Grahame convinced his listeners that he spoke several languages and had "translated one remarkable Spanish work for publication" during his time in Illinois. His brother, George, remembered him as "once a brilliant literary man and has written several plays, produced successfully at Baldwin's San Francisco theater." The records of the Library of Congress reveal that Livingston Grahame copyrighted *Perpetual Motion: A Drama in 4 Acts* in San Francisco in 1880. Unfortunately, a copy of this production has not survived.[32]

Cowlam's tales from the Civil War could also take on a literary quality. Grahame told the residents of Elgin and Capron of his exploits as a Union spy and intimated that he was a close friend of Ulysses S. Grant. The local newspaper reported that "his recital of his midnight escape from Castle Thunder with a fractured leg, was like a work of fiction." Those who had known Grahame were right to point out the fictional qualities in his wartime stories. Escape attempts from Castle Thunder were quite common but only occasionally successful. The most successful escapees donned civilian clothes and assumed a fake identity. By pretending to be a visitor, some of these inmates walked out the front door of the prison past unsuspecting guards. Others tried to climb out of windows by cutting blankets into ropes. Cowlam had likely heard stories of inmates who had sawed off bars and rappelled or jumped from the second or third story of the prison. One inmate, Alfonzo C. Webster, plotted numerous failed escape attempts from Castle Thunder, including one on March 27, 1863, where he jumped from a window onto the roof of a shed, and from there jumped fifteen feet to the ground. The fall broke both of Webster's ankles and he was quickly recaptured. If Cowlam had escaped using the same technique, one imagines that he would not have been able to make the journey from Richmond to the Union lines in Norfolk in only a week with a broken leg.[33]

Eventually Grahame wandered to Springfield, Ohio, where he lived with Mrs. Lida E. Fisher. Fisher lived and worked at 35½ Main Street, where she maintained a photo gallery and operated a business enlarging photographs. Grahame presumably assisted her as an employee. In February 1886 the pair were arrested after a disgruntled employee, J. S. Cole, complained to Fisher that he had not received his wages. Cole had worked for Fisher for five weeks, and for the first two weeks he received his pay promptly. As his wages gradually diminished he began to protest, and he ultimately confronted Fisher, who "flew at him . . . in a passionate manner and gave him to understand that he would never get his pay." Grahame took Fisher's side in the argument, and after a hostile confrontation, Cole went to the police station to make complaints against Fisher and Grahame. When the police arrived, Fisher and Grahame barricaded the door, and the pair eventually were arrested when a second officer succeeded in breaching the entrance. Fisher and Grahame reciprocated after their arrest by filing affidavits against Cole, and all three faced charges of disorderly conduct. The charges against Cole and Grahame were dismissed a few days later, and Fisher received a fine of $1 plus court costs.[34]

Fisher's financial troubles worsened through the spring of 1886, culminating in a dramatic scene that led to Grahame's admittance to the soldiers' home. When her gallery in Springfield closed, she moved to nearby Yellow Springs, where she continued to operate her photography business. As her savings dwindled, she borrowed $153 using her household effects as collateral to keep the business afloat. Fisher failed to repay the loan, and the local court allowed her creditor to recover her possessions. When an officer attempted to retrieve her property, Fisher warned that if he laid a hand on her belongings she would kill herself. The officer tried to calm Fisher, but as he began to cart her furniture outside he glanced over and noticed a bottle of laudanum between her lips. He grabbed the bottle out of her hands before she could use the opioid to commit suicide. The failure of the photography business left Fisher and Grahame destitute, and Fisher escorted Grahame to the Central Branch soldiers' home shortly after this emotional episode, where she presented herself as his cousin.[35]

Fisher told the special examiners at the Pension Bureau that Cowlam had other relatives but did not know their names or whereabouts. The examiners soon located his brother, George, and his sister Isabel, who had long assumed he was dead. George expressed his desire to visit the soldiers' home and retrieve his brother, promising that he would be made comfortable for the rest of his life. At that time George lived with his wife and three children in Madison, Indiana, and had been working for the Cumberland Railroad in Crossville, Tennessee. Isabel lived in Washington, D.C., where she worked in the Treasury Department. Charles's reappearance offered all who knew him an opportunity to reconsider his memories of the war, and to reflect on what they remembered of Livingston Grahame. His fabricated stories of espionage, prison escapes, abolitionist heroes, prominent generals, and presidents projected a view of himself that emphasized his commitment to the Union cause. More than anything Cowlam wanted to be accomplished, respected, and appreciated for his involvement in the Civil War. Even under the cover of a new identity, he was still telling the same stories that he had been relating for more than two decades. His stories seemed to represent his unrealized aspirations, and elements of his narrative resembled the experiences of his younger brother, George, who embodied everything that Charles was not.[36]

EPILOGUE

Something further may follow of this Masquerade.
—HERMAN MELVILLE, *The Confidence Man: His Masquerade* (1857)

If Charles arrived at his brother's home in Madison, Indiana, after leaving the Central Branch soldiers' home in 1886, he did not stay for long. His name never appeared with George's family in any of the Madison city directories in the years after his discharge. Charles disappeared again, just as quickly as he had been found. His first wife, Mary Ives Cowlam, began listing herself in the Detroit city directory as the widow of Charles in 1889. Although it is possible that she had received some news of Charles's death, she may have simply preferred to describe herself as a widow now that fifteen years had elapsed since he had abandoned her. As Ira Shafer noted presciently when summarizing Cowlam's life in the *Detroit Free Press* years before, "his later record is not so well known."[1]

There are certain things we cannot know about Charles Cowlam's life. Elusive figures do not make their absence known or advertise their demise. The historian Thomas Cohen notes that "the desire for an end is often frustrated in microhistory."[2] It is customary for microhistories to engage in informed speculation when the historical evidence fails to deliver closure. Cowlam may have died, or he may have changed his name once again to obscure his past and continue on as a grifter. Throughout his adult life he complained of his ill health, most likely owing to his years in confinement, which he ascribed to a variety of causes. One recollection describes him as a heavy smoker, and he often gave observers the impression that he did not have long to live. If he survived under an alias, it is possible that he continued to go by Charles but adopted a different spelling or pronunciation of his surname, as he did often, or he may have invented a more original assumed name that would have been harder to connect to his former life. If he pursued the latter course, he succeeded in remaining anonymous, for he left no trace after leaving Dayton, Ohio, in 1886.

Charles's brother, George, offers a counterpoint to his life and allows us to speculate on what type of life he might have led had he not gone to prison. George was seven years younger, having been born in Battle Creek on April 19, 1844. After their father died in 1850, George lived with Henry Izard and his family in Woodstock, Ontario, where he learned to operate a telegraph as a teenager. When the Civil War began, George traveled to New York and enlisted as a private in Company D of Elmer E. Ellsworth's Zouaves, the 11th New York Infantry. He signed his enlistment papers on April 20, 1861, little more than a week after the attack on Fort Sumter, and mustered into the unit in Washington, D.C., on May 7. In joining the army, George exaggerated his age, claiming to be twenty years old when he had really just turned seventeen. His wife, Mary S. Cowlam, would later describe him in her pension application as five feet, seven and a half inches tall, with light blue eyes, brown hair, and a light complexion.[3]

Like his brother, Charles, George also claimed a connection to Abraham Lincoln. In the last years of his life he relayed an encounter that took place when he was a sixteen-year-old telegraph operator traveling from Chicago to St. Louis on the Alton Railroad in June or early July of 1860. In George's telling, a tall man boarded and sat next to him as the car passed through Springfield, Illinois. In the course of their conversation George made his support for Lincoln known, when the gentleman "said he was a republican, but he didn't think he would vote for Lincoln." Upon hearing this George expressed his indignation and attempted to persuade him of his sense of duty. When the train reached Alton, Illinois, a new conductor boarded and recognized the presidential candidate, greeting him as "Mr. Lincoln." George made the connection himself only after the train left the station and approached East St. Louis. Looking the future president in the eye, George asked him, "is it Abe?" The answer left him in stunned silence. As the two parted, the future president invited him to visit the White House if Lincoln were elected and if George was in Washington. George claimed to have followed through on this promise early the following year. When his unit arrived in Washington,

EPILOGUE

George remembered, Lincoln, Secretary of State William Seward, and Secretary of the Navy Gideon Welles reviewed the regiment on the east Capitol grounds. George recalled that Lincoln recognized him instantly, remarking, "I knew you would be in Washington," before asking why he had not called on him at the White House.[4]

In recounting the incident more than thirty-five years later, the story sounds apocryphal. If the two met on a train in the summer of 1860, the occasion would have offered the perfect opportunity to put in a few good words for Charles's clemency. A careful look at Lincoln's movements that summer reveal that the meeting on the train likely never occurred. Lincoln remained in Springfield, Illinois, all summer awaiting news of his nomination as the Republican presidential candidate, attending to his law practice, and sitting with portrait painter John Henry Brown. The president did, however, review the 11th New York Infantry on May 7, 1861, the same day that George joined the unit, on a lot behind the Capitol with his son, Tad, and his private secretary, John Hay. It is possible that George cast eyes on Lincoln, or even shook the president's hand, but the other elements of the story are fanciful. The story demonstrates that Charles was not the only member of his family prone to imagined meetings with famous Americans.[5]

Recollections of George's military service contain some uncertainties alongside accounts that can be confirmed. Obituaries would later describe him as the chief telegrapher under General George B. McClellan and indicated that he rose to the rank of colonel by the end of the war and received a medal from Congress for gallantry. A fellow telegraph operator remembered George participating in the First Battle of Manassas in July 1861 before his superiors recognized his talents for transmitting messages over the wire. Each of these statements are unconfirmed. On the company muster rolls George appears as "absent" or "not stated" after June 30, presumably reflecting a new assignment as a telegraph operator that separated him from his unit. In January 1862 he was detached to the U.S. Military Telegraph Corps, and he received a discharge from the army in March that enabled him to serve out the remainder of the war as a civilian telegraph officer. Almost as soon as he received his assignment with the telegraph service, George witnessed the Battle of Hampton Roads, which featured the famous engagement between the ironclad USS *Monitor* and the CSS *Virginia*. The story of George's exploits at the battle first appeared two decades later, in an early history of military telegraphy based on the recollections of fellow operators. On March 8, the first day of the battle, George occupied a log cabin sheltered behind the breastworks in Newport News. As he telegraphed news of the fighting, two shells ripped through the dwelling, shattering his bunk and leaving splinters in his clothes.[6]

After the war George continued working as a telegraph operator, and he occasionally used his access to privileged information to curry favor with prominent politicians.[7] George entered Benjamin F. Butler's circle when he leaked a telegram to Butler sent from the lobbyist Sam Ward to the political economist Edward Atkinson in the fall of 1868. The telegram briefly described Ward's efforts to prevent Butler's reelection to Congress. In forwarding the message, George added that he had intercepted additional dispatches that revealed Ward's speculation in the gold market with the help of insider information from the Treasury Department. George claimed that these telegrams implicated Secretary of the Treasury Hugh McCulloch. He noted that he could not afford to travel to Boston, but proposed to share the supplementary telegrams with Butler in person when the general returned to Washington. Although George insisted that the information he offered should remain strictly confidential until the two could meet, he added that if Butler needed to "make any use of it let it be understood you picked it up in Boston."[8]

In follow-up letters George coyly distanced himself from the leak, remarking, "whoever your friend was that sent you the information regarding the Ward-Atkinson correspondence did you and your constituents a good service in informing you all what a nest you could stir up." When George's coworkers at the telegraph office began to suspect that he was the source of the leak, he pressed Butler to "correct this wrong impression." When Butler sent a telegram to George at the office of his employer, the Franklin Telegraph Company, however, company officials accused him of disclosing the earlier telegrams. George resigned rather than protest the investigations against him. He cautioned Butler to burn all of their correspondence, to contact him only through Western Union rather than Franklin Telegraph, and encouraged him to "dispossess yourself" of the incriminating Ward-Atkinson letter.[9] Through Butler's influence, George obtained positions as a congressional messenger and committee clerk, and the two maintained a friendly occasional correspondence for several years. Although no correspondence survives connecting

Charles and Butler, George almost certainly provided the conduit connecting them.[10]

George again leaked private correspondence in April 1872 when he warned Horace F. Clark, the president of the Union Pacific Railroad, that an unnamed member of Congress intended to introduce legislation that would have a ruinous effect on the company's stock price. The Union Pacific had been a frequent target of short sellers, and Clark probed George's motivations for contacting him. Without revealing any details of the plan, George explained that he was acting on his own accord as Butler's private secretary, and insisted that Clark travel to Washington at once to meet in person. Clark did not know what to make of George's cryptic telegrams, and let him know that he could not fathom how the proposed legislation could be averted "unless by the purchase or bribery of the indefatigable worker in the House to whom you refer." Avowing that he would not expend a single cent for corrupt purposes, Clark dispatched company counsel Andrew J. Poppleton to Washington once he was satisfied that George was acting unselfishly and not as a conspirator. The following Monday, Republican congressman James S. Negley of Pennsylvania proposed a resolution authorizing President Grant to appoint a commission to investigate the Union Pacific's finances and indebtedness to the federal government. As soon as he introduced the motion, Democrat James Brooks of New York objected, accusing Negley of being in the pocket of Wall Street speculators, and threatening to read the correspondence George had shared. Brooks's rebuttal prompted Negley to withdraw his motion, and rumors circulated that the Pennsylvania Railroad had orchestrated the attack on the Union Pacific.[11]

Like his older brother, Charles, George spent three years in the South, from 1876 until 1879, working as an agent for the Quartermasters Department in eastern Tennessee. Based on these experiences, George came to believe that the future of the Republican Party depended on developing the southern economy. He corresponded with James A. Garfield in 1881, cautioning the president-elect that "the South needs, not schools, but *education*. She has schools enough teaching false history and false political economy. One good factory, or mine, or railroad, with a big pay roll will correct the teaching of a hundred such schools." George believed that southerners' single-minded focus on cotton cultivation had caused their economy to languish and their natural resources to remain untapped. To draw attention to the issue, George authored two works of southern boosterism. Both *The Undeveloped South* (1887) and *The Industrial Future of the South* (1891) emphasized the unbounded potential of southern industrial growth. To illustrate his point, George noted that the mountainous region from Nashville to Charleston possessed richer deposits of coal, iron, and timber than the comparable industrial region stretching from Cincinnati to New York. Rather than urging development through individual boomtowns, he argued that the South needed rail networks to connect commodities to international markets in the same way that the railroads had stimulated the development of the West.[12]

George died on March 11, 1901, of heart failure while staying at the Cosmopolitan Hotel in New York. A stroke he suffered the previous fall had diminished his faculties. He was fifty-seven years old. Like his older brother, Charles, he had corresponded with presidents and generals, engaged in intrigues of his own, hobnobbed with the leading power brokers, and witnessed southern Reconstruction. In many ways George led the life that Charles may have wished to live. George was upstanding and respectable, associated with numerous mining and railroad interests, a noted authority on southern mineral deposits, and a genuine Union veteran. The similarities shared between the two brothers may have been the secret to Charles's success. George's life story provided material for Charles's lies. Charles borrowed and benefited from his brother's connections, access to information, expertise, and personal experiences. On at least one occasion, confusion between the brothers gave Charles an advantage. George's contacts in the telegraph industry granted Charles entry into a world of confidential correspondence. His service in the Union army, friendship with Benjamin Butler, and knowledge acquired while serving as the clerk for the Committee on Mines and Mining would have all provided information that Charles could apply for his own purposes.

In the course of my research, I searched for every conceivable alternate spelling of *Cowlam* in hopes of uncovering another alias or discovering what became of Charles after 1886. The search produced two leads, both of which are doubtful but uncertain. In 1903 the U.S. Supreme Court heard the case of *Wiser v. Lawler,* which involved the promoters of a gold mine who misled investors in their prospectus. The case originated in May 1892 in Yavapai County, Arizona, where John Lawler and Edward W. Wells offered the mine for sale for $450,000 to Hulbert Harrington Warner, a Rochester businessman who had made his fortune selling patent medicine. Rather than convey the property immediately, however, the contract specified that Lawler and Wells would retain possession of the mine while Warner made payments in installments. The contract stipulated that, in the meantime, Charles Cowland would develop and operate the mine. Warner and Cowland soon transferred ownership of the mine to a holding company, and later incorporated the Seven Stars Gold Mining Company in New Jersey, raising $2.8 million through the sale of its stock. Company advertisements lured prospective investors with promises of 15 percent dividends guaranteed for five years. Cowland also prepared and circulated an unauthorized prospectus in Great Britain without consulting either the holding company or Seven Stars. The company never delivered on its promises, and by the time investors discovered the fraud and the case appeared in federal court, Charles Cowland was deceased. While the court case contains insufficient clues to determine whether this Charles Cowland was Charles Cowlam, other evidence casts doubt on their connection.[13]

Another lead involves a transcontinental journey for the sake of marriage. Charles Cowland and Alice Horton, both of San Francisco, arrived in Camden, New Jersey, on November 8, 1894, after traversing the continent by rail. Camden was one of the few places in the United States that did not require marriage licenses, and consequently attracted the attention of couples who wished to avoid the publicity or restrictions imposed by their home jurisdictions. Justice Philip Schmitz officiated the ceremony between Cowland and Horton, and the newlyweds began the return journey the following day. Could this be Charles Cowlam? Traveling nearly three thousand miles for a wedding, only to return home the next day, sounds strangely suspicious. What lies lurking beneath this inconspicuous news story we may never know for sure.[14]

NOTES

ABBREVIATIONS

DCA   Devonshire Collection Archives, Chatsworth House, Bakewell, United Kingdom.
FLA   State Library and Archives of Florida, Tallahassee, Florida.
LAC   Library and Archives of Canada, Ottawa, Ontario, Canada.
LC   Manuscript Division, Library of Congress, Washington, D.C.
LAE   William C. Edwards and Edward Steers Jr., eds., *The Lincoln Assassination: The Evidence* (Urbana: Univ. of Illinois Press, 2009).
NACP   National Archives and Records Administration, College Park, Maryland.
NAGA   National Archives and Records Administration, Atlanta, Georgia.
NARA   National Archives and Records Administration, Washington, D.C.
OR   U.S. War Department, comp., *War of the Rebellion: A Compilation of the Official Records of the Union and Confederate Armies,* 128 vols. (Washington D.C.: Government Printing Office, 1880–1901).
PUSG   John Y. Simon, ed., *The Papers of Ulysses S. Grant,* 31 vols. (Carbondale: Southern Illinois Univ. Press, 1967–2009).
SHC   Southern Historical Collection, Wilson Library, University of North Carolina at Chapel Hill, Chapel Hill, North Carolina.
SWEM   College of William & Mary, Earl Gregg Swem Library, Special Collections Research Center, Williamsburg, Virginia.

INTRODUCTION

1. Brian P. Luskey, *Men Is Cheap: Exposing the Frauds of Free Labor in Civil War America* (Chapel Hill: Univ. of North Carolina Press, 2020), 5–6; Mark A. Lause, *Free Labor: The Civil War and the Making of an American Working Class* (Urbana: Univ. of Illinois Press, 2015), 19–22; Robert J. Steinfeld, *Coercion, Contract, and Free Labor in the Nineteenth Century* (New York: Cambridge Univ. Press, 2001), 13–14; Amy Dru Stanley, *From Bondage to Contract: Wage Labor, Marriage, and the Market in the Age of Slave Emancipation* (Cambridge: Cambridge Univ. Press, 1998), 2–17; Jonathan A. Glickstein, *Concepts of Free Labor in Antebellum America* (New Haven:

Yale Univ. Press, 1991), 11–16; Eric Foner, *Free Soil, Free Labor, Free Men: The Ideology of the Republican Party Before the Civil War* (1970; reprint, New York: Oxford Univ. Press, 1995), 11–39, 163. James L. Huston proposes an earlier periodization of the free labor ideology, dating its origins to seventeenth-century England. See James L. Huston, *The British Gentry, the Southern Planter, and the Northern Family Farmer: Agriculture and Sectional Antagonism in North America* (Baton Rouge: Louisiana State Univ. Press, 2015), xi–xvi.

2. Henry David Thoreau, *Walden*, ed. Jeffrey S. Cramer (1854; reprint, New Haven: Yale Univ. Press, 2004), 320; Brian Balogh, *A Government Out of Sight: The Mystery of National Authority in Nineteenth-Century America* (Cambridge: Cambridge Univ. Press, 2009), 277–308; Charles Sellers, *The Market Revolution: Jacksonian America, 1815–1846* (New York: Oxford Univ. Press, 1991), 3–69. On the effects of these transformations later in the century, see T. J. Jackson Lears, *No Place of Grace: Antimodernism and the Transformation of American Culture, 1880–1920* (Chicago: Univ. of Chicago Press, 1981), 4–58; Robert H. Wiebe, *The Search for Order 1877–1920* (New York: Hill and Wang, 1967), 44–75.

3. Karen Halttunen, *Confidence Men and Painted Women: A Study of Middle-Class Culture in America, 1830–1870* (New Haven: Yale Univ. Press, 1982), 1–9, 12–13, 21–25, 31, 47, 201–202; Maria Konnikova, *The Confidence Game: The Psychology of the Con and Why We Fall for It . . . Every Time* (New York: Viking, 2016), 4–10; Hugo Van Driel, "Financial Fraud, Scandals, and Regulation: A Conceptual Framework and Literature Review," *Business History* 61, no. 8 (November 2019): 1259–1299; Edward J. Balleisen, "A Profusion of Microhistories: The Historiography of American Business Fraud" (October 2017), https://sites.duke.edu/suckersandswindlers/files/2017/10/Historical-Scholarship-on-Business-Fraud-10-3-17.pdf; Michael Pettit, *The Science of Deception: Psychology and Commerce in America* (Chicago: Univ. of Chicago Press, 2013), 33–46; James W. Cook, *The Arts of Deception: Playing with Fraud in the Age of Barnum* (Cambridge: Harvard Univ. Press, 2001); John Lindbeck, "Preachers and Peddlers: Credit and Belief in the Flush Times," in *Southern Scoundrels: Grifters and Graft in the Nineteenth Century,* ed. Jeff Forret and Bruce E. Baker (Baton Rouge: Louisiana State Univ. Press, 2021), 12–36; David Walker, "The Humbug in American Religion: Ritual Theories of Nineteenth-Century Spiritualism," *Religion and American Culture* 23 (winter 2013): 30–74; Stanley J. Thayne, "Walking on Water: Nineteenth-Century Prophets and a Legend of Religious Imposture," *Journal of Mormon History* 36, no. 2 (spring 2010): 160–204. On the confidence woman, see Kathleen DeGrave, *Swindler, Spy, Rebel: The Confidence Woman in Nineteenth-Century America* (Columbia: Univ. of Missouri Press, 1995).

4. William Cronon, *Nature's Metropolis: Chicago and the Great West* (New York: Norton, 1991), 31–45; Susan E. Gray, *The Yankee West: Community Life on the Michigan Frontier* (Chapel Hill: Univ. of North Carolina Press, 1996), 1–5, 47; Bayrd Still, "Patterns of Mid-Nineteenth Century Urbanization in the Middle West," *Mississippi Valley Historical Review* 28, no. 2 (September 1941): 187–206; Sharon Hartman Strom, *Fortune, Fame, and Desire: Promoting the Self in the Long Nineteenth Century* (Lanham, Md.: Rowman and Littlefield, 2016), xiii–xiv. For confidence men in the South, see Forret and Baker, eds., *Southern Scoundrels.*

5. "A Strange History," *Detroit Free Press,* 12 December 1874, 1.

6. Ibid.

7. Two of the best-known examples of microhistory include Natalie Zemon Davis, *The Return of Martin Guerre* (Cambridge: Harvard Univ. Press, 1983), and Paul E. Johnson and Sean Wilentz, *The Kingdom of Matthias: A Story of Sex and Salvation in 19th-Century America* (New York: Oxford Univ. Press, 1994).

8. David Nash and Anne-Marie Kilday note that "court cases are themselves micro-histories of the law at work." David S. Nash and Anne-Marie Kilday, "Introduction," in *Law, Crime and Deviance Since 1700: Micro-Studies in the History of Crime,* ed. Anne-Marie Kilday and David Nash (London: Bloomsbury, 2017), 3; Thomas V. Cohen, "The Macrohistory of Microhistory," *Journal of Medieval and Early Modern Studies* 47, no. 1 (January 2017): 53–73; Alex Tepperman, "Status Quotidian: Microhistory and the Study of Crime," in *History and Crime: A Transdisciplinary Approach,* ed. Thomas J. Kehoe and Jeffrey E. Pfeifer (Bingley: Emerald Publishing, 2021), 143–156; Timothy J. Gilfoyle, *A Pickpocket's Tale: The Underworld of Nineteenth-Century New York* (New York: Norton, 2006).

9. The term "normal exception" originates in Edoardo Grendi, "Ripensare la microstoria?," *Quaderni Storici* 86, no. 2 (August 1994): 539–549.

10. Richard Bell, "Peepholes, Eels, and Pickett's Charge: Doing Microhistory Then and Now," *Journal of the Civil War Era* 12, no. 3 (September 2022): 362–387; Sigurður Gylfi Magnússon and István M. Szijártó, *What Is Microhistory?: Theory and Practice* (Abingdon: Routledge, 2013), 4–7, 50–55; Richard D. Brown, "Microhistory and the Post-Modern Challenge," *Journal of the Early Republic* 23, no. 1 (spring 2003): 1–20; Jill Lepore, "Historians Who Love Too Much: Reflections on Microhistory and Biography," *Journal of American History* 88, no. 1 (June 2001): 129–144; Carlos Ginzburg, "Microhistory: Two or Three Things That I Know About It," *Critical Inquiry* 20, no. 1 (autumn 1993): 10–35. For scoundrels that bear similarities to Cowlam's life, see William C. Davis, *Inventing Loreta Velasquez: Confederate Soldier Impersonator, Media Celebrity, and Con Artist* (Carbondale: Southern Illinois Univ. Press, 2016); Carman Cumming, *Devil's Game: The Civil War Intrigues of Charles A. Dunham* (Urbana: Univ. of Illinois Press, 2004); Ann Larabee, *The Dynamite Fiend: The Chilling Tale of a Confederate Spy, Con Artist, and Mass Murderer* (New York: Palgrave Macmillan, 2005).

11. On the history of criminal identification, see Simon A. Cole, *Suspect Identities: A History of Fingerprinting and Criminal Identification* (Cambridge: Harvard Univ. Press, 2001), 6–31; Jane Caplan and John Torpey, eds., *Documenting Individual Identity: The Development of State Practices in the Modern World* (Princeton: Princeton Univ. Press, 2001).

12. Emphasis added. Gustave de Beaumont and Alexis de Tocqueville, *On the Penitentiary System in the United States, and Its Application in France: The Complete Text,* trans. Emily Katherine Ferkaluk (1833; reprint, Cham, Switzerland: Palgrave Macmillan, 2018), 76.

13. Lawrence M. Friedman, *Crime and Punishment in American History* (New York: Basic Books, 1993), 193–210; Katherine Unterman, *Uncle Sam's Policemen: The Pursuit of Fugitives Across Borders* (Cambridge: Harvard Univ. Press, 2015), 14–74; Katherine Unterman, "Boodle Over the Border: Embezzlement and the Crisis of International Mobility, 1880–1890," *Journal of the Gilded Age and Progressive Era* 11, no. 2 (April 2012): 151–189; Benjamin P. Thomas, *Abraham Lincoln: A Biography* (1952, reprint, Carbondale: Southern Illinois Univ. Press, 2008), 37–38.

14. Yael A. Sternhell, *Routes of War: The World of Movement in the Confederate South* (Cambridge: Harvard Univ. Press, 2012), 5–11; The sociologist Lyn Lofland emphasizes the importance of spatial ordering, noting that "the modern urbanite, then, in contrast to his preindustrial counterpart, primarily uses location rather than appearance to identify the strange others who surround him. In the preindustrial city, space was chaotic, appearances were ordered. In the modern city, appearances are chaotic, space is ordered. In the preindustrial city, a man was what he wore. In the modern city, a man is where he stands." Lyn H. Lofland, *A World of Strangers: Order and Action in Urban Public Space* (New York: Basic Books, 1973), 82.

15. Michael Thomas Smith emphasizes the role of republicanism in stoking fears of corruption in the North, suggesting that the persistence of republicanism in nineteenth-century American life signifies the perseverance of pre-modern relationship and culture in the Civil War era. See Michael Thomas Smith, *The Enemy Within: Fears of Corruption in the Civil War North* (Charlottesville: Univ. of Virginia Press, 2011), 2–12; Mark Wahlgren Summers, *The Ordeal of the Reunion: A New History of Reconstruction* (Chapel Hill: Univ. of North Carolina Press, 2014), 273–297; Mark W. Summers, *The Plundering Generation: Corruption and the Crisis of the Union, 1849–1861* (New York: Oxford Univ. Press, 1987), 23–36; Eric Foner, *Reconstruction: America's Unfinished Revolution 1863–1877* (New York: Harper and Row, 1988), 347–351, 484–486, quotation 484; Margaret Susan Thompson, *The "Spider Web": Congress and Lobbying in the Age of Grant* (Ithaca: Cornell Univ. Press, 1985), 43–45, 145–176, 248–250; Margaret Susan Thompson, "Corruption—or Confusion? Lobbying and Congressional Government in the Early Gilded Age," *Congress and the Presidency* 10, no. 2 (autumn 1983): 169–193, especially 173–174, 179–181; Margaret S. Thompson, "Ben Butler versus the Brahmins: Patronage and Politics in Early Gilded Age Massachusetts," *New England Quarterly* 55, no. 2 (June 1982): 163–186.

16. After highlighting the contributions of the New History of Capitalism, Jeffrey Broxmeyer emphasizes that as "yet no studies have examined how political parties, specifically, transform into circuits of accumulation. Surprisingly little is written in American political development on how 'coalition merchants' constructed the machinery of partisan conflict." Jeffrey D. Broxmeyer, *Electoral Capitalism: The Party System in New York's Gilded Age* (Philadelphia: Univ. of Pennsylvania Press, 2020), 1–25, quotation 5; Jeffrey D. Broxmeyer, "Bringing The 'Ring' Back In: The Politics of Booty Capitalism," *Journal of the Gilded Age and Progressive Era* 19 (2020): 235–245; Ian Klaus, *Forging Capitalism: Rogues, Swindlers, Frauds, and the Rise of Modern Finance* (New Haven: Yale Univ. Press, 2014), 5; Forret and Baker, eds., *Southern Scoundrels*, 4–8, quotation 6. Baker has argued elsewhere that "capitalists need criminals" because crime offers a diagnostic test that reveals weak points in a system in need of strengthening. Bruce E. Baker, "Fires on Shipboard: Sandbars, Salvage Fraud, and the Cotton Trade in New Orleans in the 1870s," *Journal of Southern History* 86, no. 3 (August 2020): 602–603. On the negligible distinctions between legitimate and illegitimate commerce, see Brian P. Luskey and Wendy A. Woloson, eds., *Capitalism by Gaslight: Illuminating the Economy of Nineteenth-Century America* (Philadelphia: Univ. of Pennsylvania Press, 2015), 5–8; Stephen Mihm, *A Nation of Counterfeiters: Capitalists, Con Men, and the Making of the United States* (Cambridge: Harvard Univ. Press, 2007), 1–20, 360–365. On the history of

American business fraud, see Edward J. Balleisen, *Fraud: An American History from Barnum to Madoff* (Princeton: Princeton Univ. Press, 2017), 107–173.

17. Mark Summers argues that corruption was just as common in the decade before the Civil War as in the decade that followed, noting that "the further one looks at some postwar scandals, the more ambiguous the evidence appears." Mark Summers, *The Plundering Generation*, xii–xiii, 14–19; David Roth Singerman, "Science, Commodities, and Corruption in the Gilded Age," *Journal of the Gilded Age and Progressive Era* 15, no. 3 (July 2016): 278–293; Mark Wahlgren Summers, *The Era of Good Stealings* (New York: Oxford Univ. Press, 1993), x; quotation from Mark W. Summers, "The Press Gang: Corruption and the Independent Press in the Grant Era," *Congress and the Presidency* 17, no. 1 (spring 1990): 29–44; Richard White, "Information, Markets, and Corruption: Transcontinental Railroads in the Gilded Age," *Journal of American History* 90, no. 1 (June 2003): 19–43. On machine politics in this era, see Peter McCaffery, *When Bosses Ruled Philadelphia: The Emergence of the Republican Machine, 1867–1933* (University Park: Penn State Univ. Press, 1993), 17–76.

18. Michael Zakim, *Accounting for Capitalism: The World the Clerk Made* (Chicago: Univ. of Chicago Press, 2018); Brian P. Luskey, *On the Make: Clerks and the Quest for Capital in Nineteenth-Century America* (New York: New York Univ. Press, 2010), 46; Michael Zakim, "The Business Clerk as Social Revolutionary; or, a Labor History of the Nonproducing Classes," *Journal of the Early Republic* 26, no. 4 (winter 2006): 563–603, especially 575–576; Stephen Mihm, "Clerks, Classes, and Conflicts," *Journal of the Early Republic* 26, no. 4 (winter 2006): 605–615, especially 613–614; Heath J. Bowen, "Your Obedient Servant: Government Clerks, Officeseeking, and the Politics of Patronage in Antebellum Washington City" (Ph.D. diss., Michigan State University, 2011); Jerome P. Bjelopera, *City of Clerks: Office and Sales Workers in Philadelphia, 1870–1920* (Urbana: Univ. of Illinois Press, 2005), 126–128; Thomas Augst, *The Clerk's Tale: Young Men and Moral Life in Nineteenth-Century America* (Chicago: Univ. of Chicago Press, 2003), 24–32; Karen Halttunen notes that "ironically, the new law enforcement officer who emerged during this period to handle this sophisticated new breed of urban crime himself often resorted to the arts of the confidence man." Halttunen, *Confidence Men and Painted Women*, 7.

19. Gary Lindberg, *The Confidence Man in American Literature* (New York: Oxford Univ. Press, 1982), 3–9; Halttunen, *Confidence Men and Painted Women*, 153–190; Friedman, *Crime and Punishment in American History*, 207.

20. Lindberg, *The Confidence Man in American Literature*, 15–47, quotation 19–20; Johannes Dietrich Bergmann, "The Original Confidence Man," *American Quarterly* 21, no. 3 (August 1969): 560–577.

21. Peter Arnade and Elizabeth Colwill describe pardon cases as "a microhistory that reveals riches but conceals more, confounding us all with its trickster sources and troublous pasts." Peter Arnade and Elizabeth Colwill, "Crime and Testimony: Life Narratives, Pardon Letters, and Microhistory," *Journal of Medieval and Early Modern Studies* 47, no. 1 (January 2017): 147–166, quotation 163; Natalie Zemon Davis, *Fiction in the Archives: Pardon Tales and Their Tellers in Sixteenth-Century France* (Stanford: Stanford Univ. Press, 1987), 3–6.

1. CONVICT

1. J. M. Cooper to Edward Bates, 12 April 1861, RG 204, entry 1a: Pardon Case Files, 1853–1946, NACP.

2. Pardon of Charles Cowlam, RG 59, entry 902: Appointment Records, General Pardon Records, Requisitions for Pardons, 1858–1862, NACP, box 7; Pardon of Charles Cowlam, RG 59, entry 897: Appointment Records, General Pardon Records, Pardons and Remissions, NACP; Samuel Bassett French to Abraham Lincoln, 7 June 1861, RG 59, entry 902: Appointment Records, General Pardon Records, Requisitions for Pardons, 1858–1862, NACP, box 7; *Boston Morning Journal,* 11 July 1861, 2.

3. For recent examples, see Evan A. Kutzler, *Living by Inches: The Smells, Sounds, Tastes, and Feeling of Captivity in Civil War Prisons* (Chapel Hill: Univ. of North Carolina Press, 2019); Michael P. Gray, ed., *Crossing the Deadlines: Civil War Prisons Reconsidered* (Kent, Ohio: Kent State Univ. Press, 2018); Timothy J. Williams and Evan A. Kutzler, eds., *Prison Pens: Gender, Memory, and Imprisonment in the Writings of Mollie Scollay and Wash Nelson, 1863–1866* (Athens: Univ. of Georgia Press, 2018); Chris Barr, David R. Bush, et al., "Civil War Incarceration in History and Memory: A Roundtable," *Civil War History* 63, no. 3 (September 2017): 295–319; Lorien Foote, *The Yankee Plague: Escaped Union Prisoners and the Collapse of the Confederacy* (Chapel Hill: Univ. of North Carolina Press, 2016); Paul J. Springer and Glenn Robins, *Transforming Civil War Prisons: Lincoln, Lieber, and the Politics of Captivity* (New York: Routledge, 2015); Roger Pickenpaugh, *Captives in Blue: The Civil War Prisons of the Confederacy* (Tuscaloosa: Univ. of Alabama Press, 2013); Benjamin G. Cloyd, *Haunted by Atrocity: Civil War Prisons in American Memory* (Baton Rouge: Louisiana State Univ. Press, 2010); Charles W. Sanders Jr., *While in the Hands of the Enemy: Military Prisons of the Civil War* (Baton Rouge: Louisiana State Univ. Press, 2005).

4. Angela M. Zombek is among the first to bridge these two parallel literatures. See Angela M. Zombek, *Penitentiaries, Punishment, and Military Prisons: Familiar Responses to an Extraordinary Crisis During the American Civil War* (Kent, Ohio: Kent State Univ. Press, 2018), 1–51. See also Henry Kamerling, *Capital and Convict: Race, Region, and Punishment in Post–Civil War America* (Charlottesville: Univ. of Virginia Press, 2017); Edward L. Ayers, *Vengeance and Justice: Crime and Punishment in the Nineteenth-Century American South* (New York: Oxford Univ. Press, 1984), 34–105.

5. Jonathan White, "The Presidential Pardon Records of the Lincoln Administration," *Journal of the Abraham Lincoln Association* 39, no. 2 (summer 2018): 55–65; P. S. Ruckman Jr. and David Kincaid, "Inside Lincoln's Clemency Decision Making," *Presidential Studies Quarterly* 29, no. 1 (March 1999): 84–99; Jonathan Truman Dorris, *Pardon and Amnesty under Lincoln and Johnson: The Restoration of the Confederates to Their Rights and Privileges, 1861–1898* (Chapel Hill: Univ. of North Carolina Press, 1953), 74–80; J. T. Dorris, "President Lincoln's Clemency," *Journal of the Illinois State Historical Society* 20, no. 4 (January 1928): 547–568; Laura Stedman and George Milbry Gould, *Life and Letters of Edmund Clarence Stedman* (New York: Moffat, Yard, 1910), 1:265; Jonathan W. White, ed., *To Address You as My Friend: African Americans' Letters to Abraham Lincoln* (Chapel Hill: Univ. of North Carolina Press, 2021), 9–32.

6. *CIS Index to Presidential Executive Orders and Proclamations: Part I: April 30, 1789 to March 4, 1921 George Washington to Woodrow Wilson* (Washington, D.C.: Congressional Information Service, 1987), 424.

7. Ruckman Jr. and Kincaid, "Inside Lincoln's Clemency Decision Making," 84–99; Daniel Ringo to James Buchanan, 22 June 1860, RG 59, entry 902, Requisitions for Pardons, NACP, box 7; J. M. Cooper to Edward Bates, 17 May 1861, Pardon File of John A. Willson, RG 204, entry 1a: Pardon Case Files, 1853–1946, NACP; Pardon of John A. Willson, RG 59, entry 897: Appointment Records, General Pardon Records, Pardons and Remissions, NACP.

8. Cynthia Nicoletti, "William Henry Trescot, Pardon Broker," *Journal of the Civil War Era* 11, no. 4 (December 2021): 484; Davis, *Fiction in the Archives*, 3–6.

9. Faustin Guillot to Abraham Lincoln, 15 July 1861, RG 204, entry 1a: Pardon Case Files, 1853–1946, NACP; "Crimes and Casualties," *Sacramento Daily Union*, 18 January 1860, 5; "Correspondence of the Mercury," *Charleston (S.C.) Mercury*, 13 December 1859, 1.

10. Gray, *The Yankee West*, 48–50, 71–75, 122–123; Robert H. Churchill, *The Underground Railroad and the Geography of Violence in Antebellum America* (Cambridge: Cambridge Univ. Press, 2020), 121–127; Carlisle G. Davidson, "A Profile of Hicksite Quakerism in Michigan, 1830–1860," *Quaker History* 59, no. 2 (autumn 1970): 111; Sixth Census of the United States, 1840, Records of the Bureau of the Census, RG 29, NARA, York, Washtenaw, Michigan, microfilm reel 211, 133, Family History Library Film: 0014797.

11. Registers of Births, Marriages and Deaths Surrendered to the Non-Parochial Registers Commissions of 1837 and 1857, National Archives of the UK, Class Number: RG 4, Piece Number: 1318, Market Rasen, Catholic Chapel, Lincolnshire, 19.

12. Franklin Ellis, *History of Livingston County, Michigan: With Illustrations and Biographical Sketches of Its Prominent Men and Pioneers* (Philadelphia: Everts and Abbott, 1880), 50; Carol E. Mull, *The Underground Railroad in Michigan* (Jefferson, N.C.: McFarland, 2010), 75; "Livingston Liberty Convention," *Ann Arbor Signal of Liberty*, 31 October 1846, 3.

13. Silas F. Mead to Abigail J. Mead, 9 July 1840, reprinted in Marty Carr, "A Fourth of July Celebration, 1840," *Family History Capers*, Genealogical Society of Washtenaw County, Michigan, 10, no. 4 (spring 1987): 79–82, quotation 81.

14. It is not clear how much contact Elsie had with her half-siblings. She married in 1852, had two children who died in infancy, and she died in 1856. She was not in the same household in the census of 1850.

15. Henry Wyles Cushman, *A Historical and Biographical Genealogy of the Cushmans: The Descendants of Robert Cushman the Puritan from the Year 1617 to 1855* (Boston: Little, Brown, 1855), 180–181, 337; Gray, *The Yankee West*, 119–138. On the Second Great Awakening, see Brett Malcolm Grainger, *Church in the Wild: Evangelicals in Antebellum America* (Cambridge: Harvard Univ. Press, 2019), 18–60; Paul E. Johnson, *A Shopkeeper's Millennium: Society and Revivals in Rochester, New York, 1815–1837*, Twenty-Fifth Anniversary ed. (1978; reprint, New York: Hill and Wang, 2004), 3–14.

16. Michel Ducharme argues that the rebellions of 1837–1838 are best understood in the context of the larger Atlantic Revolution taking place in the late eighteenth century. Michel

Ducharme, "Closing the Last Chapter of the Atlantic Revolution: The 1837–38 Rebellions in Upper and Lower Canada," *Proceedings of the American Antiquarian Society* 116, no. 2 (October 2006): 413–430; Albert Schrauwers, *"Union Is Strength": W.L. Mackenzie, the Children of Peace, and the Emergence of Joint Stock Democracy in Upper Canada* (Toronto: Univ. of Toronto Press, 2009), 151–175.

17. The Treaty of Chicago signed in 1833 required the Potawatomi to relocate within three years of ratification. The U.S. Senate ratified in the treaty in 1835. William D. Reid, *Death Notices of Ontario* (Lambertville, N.J.: Clearfield, 1997), 111; Cushman, *A Historical and Biographical Genealogy of the Cushmans,* 337; Ontario, Canada, Select Marriages, Archives of Ontario, Toronto District Marriage Registers, 1801–1858, microfilm reel 3; John P. Bowes, *Land Too Good for Indians: Northern Indian Removal* (Norman: Univ. of Oklahoma Press, 2016), 149–181; Charles E. Cleland, *Rites of Conquest: The History and Culture of Michigan's Native Americans* (Ann Arbor: Univ. of Michigan Press, 1992), 218–225; Record book, Dec. 1830–May 1839, 31 March 1838, First Baptist Church Records, 1830–1920 and 1956, Saline, Michigan, Bentley Historical Collection, University of Michigan.

18. Charles E. Barnes, "Battle Creek as a Station on the Underground Railway," in *Historical Collections: Collections and Researches Made by the Michigan Pioneer and Historical Society,* 40 vols. (Lansing: Wynkoop Hallenbeck Crawford, 1912), 38:279–285, especially 280; Washington Gardner, *History of Calhoun County, Michigan: A Narrative Account of Its Historical Progress, Its People, and Its Principal Interests,* 2 vols. (Chicago: Lewis, 1913), 2:293.

19. Mariette's name appears under a variety of spellings, but Charles used this version in a letter to his sister Sarah.

20. Given the family's social standing and household possessions there is no reason to believe that the elder Charles was illiterate. Estate of Charles Cowlam, Michigan County, District and Probate Courts, Calhoun County Probate Packets, 1850, 156–197; Estate of Charles Cowlam, Illinois County, District and Probate Courts, Lake County Probate Packets, 1840–1900, Probate Case Files, box no.1, files 118, to box no.2, file 214, 1849–1852.

21. On mechanics, workingmen, and the free labor ideology, see Seth Rockman, *Scraping By: Wage Labor, Slavery, and Survival in Early Baltimore* (Baltimore: Johns Hopkins Univ. Press, 2009), 45–74; Daniel Walker Howe, *What Hath God Wrought: The Transformation of America, 1815–1848* (New York: Oxford Univ. Press, 2007), 536–546; Sean Wilentz, *Chants Democratic: New York City and the Rise of the American Working Class, 1788–1850,* Twentieth Anniversary ed. (New York: Oxford Univ. Press, 2004), 23–60; Sellers, *The Market Revolution,* 24–26; Luskey, *Men Is Cheap,* 5–6; Lause, *Free Labor,* 19–22; Steinfeld, *Coercion, Contract, and Free Labor in the Nineteenth Century,* 13–14; Glickstein, *Concepts of Free Labor in Antebellum America,* 11–16; Foner, *Free Soil, Free Labor, Free Men,* 11–39, 163.

22. Elizabeth Husted Cotter to Stuart Hay Chamberlain, 3 June 1981, courtesy of Sarah Dolley and Mary Postellon.

23. "Visits City After an Absence of Over 66 Years," *Libertyville (Ill.) Lake County Independent,* 4 June 1915, 5.

24. *The People v. Charles Cowlam,* Archives of Michigan, Criminal Calendar, Calhoun County, Clerk, RG 2017-111, vol. 41, 149; "Schedule A: Abstracts of Reports of Prosecuting Attorneys," "Annual Report of the Attorney General," in *Joint Documents of the State of Michigan for the Year 1853* (Lansing, Mich.: Peck, 1854), document 6, 9.

25. "A Strange History," *Detroit Free Press,* 12 December 1874, 1; *New York Daily Herald,* 2 January 1875, 1.

26. "Robbery and Arrest," *Richmond Dispatch,* 29 November 1854, 1; "Recognized as an Old Hand at the Bellows," *Richmond Dispatch,* 10 November 1857, 1.

27. "The Post Office Robbery at Portsmouth," *Baltimore Sun,* 25 June 1857, 2; "Important Arrest at Portsmouth," *Wilmington (N.C.) Tri-Weekly Commercial,* 25 June 1857, 2; "Mail Robber Arrested," *Charlotte (N.C.) Democrat,* 30 June 1857, 3.

28. The petition is not included among the documents in support of Cowlam's application in the National Archives. "The Penalty of Stealing Money from the United States Mail," *Wilmington (N.C.) Tri-Weekly Commercial,* 14 November 1857, 2; "The Richmond Papers," *Washington (D.C.) Evening Star,* 11 November 1857, 2; "U.S. Court," *Norfolk Day Book,* 4 November 1857, 3; Peter Graham Fish, *Federal Justice in the Mid-Atlantic South: United States Courts from Maryland to the Carolinas, 1836–1861* (Durham: Carolina Academic Press, 2015), 102; John O. Peters, *From Marshall to Moussaoui: Federal Justice in the Eastern District of Virginia* (Petersburg, Va.: Dietz Press, 2013), 55–57.

29. "U.S. Court," *Norfolk Day Book,* 4 November 1857, 4; "U.S. Court Yesterday," *Norfolk Day Book,* 7 November 1857, 4; Proverbs 13:15 (KJV).

30. "In the Penitentiary," *Richmond Dispatch,* 9 November 1857, 2; "Attempted Suicide," *Norfolk Day Book,* 7 November 1857, 4; "Recognized as an Old Hand at the Bellows," *Richmond Dispatch,* 10 November 1857, 1.

31. Zombek, *Penitentiaries, Punishment, and Military Prisons,* 24, 77; Sanders, *While in the Hands of the Enemy,* 163–164; James F. Pendleton, *Annual Report of the Board of Directors of the Penitentiary Institution, Year Ending September 30, 1859,* Document no. XIII (Richmond, Va., 1859), 6, 8, 39–40.

32. Records of the Virginia Penitentiary, 1798–1869, APA 131, Library of Virginia, box 6–7; *Annual Reports of Officers, Boards and Institutions of the Commonwealth of Virginia* Part 5 (Richmond, Va.: Ritchie, 1858), 13; Samuel D. Denoon, *Annual Report of the Board of Directors of the Penitentiary Institution, Year Ending September 30, 1862,* Document no. VI (Richmond, Va., 1862), 5, 18, 33; Charles S. Morgan, *Annual Report of the Board of Directors of the Penitentiary Institution, 1857,* Document no. XIII (Richmond, Va., 1857), v, xii; Charles S. Morgan, *Annual Report of the Board of Directors of the Penitentiary Institution, Year Ending September 30, 1858,* Document no. XIII (Richmond, Va., 1858), 6, 8, 27, 30–31.

33. "Hiring of Convicts from Penitentiary, 4 May 1858 to 1 July 1863," Records of the Virginia Penitentiary, Library of Virginia, Series I, Subseries F, box 6, folder 14; Morgan, *Annual Report of the Board of Directors of the Penitentiary Institution, Year Ending September 30, 1858,* 6, 8, 27, 30–31; Zombek, *Penitentiaries, Punishment, and Military Prisons,* 95.

34. Paul W. Keve, *The History of Corrections in Virginia* (Charlottesville: Univ. Press of Virginia, 1986), 39, 43–44, 54–57, quotation 44.

35. Diane Miller Sommerville, *Aberration of Mind: Suicide and Suffering in the Civil War-Era South* (Chapel Hill: Univ. of North Carolina Press, 2018), 15–16; Richard Bell, *We Shall Be No More: Suicide and Self-Government in the Newly United States* (Cambridge: Harvard Univ. Press, 2012), 151–159.

36. Charles S. Morgan to James Buchanan, 9 November 1857, RG 59, entry 902, Requisitions for Pardons, NACP, box 7.

37. Sarah Cowlam to James Buchanan, 17 July 1859, RG 59, entry 902, Requisitions for Pardons, NACP, box 7. In his study of sibling relationships, C. Dallett Hemphill notes that older sisters emerged as a source of moral authority in the nineteenth century, with older sisters often exhibiting a "sort of auxiliary motherhood." C. Dallett Hemphill, *Siblings: Brothers and Sisters in American History* (New York: Oxford Univ. Press, 2011), 162–174, quotation 166.

38. Elizabeth Husted Cotter to Stuart Hay Chamberlain, 3 June 1981, courtesy of Sarah Dolley and Mary Postellon.

39. "Memorial of N.P. Tallmadge and Others, Citizens of the US Praying the Appointment of a Scientific Commission to Investigate Certain Physical and Mental Phenomena of Questionable Origin and Mysterious Import that have of Late Occurred in this Country and in Europe," 17 April 1854, 33rd Congress, 1st Session, http://iapsop.com/spirithistory/signatures_on_the_congressional_petition.html; "Spiritualist Manifestations," *Congressional Globe*, Senate, 33rd Congress, 1st Session, 923–924; Hobart and Mather, *Biographical Review of Calhoun County, Michigan: Containing Historical, Biographical and Genealogical Sketches of Many of the Prominent Citizens of To-day and Also of the Past* (Chicago: Hobart and Mather, 1904), 523. On spiritualism, see Mark A. Lause, *Free Spirits: Spiritualism, Republicanism, and Radicalism in the Civil War Era* (Champaign: Univ. of Illinois Press, 2016), 5–8; Erik R. Seeman, *Speaking with the Dead in Early America* (Philadelphia: Univ. of Pennsylvania Press, 2019), 263–269; Simone Natale, *Supernatural Entertainments: Victorian Spiritualism and the Rise of Modern Media Culture* (University Park: Penn State Univ. Press, 2016), 1–17.

40. A nineteenth-century history of the telegraph service notes that George trained under James Izard in Woodstock in 1859. William R. Plum, *The Military Telegraph During the Civil War in the United States*, 2 vols. (Chicago: Jansen, McClurg, 1882), 2:79. Elizabeth Husted Cotter listed the "Izzards" among the "Michigan relatives" whom the Cowlam children lived with after their mother's death. Elizabeth Husted Cotter to Stuart Hay Chamberlain, 3 June 1981, courtesy of Sarah Dolley and Mary Postellon.

41. The passage "he is thy brother" appears twice in the King James Version of the Old Testament, most notably in Deuteronomy 23:7, "Thou shalt not abhor an Edomite; for he is thy brother: thou shalt not abhor an Egyptian; because thou wast a stranger in his land."

42. Sarah Cowlam to James Buchanan, 17 July 1859, RG 59, entry 902, Requisitions for Pardons, NACP, box 7.

43. Charles Cowlam to Sarah Cowlam, Undated, RG 59, entry 902, Requisitions for Pardons, NACP, box 7.

44. Sarah Cowlam to James Buchanan, 20 March 1860, RG 59, entry 902, Requisitions for Pardons, NACP, box 7.

45. The petition describes Cowlam as "now about twenty-three years old," indicating that the petition originated in the fall of 1860. Petition of Charles E. Stuart and other to James Buchanan, Undated, RG 59, entry 902, Requisitions for Pardons, NACP, box 7.

46. Francis W. Kellogg to Lewis Cass, 7 May 1860, RG 59, entry 902, Requisitions for Pardons, NACP, box 7.

47. William Wells Brown, *The American Fugitive in Europe: Sketches of Places and People Abroad* (Boston: Jewett, 1855), 296–297; Howard Glyndon, *Notable Men in "The House": A Series of Sketches of Prominent Men in the House of Representatives, Members of the Thirty-Seventh Congress* (New York: Baker and Goodwin, 1862), 29–30; Timothy Hopkins, *The Kelloggs in the Old World and the New*, 3 vols. (San Francisco: Sunset Press and Photo Engraving Co., 1903), 1:294, 650, 562.

48. Francis W. Kellogg to Abraham Lincoln, undated April 1861, RG 59, entry 902: Appointment Records, General Pardon Records, Requisitions for Pardons, 1858–1862, NACP, box 7.

49. Petition of Leonard H. Stewart and others to Abraham Lincoln, undated April 1861, RG 59, entry 902: Appointment Records, General Pardon Records, Requisitions for Pardons, 1858–1862, NACP, box 7.

50. Francis W. Kellogg to Edward Bates, 18 and 21 April 1861, RG 59, entry 902, Requisitions for Pardons, NACP, box 7.

51. William H. Seward to John Letcher, 28 May 1861, private collection; Pardon of Charles Cowlam, 28 May 1861, private collection; Edward Bates to William H. Seward, Francis W. Kellogg to Charles Cowlam, 27 May 1861, RG 59, entry 902, Requisitions for Pardons, NACP, box 7.

2. SPY

1. Bennett Hoskin Hill to James B. Fry, 16 April 1865, James B. Fry to John A. Foster, 27 April 1865, *LAE*, 693, 578.

2. Charles Cowlam, 19 April 1865, *LAE*, 388–390.

3. Wade Keyes to Jefferson Davis, 26 August 1863, in Rembert W. Patrick, ed., *The Opinions of the Confederate Attorneys General, 1861–1865* (Buffalo: Dennis, 1950), 325–327; William M. Robinson Jr., *Justice in Grey: A History of the Judicial System of the Confederate States of America* (Cambridge: Harvard Univ. Press, 1941), 206n, 207.

4. The pardon book describes the pardon as being issued on August 28, 1863, but an article in the *Richmond Examiner* suggests that it was exercised September 2. Pardon Record Book 1862–1864, Records of the Confederate States of America, LC, box 38, microfilm reel 21, 7; Lynda Lasswell Crist et al., eds., *The Papers of Jefferson Davis*, 14 vols. (Baton Rouge: Louisiana State Univ. Press, 1997), 9:361; "Pardoned," *Richmond Examiner*, 3 September 1863, 1.

5. Constitution of the Confederate States of America, 11 March 1861, Article II, Section 2(1).

6. Mark Neely notes that much of the scholarship on the Confederacy has ignored constitutional issues, and "the history of the Confederate bench and bar remains largely undeveloped." Mark E. Neely Jr., *Southern Rights: Political Prisoners and the Myth of Confederate Constitution-*

alism (Charlottesville: Univ. of Virginia Press, 1999), 7, 45; Marshall L. DeRosa, *The Confederate Constitution of 1861: An Inquiry into American Constitutionalism* (Colombia: Univ. of Missouri Press, 1991), 145. On Davis's creative interpretations of executive power, see David P. Currie, "Through the Looking-Glass: The Confederate Constitution in Congress, 1861–1865," *Virginia Law Review* 90, no. 5 (September 2004): 1344–1358.

7. Pardon Record Book 1862–1864, Records of the Confederate States of America, LC, box 38, microfilm reel 21, 1–17.

8. Richard R. John, *Spreading the News: The American Postal System from Franklin to Morse* (Cambridge: Harvard Univ. Press, 1995), 54–55; David M. Henkin, *The Postal Age: The Emergence of Modern Communications in Nineteenth-Century America* (Chicago: Univ. of Chicago Press, 2006), 47–53; Cameron Blevins, *Paper Trails: The US Post and the Making of the American West* (New York: Oxford Univ. Press, 2021), 59.

9. Mark Neely notes that among political prisoners "there was little mystery about the system, and prisoners found that they could get out of prison if they would go into the army." Neely, *Southern Rights*, 112; Pardon Record Book 1862–1864, Records of the Confederate States of America, LC, box 38, microfilm reel 21, 2, 7, 11–12; "Arrest on Charge of Mail Robbing," *Montgomery (Ala.) Daily Confederation*, 18 April 1860, 2; "Mail Robber Arrested," *Wilmington (N.C.) Journal*, 28 June 1860, 2; "Convicted of Embezzling Letters," *Vicksburg Whig*, 29 August 1860, 1.

10. *Martin V. Brantley v. State of Georgia*, A-03652, Georgia Supreme Court Case Files, RG 092-01-001, Georgia Archives; "A Novel 'Secession' Question. Trial of an U.S. Prisoner in the Georgia Penitentiary. Important Decision by Judge Harris," *New York Irish American*, 16 February 1861, 1; Constitution of Georgia, 23 March 1861, Article III, Section 2, clause 2.

11. There was significant continuity between the U.S. courts and the Confederate courts. As Alison LaCroix notes, "the predominant mode of constitutional interpretation in the Confederacy was to incorporate U.S. law into the new regime except where it had been specifically rejected." Confederate judges continued to hear cases that had been pending in the U.S. courts before secession, and only two states modified the structure of their state courts. See Alison L. LaCroix, "Continuity in Secession: The Case of the Confederate Constitution," in *Nullification and Secession in Modern Constitutional Thought*, ed. Sanford Levinson (Lawrence: Univ. Press of Kansas, 2016), 274–293, quotation 289; G. Edward White, "Recovering the Legal History of the Confederacy," *Washington and Lee Law Review* 68, no. 2 (spring 2011): 509–512; Richard Franklin Bensel, *Yankee Leviathan: The Origins of Central State Authority in America, 1859–1877* (New York: Cambridge Univ. Press, 1990), 101–103, 132–135; Robinson, *Justice in Grey*, 182, 70; Curtis Arthur Amlund, *Federalism in the Southern Confederacy* (Washington, D.C.: Public Affairs Press, 1966), 80–93; J. G. de Roulhac Hamilton, "The State Courts and the Confederate Constitution," *Journal of Southern History* 4, no. 4 (November 1938): 425–448; Sidney D. Brummer, "The Judicial Interpretation of the Confederate Constitution," *Lawyer and Banker and Southern Bench and Bar Review* 8, no. 6 (December 1915): 407–409.

12. "Georgia. Trial of a United States Prisoner in a Georgia Court—the Case Brought up on a Writ of Habeas Corpus—Important Decision by Judge Harris, Etc.," *New York Daily Herald*, 5 February 1861, 1.

13. Mark Neely notes that southern lawyers "sometimes appeared ready to take cases that involved veiled political opposition to the government in Richmond." Neely, *Southern Rights*, 56; "United States Prisoners in Seceded States," *New York Times*, 6 February 1861, 4.

14. Denoon, *Annual Report of the Board of Directors of the Penitentiary Institution, Year Ending September 30, 1862*, 5, 18, 33; James F. Pendleton, *Annual Report of the Board of Directors of the Penitentiary Institution, Year Ending September 30, 1861*, Document no. XIII (Richmond, Va., 1861), 5; Dale M. Brumfield, *Virginia State Penitentiary: A Notorious History* (Charleston, S.C.: History Press, 2017), 63; Robinson, *Justice in Grey*, 146.

15. John Letcher to Robert E. Lee, 20 February 1863, Letter of Governor John Letcher, Library of Virginia, box 1, folder 25, Accession 23476ai; Zombek, *Penitentiaries, Punishment, and Military Prisons*, 24, 77; Sanders, *While in the Hands of the Enemy*, 163–164; Angela M. Zombek, "Transcending Stereotypes: A Study of Civil War Military Prisons in the Context of Nineteenth-Century Penitentiaries and Penal Development at the Ohio, Virginia, and D.C. Penitentiaries and at Camp Chase, Castle Thunder, and Old Capitol Military Prisons" (Ph.D. diss., University of Florida, 2012), 186.

16. J. B. Jones, *A Rebel War Clerk's Diary: At the Confederate States Capital*, vol. 2, *August 1863–April 1865*, edited by James I. Robertson Jr. (Lawrence: Univ. Press of Kansas, 2015), 2:12; *OR*, Series IV, 2:709–710.

17. Jack Friend, *West Wind, Flood Tide: The Battle of Mobile Bay* (Annapolis: Naval Institute Press, 2004), 238–240.

18. Stephen V. Ash, *Rebel Richmond: Life and Death in the Confederate Capital* (Chapel Hill: Univ. of North Carolina Press, 2019), 19–36, 147–150; Charles Cowlam, 19 April 1865, *LAE*, 388–389.

19. Charles Cowlam, 19–21 April 1865, *LAE*, 389–390.

20. Charlotte Corday murdered Jean-Paul Marat during the French Revolution. William Tell was a Swiss folk hero who assassinated Albrecht Gessler in the fourteenth century. John Felton killed George Villiers, the unpopular 1st Duke of Buckingham in seventeenth-century England.

21. Charles Cowlam, 21 April 1865, *LAE*, 392.

22. David C. Keehn, *Knights of the Golden Circle: Secret Empire, Southern Secession, Civil War* (Baton Rouge: Louisiana State Univ. Press, 2013), quotations 179, 4; Frank L. Klement, *Dark Lanterns: Secret Political Societies, Conspiracies, and Treason Trials in the Civil War* (Baton Rouge: Louisiana State Univ. Press, 1984), 218–222; Elizabeth D. Leonard, *Lincoln's Avengers: Justice, Revenge, and Reunion after the Civil War* (New York: Norton, 2004), 34–35.

23. For Confederate clandestine operations in Canada, see Oscar A. Kinchen, *Confederate Operations in Canada and the North* (North Quincy, Mass.: Christopher, 1970); for operations in the Midwest, see Stephen E. Towne, *Surveillance and Spies in the Civil War: Exposing Confederate Conspiracies in America's Heartland* (Athens: Ohio Univ. Press, 2015), 307–313.

24. Charles Cowlam, 19–21 April 1865, *LAE*, 388–393; John Bell, *Confederate Seadog: John Taylor Wood in War and Exile* (Jefferson, N.C.: McFarland, 2002), 38–44.

25. "Committed to Castle Thunder," *Richmond Dispatch*, 23 December 1864, 1; Frances H. Casstevens, *George W. Alexander and Castle Thunder* (Jefferson, N.C.: McFarland, 2004), 36–38, 46–49, 147; "Old Castle Thunder," *Richmond Dispatch*, 3 March 1895, 2.

26. Sanders, *While in the Hands of the Enemy*, 184–196, 266–271; Lonnie R. Speer, *Portals to Hell: Military Prisons of the Civil War* (Mechanicsburg, Pa.: Stackpole Books, 1997), 93–95, 124–126; Casstevens, *George W. Alexander and Castle Thunder*, 46–49, quotation 47.

27. *OR*, Series IV, 2:578–579; Robert D. Carlson, "Breach of Faith: Conscription in Confederate Georgia" (Ph.D. diss., Emory University, 2009), 147.

28. Reports on Prisoners Brought Before Commissioners Vowles and Sands, Richmond, Virginia, 1864, NARA, RG 109, chapter IX, vol. 229, 42; Ash, *Rebel Richmond*, 22; William A. Tidwell, *Come Retribution: The Confederate Secret Service and the Assassination of Abraham Lincoln* (Jackson: Univ. Press of Mississippi, 1988), 110, 116–118; William A. Tidwell, *April '65: Confederate Covert Action in the American Civil War* (Kent, Ohio: Kent State Univ. Press, 1995), 45–47.

29. Miscellaneous Records, NARA, RG 109, box 9, entry 183, Manuscript 939; Chas. Cowlan, Unfiled Papers and Slips Belonging in Confederate Compiled Service Records, NARA, RG 109, Papers of and Relating to Military and Civilian Personnel, 1874–1899, microfilm reel 87; Charles Cowlam, 21 April 1865, *LAE*, 392. On the fall of Richmond, see Mary A. DeCredico, *Confederate Citadel: Richmond and Its People at War* (Lexington: Univ. Press of Kentucky, 2020), 101–152.

30. A "Mary Ann Sands" appears in the Census of 1860 and 1870 from Nashville, but there is no other evidence connecting her to Cowlam.

31. The town name is transcribed Claimwell by mistake in *LAE*. See Charles Cowlam, 21 April 1865, *LAE*, 390–391.

32. The scrap of paper contains the notation "21st Mar. to Col. B.H. Hill" that is not transcribed. See Charles Cowlam, "Scrap of Paper Containing Names," *LAE*, 394.

33. On the similarities between spycraft and con artistry, see Christopher Grasso, *Teacher, Preacher, Soldier, Spy: The Civil Wars of John R. Kelso* (New York: Oxford Univ. Press, 2021), 96–97; Joseph M. Beilein Jr., *A Man by Any Other Name: William Clarke Quantrill and the Search for American Manhood* (Athens: Univ. of Georgia Press, 2023), 93–117.

34. On the rumors circulating after Lincoln's death, see Martha Hodes, *Mourning Lincoln* (New Haven: Yale Univ. Press, 2015), 43–67.

35. Accounts of Secret Service Agents, 1861–1870, NARA, RG 110 NM-65, part 1, entry 95, box 7, receipts 17–19, of Miscellaneous Account of H.S. Olcott.

36. Bennett Hoskin Hill to James B. Fry, 16 April 1865, *LAE*, 693; Cowlam's supervisor, Henry Steel Olcott, was also a practicing spiritualist. See Lause, *Free Spirits*, 73, 84.

37. Thomas P. Lowry, *The Story the Soldiers Wouldn't Tell: Sex in the Civil War* (Mechanicsburg, Pa.: Stackpole Books, 1994), 62.

38. The story of Lizzie Murtry attempting to spit on Lincoln's head is retold in Stanley Kimmel, *Mr. Lincoln's Washington* (New York: Coward-McCann, 1957), 172; Charles Cowlam, 26 April 1865, *LAE*, 394–395. H. S. Benson was the hotel's proprietor. See Andrew Boyd, *Boyd's Washington and Georgetown Directory of Washington, Containing also a Business Directory of Washington, Georgetown and Alexandria* (Washington, D.C.: Hudson Taylor, 1864), 220. On Lincoln's speech, see "Presentation of a Rebel Flag," *Washington (D.C.) Evening Star*, 18 March 1865, 3; Edward Steers Jr., *Blood on the Moon: The Assassination of Abraham Lincoln* (Lexington: Univ. Press of Kentucky, 2001), 87; Tidwell, *Come Retribution*, 416.

39. James B. Fry to John A. Foster, 26 April 1865, *LAE*, 393–394, 578.
40. List of Papers and Letters Held by Burnett, *LAE*, 228–229, 540.
41. Henry S. Olcott to H. L. Burnett, 17 May 1865, *LAE*, 1011, 1136n.
42. Tidwell, *Come Retribution*, 12, 37–39, 124, quotation 43; Tidwell, *April '65*, 30–56.
43. Theodore Roscoe, *The Web of Conspiracy: The Complete Story of the Men Who Murdered Abraham Lincoln* (Englewood Cliffs, N.J.: Prentice Hall, 1959), 504; Don Thomas, "How They Got Away with Murder," https://reasonlincoln.com/wp-content/uploads/2017/09/New-How-They-Got-Away-with-Murder.pdf. On the rumors that circulated after the assassination, and the conspiracy theories advanced in later years, see Thomas R. Turner, "Writing History in a Vacuum: The Lincoln Assassination," in *The Lincoln Assassination: Crime and Punishment, Myth and Memory*, ed. Harold Holzer et al. (New York: Fordham Univ. Press, 2010), 157–171.
44. Michigan County Marriages, Allegan County, Marriage Certificates, 1847–1866, 2:374–375.
45. Michigan County Marriages, Wayne County, Marriage Certificates, 1865–1887, microfilm reel 1377622, v. F, 54; "Married," *Chicago Times*, 8 March 1866, 5.
46. Charles is not mentioned in the marriage record, but newspaper sources place him in Milwaukee. "Cowlam & Co.," *Daily Milwaukee News*, 10 October 1865, 5; Michigan Marriage Records, Wayne County, microfilm reel 927488, v. 3–4, 13.

3. DETECTIVE

1. "Advertising Through Correspondence—So-Called," *Cincinnati Semi-Weekly Gazette*, 28 August 1868, 1; "A Puffing Circular," *New York Times*, 15 August 1868, 5; "A New Way to Raise the Wind," *Charleston (S.C.) Mercury*, 20 August 1868, 4; "An Evident Swindle," *Windsor Vermont Journal*, 22 August 1868, 2.
2. Charles's younger brother, George, offered a testimonial of his own in the *Chicago Tribune* two years before. On the history of puff pieces and "reading notices," see Linda Lawson, "Advertisements Masquerading as News in Turn-of-the-Century American Periodicals," *American Journalism* 5, no. 2 (spring 1988): 81–96; Gerald J. Baldasty, *The Commercialization of the News in the Nineteenth Century* (Madison: Univ. of Wisconsin Press, 1992), 66–74; "More Evidences of the Success of Dr. Lighthill in Deafness and Discharges from the Ear," *Chicago Tribune*, 3 July 1866, 1.
3. Cowlam had made an earlier effort to establish a news business, Cowlam & Co., which he sold to a Chicago firm in early 1866. The *Daily Milwaukee News* reported that Cowlam was "an energetic business man, and since his residence here has made many friends." "Closed Up," *Daily Milwaukee News*, 15 January 1866, 5. For an example of another swindler who employed a similar news bureau, see T. D. Thornton, *My Adventures with Your Money: George Graham Rice and the Golden Age of the Con Artist* (New York: St. Martin's Press, 2015).
4. One contemporary defined the Bohemian as "a man who refuses fifty dollars a week for a thousand dollars now and then." See "The Alleged Blackmailers," *Chicago Tribune*, 8 February 1869, 2, quoted in Mark Wahlgren Summers, *The Press Gang: Newspapers and Politics, 1865–1878* (Chapel Hill: Univ. of North Carolina Press, 1994), 12–15, 70, 87, 103, 149, quotation 117. On the

detective profession in the Gilded Age, see Jonathan Obert, "The Coevolution of Public and Private Security in Nineteenth-Century Chicago," *Law and Social Inquiry* 43, no. 3 (summer 2018): 827–861; William R. Hunt, *Front-Page Detective: William J. Burns and the Detective Profession, 1880–1930* (Bowling Green, Ky.: Bowling Green State Univ. Popular Press, 1990), 1–20; Frank Morn, *The Eye That Never Sleeps: A History of the Pinkerton National Detective Agency* (Bloomington: Indiana Univ. Press, 1982).

5. Charles Cowlam, memorandum, April 1868, John A. Macdonald Papers, LAC, MG26-A, vol. 240, microfilm reel C-1666, 106664–106667.

6. Curiously, the news business Cowlam & Co. advertised the arrival of J. W. McCartney's dime novel *The Fenians, or, Neil O'Connor's Triumph: A Story of Old Ireland and Young America* in October 1865. "Personal," *Daily Milwaukee News,* 22 December 1865, 5.

7. David Wilson offers the most thorough analysis of Whelan's trial and summarizes the case against him, observing, "Taking the trial alone and using the criminal law criterion of reasonable doubt, he should have been acquitted. Taking all the available evidence and using the civil law criterion of the balance of probabilities, he was involved in the murder of Thomas D'Arcy McGee, either as the assassin himself or as an accomplice of the assassin, and he should have been found guilty." Christopher Klein, *When the Irish Invaded Canada: The Incredible True Story of the Civil War Veterans Who Fought for Ireland's Freedom* (New York: Doubleday, 2019), 172–177; David A. Wilson, *Thomas D'Arcy McGee*, vol. 2, *The Extreme Moderate, 1857–1868* (Montreal: McGill-Queen's Univ. Press, 2011), 341–347, 376–383, quotation 383; David A. Wilson, "Was Patrick James Whelan a Fenian and Did He Assassinate Thomas D'Arcy McGee?" in *Irish Nationalism in Canada,* ed. David A. Wilson (Montreal: McGill-Queens Univ. Press, 2009), 52–82.

8. Macdonald's letter has not been found, but it reached McMicken on April 15. See Gilbert McMicken to John A. Macdonald, 16 April 1868, John A. Macdonald Papers, LAC, MG26-A, vol. 240, microfilm reel C-1666, 106750.

9. David Wilson notes that, among the Canadian secret police, "Some of the detectives were astute, others were gullible, and a few were incompetent; all found it difficult to sort out fact from fiction." David A. Wilson, *Canadian Spy Story: Irish Revolutionaries and the Secret Police* (Montreal: McGill-Queen's Univ. Press, 2022), 38–45, 103–116, 245–254, quotations 41, 43; Hereward Senior, *The Last Invasion of Canada: The Fenian Raids, 1866–1870* (Toronto: Dundurn Press, 1991), 133; Andrew Parnaby and Gregory S. Kealey, "The Origins of Political Policing in Canada: Class, Law, and the Burden of Empire," *Osgoode Hall Law Journal* 41, no. 2/3 (summer 2003): 211–240; Reginald Whitaker, Gregory S. Kealey, and Andrew Parnaby, *Secret Service: Political Policing in Canada from the Fenians to Fortress America* (Toronto: Univ. of Toronto Press, 2012), 19–37.

10. Account of Disbursements for Special Service in month of April 1868, attached to McMicken to Macdonald, 8 May 1868, John A. Macdonald Papers, LAC, MG26-A, vol. 240, microfilm reel C-1666, 106851–106853.

11. See the annotations on the back of Edwin Frederick Thomas Brokovski to John A. Macdonald, 11 May 1868, John A. Macdonald Papers, LAC, MG26-A, vol. 240, microfilm reel C-1666, 106867. Jeff Keshen observes, "In his desperation to find out about Fenian plans, McMicken gave serious audience to questionable sources of information." Jeff Keshen, "Cloak and Dagger: Canada

West's Secret Police, 1864–1867," *Ontario History* 79, no. 4 (December 1987): 371; Wilson, *Thomas D'Arcy McGee*, 2:346–347.

12. Cowlam and Macdonald were mistaken in believing that McGee's assassination had emanated from the Fenian headquarters. O'Neill denounced the assassination publicly soon after it occurred, and McMicken's detectives confirmed O'Neill's sentiments privately. Wilson, *Canadian Spy Story*, 249–250.

13. Wilson, *Thomas D'Arcy McGee*, 2:347.

14. Charles Cowlam to Gilbert McMicken, 26 May 1868, John A. Macdonald Papers, LAC, MG26-A, vol. 240, microfilm reel C-1666, 106961–106964; Wilson, *Canadian Spy Story*, 147, 165, 378–379, quotation 379.

15. The letter is unsigned, but the handwriting is Cowlam's. Charles Cowlam to Gilbert McMicken, 30 May 1868, John A. Macdonald Papers, LAC, MG26-A, vol. 240, microfilm reel C-1666, 107000–107002.

16. Charles Cowlam to Gilbert McMicken, 13 June 1868, John A. Macdonald Papers, LAC, MG26-A, vol. 241, microfilm reel C-1666, 107067–107073; Wilson, *Canadian Spy Story*, 180–185.

17. I have not found any family connection linking the Izards to the Cowlam family. It is likely that Charles considered the Izards to be cousins for taking George into their home after their mother's death. "A Presentation," *New York Telegrapher* 2, no. 29 (1 June 1866): 126; James Hedley, *A Sketch of the Canadian Telegraph System, Its Rise and Development* (Toronto: Roddy and Nurse, 1883), 38.

18. Cowlam to McMicken, 13 June 1868, John A. Macdonald Papers, LAC, MG26-A, vol. 241, microfilm reel C-1666, 107067–107073.

19. Charles Cowlam to Gilbert McMicken, 28 August 1868, John A. Macdonald Papers, LAC, MG26-A, vol. 241, microfilm reel C-1666, 107420–107421.

20. Cowlam does not appear among the name index of U.S. Secret Service agents and reports at the National Archives. Name Index to Registers of Reports, RG 87, entry A1/E.1-A, NACP, vol. 1; Record of Secret Service Operatives Employed 1865–1871, RG 87, entry A-1 51, NACP, box 1. On the fragmented nature of federal law enforcement during this period, see Jonathan Obert, "A Fragmented Force: The Evolution of Federal Law Enforcement in the United States, 1870–1900," *Journal of Policy History* 29, no. 4 (October 2017): 640–675.

21. Internal Revenue Secret Service Record, 1865–1881, RG 58, entry 317-A, NACP, vol. 1, 49; "A Strange History," *Detroit Free Press*, 12 December 1874, 1.

22. Charles Cowlam to Edward A. Rollins, 28 February 1869, Letters Received by the Attorney General, 1809–1870: Federal Government Correspondence, NARA, microfilm reel 8:0164–0171.

23. Mark Summers finds numerous examples of revenue collectors vanishing with public money in the 1850s. See Summers, *The Plundering Generation*, 30.

24. Charles Cowlam to Edward A. Rollins, 7 March 1869, Letters Received by the Attorney General, 1809–1870: Federal Government Correspondence, NARA, microfilm reel 8:0150–0158; "The Disappearance of United States Marshal William G. Dickson—A Few Thousand Dollars Also Missing," 17 March 1869, *Augusta (Ga.) Daily Constitutionalist*, 1.

25. The *Daily Columbus (Ga.) Enquirer* described Bigelow as the leader of the group. Robinson owned a store where the liquor was kept, Edmunds was a prominent merchant, Williams

was a revenue inspector, and Alder was believed to be a detective. *United States v. Albert S. Bigelow and Others*, NAGA, U.S. District Court of Georgia, Southern District, Savannah Division, Mixed Case Files 1866–1900, box 6; "The Whiskey Ring," *Daily Columbus (Ga.) Enquirer*, 14 May 1869, 2; *Nashville Union and American*, 16 April 1869, 1; "Whiskey Ring," *Augusta (Ga.) Daily Constitutionalist*, 15 May 1869, 2.

26. Stephen Ward Angell, *Bishop Henry McNeal Turner and African-American Religion in the South* (Knoxville: Univ. of Tennessee Press, 1992), 94–96; E. Merton Coulter, "Henry M. Turner: Georgia Negro Preacher-Politician During the Reconstruction Era," *Georgia Historical Quarterly* 48, no. 4 (December 1964): 389–394; "The Turner Case. Preliminary Examination Before U.S. Commissioner Morrill," *Augusta (Ga.) Daily Constitutionalist*, 22 July 1869, 3; "The Turner Case in Macon, Ga.," *New York Herald*, 26 July 1869, 9; "The Turner Case," *Rome (Ga.) Weekly Courier*, 30 July 1869, 1; "Trial of Turner" and "Marriam Harris," *Macon Georgia Journal and Messenger*, 27 July 1869, 1.

27. On whiskey raids in the South, see Wilbur R. Miller, *Revenuers and Moonshiners: Enforcing Federal Liquor Law in the Mountain South, 1865–1900* (Chapel Hill: Univ. of North Carolina Press, 1991), 15–39, 61–81; Stephen Cresswell, *Mormons and Cowboys, Moonshiners and Klansmen: Federal Law Enforcement in the South and West, 1870–1893* (Tuscaloosa: Univ. of Alabama Press, 1991), 133–180; Frederick S. Calhoun, *The Lawmen: United States Marshals and Their Deputies, 1789–1989* (Washington, D.C.: Smithsonian Institution Press, 1989), 130–136; "Distillery Troubles in Georgia," *Washington (D.C.) Evening Star*, 29 January 1870, 2; "Whiskey Raid in Georgia," *New York Times*, 6 February 1870, 4.

28. James S. Pula, *For Liberty and Justice: The Life and Times of Wladimir Krzyżanowski* (Chicago: Polish American Congress Charitable Foundation, 1978), 173–181.

29. The article confuses Charles with his brother, George, throughout, attributing Charles's exploits under George's name. At one point the article combines both brothers' deeds into one, noting that "after this little episode he became interested in an effort to break up whiskey distilleries in the Northern part of this State, but finding certain localities two [*sic*] hot for his precious skin, he maneuvered out the detective service into the more peaceful but less profitable position of clerk of a Congressional committee, where he now labors." "A Loyal Detective: Another $500 Transaction," *Savannah Daily Advertiser*, 5 April 1871, 3.

30. *United States v. One Pipe of Cherries and Bitters and Other Property, J.N. Muller, Claimant*, NAGA, U.S. District Court of Georgia, Southern District, Savannah Division; *United States v. One Pipe of Cherries and Bitters and Other Property, J.N. Muller, Claimant*, NAGA, U.S. District Court of Georgia, Southern District, Savannah Division, General Minutes, 1869–1871, Retrieval #10.

31. Gould would later abscond with an estimated $30,000 to $100,000 of the Treasury's money. See "Defaulting Government Officers," *New York Herald*, 5 April 1871, 13; "When the Swallows Homeward Fly," *Macon Georgia Weekly Telegraph, Journal and Messenger*, 4 April 1871, 8; "The Defaulting Internal Revenue Collector," *Savannah Daily Advertiser*, 9 April 1871, 3.

32. "The Little Game. Extensive Blackmailing—More Revenue Swindling," *Savannah Morning News*, 4 April 1871.

NOTES TO PAGES 64–67

33. William H. Boyd, *Boyd's Directory of Washington, Georgetown, and Alexandria* (Washington, D.C.: William H. Boyd, 1871), 77; Census of 1870, Ward 7, Washington, District of Columbia, microfilm reel M593_126, 330B.

34. "List of Cabin Passengers Per Inman Royal Mail Steamer City of Brooklyn," *Belfast (Ireland) News-Letter*, 9 December 1870, 4; U.S. Passport Applications, 1795–1925, NARA, microfilm reel 169, 01 Oct 1870–30 Nov 1870; *The ABC Court Directory and Fashionable Guide for 1871* (London: Effingham Wilson, 1871), 117.

35. Patrick Quinlivan and Paul Rose, *The Fenians in England 1865–1872: A Sense of Insecurity* (London: John Calder, 1982), 150–153; "Alarming Riots in Dublin," *Belfast (Ireland) News-Letter*, 7 August 1871, 3; "The Political Prisoners," *Freeman's Journal* (Dublin, Ireland), 7 August 1871, 3.

36. Mitchell Snay and Christian Samito have explored the connections between Irish nationalism and American Reconstruction. See Mitchell Snay, *Fenians, Freedmen, and Southern Whites: Race and Nationality in the Era of Reconstruction* (Baton Rouge: Louisiana State Univ. Press, 2007), 6–17; Christian G. Samito, *Becoming American Under Fire: Irish Americans, African Americans, and the Politics of Citizenship During the Civil War Era* (Ithaca: Cornell Univ. Press, 2009), 155–158, 179–216.

37. Francis W. Kellogg to Spencer Compton Cavendish, 12 August 1871, Papers of Spencer Compton Cavendish, 8th Duke of Devonshire, DCA, DF6/1/2/1/4.

38. J. H. Kidd, *Personal Recollections of a Cavalryman with Custer's Michigan Cavalry Brigade in the Civil War* (Ionia, Mich.: Sentinel Printing Company, 1908), 31.

39. Francis W. Kellogg to Spencer Compton Cavendish, 12 August 1871, Papers of Spencer Compton Cavendish, 8th Duke of Devonshire, DCA, DF6/1/2/1/4.

40. Patrick Jackson, *The Last of the Whigs: A Political Biography of Lord Hartington, Later Eighth Duke of Devonshire (1833–1908)* (London: Associated Univ. Presses, 1994), 15–28, 43–44, 46; Bernard Holland, *The Life of Spencer Compton, Eighth Duke of Devonshire*, 2 vols. (London: Longmans, Green, 1911), 1:39–54.

41. Lord Spencer to Lord Hartington, 25 April 1871, in *The Red Earl: The Papers of the Fifth Earl Spencer 1835–1910*, ed. Peter Gordon. 2 vols. (Northampton: Northamptonshire Record Society, 1981), 1:92.

42. J. J. Golden, "The Protestant Influence on the Origins of Irish Home Rule, 1861–1871," *English Historical Review* 128, no. 535 (December 2013): 1483–1516; David Thornley, "The Irish Conservatives and Home Rule, 1869–73," *Irish Historical Studies* 11, no. 43 (March 1959): 200–222; Lord Spencer to Lord Hartington, 25 April 1871, in *The Red Earl: The Papers of the Fifth Earl Spencer 1835–1910*, ed. Peter Gordon. 2 vols. (Northampton: Northamptonshire Record Society, 1981), 1:87.

43. Padraic Kennedy argues that Britain's underdeveloped intelligence apparatus can be explained by the paucity of sustained and credible threats to national security. Phillip Smith and Christopher Andrew emphasize the inexperience of English detectives compared to their Irish counterparts, while Brian Jenkins and Bernard Porter argue that British authorities eschewed engaging in political espionage because it undermined Victorian values. See Brian Jenkins, *The Fenian*

Problem: Insurgency and Terrorism in a Liberal State, 1858–1874 (Montreal: McGill-Queens Univ. Press, 2008), 5–7; Padraic C. Kennedy, "The Secret Service Department: A British Intelligence Bureau in Mid-Victorian London, September 1867 to April 1868," *Intelligence and National Security* 18, no. 3 (autumn 2003): 100–127, especially 101, 122; Phillip Thurmond Smith, *Policing Victorian London: Political Policing, Public Order, and the London Metropolitan Police* (Westport: Greenwood Press, 1985), 183–199; Christopher Andrew, *Secret Service: The Making of the British Intelligence Community* (London: Sceptre, 1986), 15–17; Bernard Porter, *The Origins of the Vigilant State: The London Metropolitan Police Special Branch Before the First World War* (1987; reprint, Woodbridge, UK: Boydell Press, 1991), 1–18. On the Dublin Metropolitan Police, see Anastasia Dukova, *A History of the Dublin Metropolitan Police and Its Colonial Legacy* (London: Palgrave MacMillan, 2016), 59–60; Quinlivan and Rose, *The Fenians in England,* 159.

44. Cavendish to Kellogg, 20 August 1871, Kellogg to Cavendish, 22 August 1871, Papers of Spencer Compton Cavendish, 8th Duke of Devonshire, DCA, DF6/1/2/1/4.

45. It is not clear how this letter ended up in the Devonshire Collection Archives, unless Hartington requested to see it. Francis W. Kellogg to Charles Cowlam, 23 August 1871, Papers of Spencer Compton Cavendish, 8th Duke of Devonshire, DCA, DF6/1/2/1/4.

46. Young did not arrive in Canada to serve as governor general until November 1868. While I have not located any Cowlam correspondence with Canadian authorities after August 28, 1868, he may have sent additional letters or his earlier messages may have been shared with Young after his arrival. Two volumes of the governor general's papers from this period are still restricted (classified) in the Library and Archives of Canada. Joel Kropf has submitted an Access to Information and Privacy request to make them publicly available. Charles Cowlam to Spencer Compton Cavendish, 30 August 1871, Papers of Spencer Compton Cavendish, 8th Duke of Devonshire, DCA, DF6/1/2/1/4.

47. Schenck had endorsed, along with Benjamin Butler, William E. Chandler, and Samuel Pomeroy, George's application for a clerkship in the State Department under Elihu Washburne. The application came to nothing when Washburne resigned his position as secretary of state less than a week later. George B. Cowlam to Hamilton Fish, 22 March 1869, Letters of Application and Recommendation During the Administration of U. S. Grant, 1869–1877, NARA, M698, microfilm reel 12; Robert Schenck to Spencer Compton Cavendish, 3 October and 5 October 1871, Memoranda of a Conversation with General Schenck, 14 November 1871, Charles Cowlam to Spencer Compton Cavendish, 9 October and 16 November 1871, Papers of Spencer Compton Cavendish, 8th Duke of Devonshire, DCA, DF6/1/2/1/4.

48. *Belfast (Ireland) News-Letter,* 14 October 1871, 3.

49. "The Chicago Sufferers," *North-Eastern Daily Gazette* (Middlesbrough, England), 24 October 1871, 3; "The Burning of Chicago," *Guardian* (London, UK), 14 October 1871, 9.

50. "The Chicago Sufferers," *Lancaster (England) Gazette,* 28 October 1871, 4.

51. "The Chicago Relief Fund," *Times* (London, UK), 31 October 1871, 5; "The Fire in Chicago," *Times* (London, UK), 7 November 1871, 6.

52. Charles Cowlam to Spencer Compton Cavendish, 2 December 1871, E. A. Rollins to Charles Cowlam, 5 March 1869, Papers of Spencer Compton Cavendish, 8th Duke of Devonshire, DCA, DF6/1/2/1/4. In the course of my research there were a couple occasions where I compared

handwriting to ensure that Cowlam had not forged a letter. The letter from Rollins is genuine; it is in the commissioner's handwriting.

53. "Fashion and Varieties," *Freeman's Journal* (Dublin, Ireland), 4 January 1872, 3; Spencer Compton Cavendish to Robert Henry Hobart, 5 January 1872, Papers of Spencer Compton Cavendish, 8th Duke of Devonshire, DCA, DF6/1/2/1/4.

54. Henry Atwell Lake to Spencer Compton Cavendish, 31 January 1872, Papers of Spencer Compton Cavendish, 8th Duke of Devonshire, DCA, DF6/1/2/1/4.

55. Henry Atwell Lake to Spencer Compton Cavendish, 3 February 1872, Papers of Spencer Compton Cavendish, 8th Duke of Devonshire, DCA, DF6/1/2/1/4.

56. Michael Hurst argues that "the Ballot Act was a minor matter in the history of Irish nationalism." Michael Hurst, "Ireland and the Ballot Act of 1872," *Historical Journal* 8, no. 3 (1965): 326–352, quotation 352; Henry Atwell Lake to Spencer Compton Cavendish, and enclosure from Charles Cowlam, 18 February 1872, Papers of Spencer Compton Cavendish, 8th Duke of Devonshire, DCA, DF6/1/2/1/4.

57. "Murder of a Sweetheart," *Belfast (Ireland) News-Letter*, 15 July 1871, 3; "Trial for Murder," *Belfast (Ireland) News-Letter*, 28 March 1872, 4; "The Queen v. Hugh Fay," *Belfast (Ireland) News-Letter*, 5 June 1872, 4; Henry Atwell Lake to Spencer Compton Cavendish, 20 and 22 November 1871, Papers of Spencer Compton Cavendish, 8th Duke of Devonshire, DCA, DF6/1/2/1/4.

58. On Fenianism and the home rule movement in County Kerry, see Donnacha Seán Lucey, *Land, Popular Politics and Agrarian Violence in Ireland: The Case of County Kerry, 1872–86* (Dublin: Univ. College Dublin Press, 2011), 19–31; Brendán Ó Cathaoir, "The Kerry 'Home Rule' By-Election, 1872," *Journal of the Kerry Archaeological and Historical Society* 3 (1970): 154–177.

59. "Murder of a Lady in Dublin," *Manchester (UK) Guardian*, 29 May 1872, 8; "Murder of a Lady in Dublin," *Belfast (Ireland) News-Letter*, 28 May 1872, 3; Charles Cowlam, Dispatch "No. 29," Henry Atwell Lake to Spencer Compton Cavendish, 31 May 1872, Papers of Spencer Compton Cavendish, 8th Duke of Devonshire, DCA, DF6/1/2/1/4.

60. Thomas Henry Burke to Spencer Compton Cavendish, 5 March 1872, Papers of Spencer Compton Cavendish, 8th Duke of Devonshire, DCA, DF6/1/2/1/4.

61. Thomas Henry Burke to Spencer Compton Cavendish, 22 March 1872, Papers of Spencer Compton Cavendish, 8th Duke of Devonshire, DCA, DF6/1/2/1/4; Kennedy, "The Secret Service Department," 113–118.

62. Charles Cowlam, Dispatch "No. 29," Henry Atwell Lake to Spencer Compton Cavendish, 31 May 1872, Papers of Spencer Compton Cavendish, 8th Duke of Devonshire, DCA, DF6/1/2/1/4.

63. Henry Atwell Lake to Charles Cowlam, 3 June 1872, Papers of Spencer Compton Cavendish, 8th Duke of Devonshire, DCA, DF6/1/2/1/4.

4. CANDIDATE

1. Canter Brown Jr., "Carpetbagger Intrigues, Black Leadership, and a Southern Loyalist Triumph: Florida's Gubernatorial Election of 1872," *Florida Historical Quarterly* 72, no. 3 (January

1994): 275–301; Cortez A. M. Ewing, "Florida Reconstruction Impeachments: Impeachment of Governor Harrison Reed," *Florida Historical Quarterly* 36, no. 4 (April 1958): 299–318; William Watson Davis, *The Civil War and Reconstruction in Florida* (New York: Colombia University, 1913), 528.

2. Edward Carrington Cabell to Harrison Reed, 25 November 1871, John Tyler Jr. Papers, Group A, SWEM, box 4, folder 5.

3. On the history of voter suppression and efforts to defend the Enforcement Acts in the South, see Robert J Kaczorowski, *The Politics of Judicial Interpretation: The Federal Courts, Department of Justice, and Civil Rights, 1866–1876* (New York: Fordham Univ. Press, 2005), 99–107; Robert M. Goldman, *"A Free Ballot and a Fair Count": The Department of Justice and the Enforcement of Voting Rights in the South, 1877–1893* (1990; reprint, New York: Fordham Univ. Press, 2001), 25–47; Cresswell, *Mormons and Cowboys, Moonshiners and Klansmen*, 19–78.

4. Canter Brown Jr., *Ossian Bingley Hart: Florida's Loyalist Reconstruction Governor* (Baton Rouge: Louisiana State Univ. Press, 1997), 258, 266; Brown, "Carpetbagger Intrigues, Black Leadership, and a Southern Loyalist Triumph," 275–301; Peter D. Klingman, *Josiah Walls: Florida's Black Congressman of Reconstruction* (1976; reprint, Gainesville: Univ. Press of Florida, 2017), 49; Jerrell H. Shofner, *Nor Is It Over Yet: Florida in the Era of Reconstruction, 1863–1877* (Gainesville: Univ. Presses of Florida, 1974), 283–285; Jerrell H. Shofner, "Political Reconstruction in Florida," *Florida Historical Quarterly* 45, no. 2 (October 1966): 160–161.

5. Andrew Slap finds that the Liberal Republicans cultivated their political outlook after spending their formative years as Free Soilers or Democrats, rather than in the Whig Party, which produced most mainstream Republicans. Although some Liberal Republicans did align with Whigs temporarily, these adherents generally left the Whig Party in disillusionment in the early 1850s due to their antislavery and antinativist leanings. Andrew L. Slap, *The Doom of Reconstruction: The Liberal Republicans in the Civil War Era* (New York: Fordham Univ. Press, 2006), xi–xxv, 33–38; Adam-Max Tuchinsky, *Horace Greeley's New-York Tribune: Civil War-Era Socialism and the Crisis of Free Labor* (Ithaca: Cornell Univ. Press, 2009), 212–215, 228–242; James M. McPherson, "Grant or Greeley? The Abolitionist Dilemma in the Election of 1872," *American Historical Review* 71, no. 1 (October 1965): 43–61; Patrick W. Riddleberger, "The Break in the Radical Ranks: Liberals vs Stalwarts in the Election of 1872," *Journal of Negro History* 44, no. 2 (April 1959): 136–157; "Grant Prospects in Alachua," *Jacksonville (Fla.) Tri-Weekly Union*, 2 July 1872, 2.

6. Mark Summers describes the impeachment proceedings against Reed as politically motivated and lacking in substance, noting that aside from a "trumped-up letter extorted from railroad promoter Milton S. Littlefield," Reed's opponents "never offered a scintilla of evidence for any of their allegations." Brown, *Ossian Bingley Hart*, 231–237, 251–257; Summers, *The Era of Good Stealings*, 160; Ewing, "Florida Reconstruction Impeachments," 299–318; Shofner, *Nor Is It Over Yet*, 219–222.

7. Wilbur Fisk Rice to Thomas Rice, 22 April 1872, Rice, Thompson, and Winbourne Family Papers, 1838–1972, SHC, Collection 5662, folder 5; Summers, *The Ordeal of the Reunion*, 291; Davis, *The Civil War and Reconstruction in Florida*, 632–636.

8. William J. Purman to William E. Chandler, 22 August 1872, William E. Chandler Papers, LC, vol. 28.

9. Romulus C. Loveridge to Jonathan C. Gibbs, 20 May 1872, FLA, S1325, box 4, folder 4.

10. "Gov. Reed on the Stump," *Jacksonville (Fla.) Tri-Weekly Union*, 9 July 1872, 1.

11. Reed initially proposed Thomas P. Robb for U.S. marshal and Jedediah Philo Clark Emmons for U.S. attorney. Robb had served previously in the custom house in Savannah, and Emmons was the state attorney general. "One of the Governor's Letters," *Jacksonville (Fla.) Tri-Weekly Union*, 1 June 1872, 1; Brown, *Ossian Bingley Hart*, 258.

12. Harrison Reed to Ulysses S. Grant, 24 January and 19 February 1870, *PUSG*, 23:259n, 262n; Horatio Bisbee to Ebenezer R. Hoar, 5 April 1870, Bisbee to Amos T. Akerman, 1 July 1870, both in RG 60, Letters Received by the Attorney General, NACP.

13. Purman had previously been involved in a scheme to cede much of West Florida to Alabama. Hugh C. Bailey, "Alabama and West Florida Annexation," *Florida Historical Quarterly* 35, no. 3 (January 1957): 219–232; "Assessor of Internal Revenue," *Jacksonville (Fla.) Tri-Weekly Union*, 27 July 1872, 2; "Federal Appointments," *Jacksonville (Fla.) Tri-Weekly Union*, 27 July 1872, 2; Harrison Reed to Ulysses S. Grant, 6 July 1872, John Tyler Jr. Papers, Group A, SWEM, box 5, folder 4.

14. S. B. Conover to Ulysses S. Grant, 13 July 1872, John Tyler Jr. Papers, Group A, SWEM, box 5, folder 4.

15. Attorney General George H. Williams wrote to Osborn on August 1 reassuring him that the rumor that several federal appointees would be removed in Florida had no merit. Williams promised to consult with Osborn before making any removals. George H. Williams to Thomas W. Osborn, 1 August 1872, RG 60, entry 80, Letters Sent by the Department of Justice to Executive Officers and to Members of Congress, NARA, microfilm reel 1, vol. A, 754.

16. Crist et al., eds., *The Papers of Jefferson Davis*, 10:323; "President Tyler's Son Dead," *Lancaster (Pa.) Inquirer*, 8 February 1896, 7.

17. Purman mistakenly believed that Osborn, rather than Reed, had prompted his removal, and Jerrell Shofner notes that Purman denounced Osborn repeatedly in his campaign speeches that fall. See Thomas W. Osborn to William E. Chandler, 11–12 July 1872, William E. Chandler Papers, LC, vol. 24; Thomas W. Osborn to William E. Chandler, 5 August 1872, William E. Chandler Papers, LC, vol. 26; William J. Purman to William E. Chandler, 22 August 1872, William E. Chandler Papers, LC, vol. 28; Shofner, *Nor Is It Over Yet*, 277–284.

18. On southern Unionists during Reconstruction, see Clayton J. Butler, *True Blue: White Unionists in the Deep South during the Civil War and Reconstruction* (Baton Rouge: Louisiana State Univ. Press, 2022), chapter 5.

19. "Republican State Convention," *Jacksonville (Fla.) Tri-Weekly Union*, 10 August 1872, 2; "Republican State Convention," *Jacksonville (Fla.) Tri-Weekly Union*, 13 August 1872, 2; Shofner, *Nor Is It Over Yet*, 278–280; Brown, *Ossian Bingley Hart*, 260–263.

20. Thomas W. Osborn to William E. Chandler, 17 August 1872, William E. Chandler Papers, LC, vol. 27; Charles Cowlam to John Tyler Jr., 22 August 1872, John Tyler Jr. Papers, Group A,

SWEM, box 5, folder 6; John Allen Meador, "Florida Political Parties, 1865–1877" (Ph.D. diss., University of Florida, 1964), 27–28.

21. Charles Cowlam to John Tyler Jr., 22 August 1872, John Tyler Jr. Papers, Group A, SWEM, box 5, folder 6; Klingman, *Josiah Walls,* 30–51.

22. "The Democratic Convention," *Jacksonville (Fla.) Tri-Weekly Union,* 17 August 1872, 3.

23. Charles Cowlam to John Tyler Jr., 23 August 1872, John Tyler Jr. Papers, Group A, SWEM, box 5, folder 6.

24. Harrison Reed to John Tyler Jr., 22 and 23 August 1872, John Tyler Jr. Papers, Group A, SWEM, box 5, folder 6.

25. Charles Cowlam to John Tyler Jr., 26 August 1872, John Tyler Jr. Papers, Group A, SWEM, box 5, folder 6.

26. Thomas W. Osborn to William E. Chandler, 27 August 1872, William E. Chandler Papers, LC, vol. 28.

27. Harrison Reed to John Tyler Jr., 3 September 1872, John Tyler Jr. Papers, Group A, SWEM, box 5, folder 7.

28. Harrison Reed to John Tyler Jr., 5 September 1872, John Tyler Jr. Papers, Group A, SWEM, box 5, folder 7.

29. Harrison Reed to John Tyler Jr., 11 September 1872, John Tyler Jr. Papers, Group A, SWEM, box 5, folder 7.

30. An article in the *Jacksonville (Fla.) Tri-Weekly Union* was almost certainly the work of Cowlam. The article reports a letter from U.S. Attorney Horatio Bisbee encouraging a friend not to vote for Greeley, noting that the election in Maine will soon confirm the magnitude of Grant's support. The article also mentioned that the letter's recipient had in his possession a letter from Battle Creek, Michigan, stating that Grant will carry the state by a thirty thousand-vote majority. John Tyler Jr. to James M. Ray, 13 September 1872, John Tyler Jr. Papers, Group A, SWEM, box 5, folder 7; "Not for Horace," *Jacksonville (Fla.) Tri-Weekly Union,* 12 September 1872, 3.

31. William E. Chandler to Harrison Reed, 15 September 1872, William E. Chandler Papers, LC, vol. 30.

32. Harrison Reed to John Tyler Jr., 18 September 1872, John Tyler Jr. Papers, Group A, SWEM, box 5, folder 7; Charles H. Summers to Edward M. L'Engle, 9 September 1872, Edward M. L'Engle Papers, #425, SHC, box 4, folder 65.

33. Reed was evidently unfamiliar with Basnett. His real name was Arthur D. Basnett, and he was a twenty-four-year-old Jacksonville attorney who practiced law with Wilkinson Call. Basnett was born in Indiana and had only recently arrived in Florida in the preceding months. His name appears under various initials and spellings in newspaper sources, and in histories of Florida politics. It is remarkable to consider that Grant issued an appointment under a mistaken name to a newcomer with no Republican connections solely on the governor's recommendation.

34. Harrison Reed to William E. Chandler, 18 September 1872, and Harrison Reed to Charles Cowlam, 19 September 1872, both in William E. Chandler Papers, LC, vol. 31.

35. William E. Chandler to Ulysses S. Grant, 23 September 1872, William E. Chandler Papers, LC, vol. 31; William E. Chandler to George H. Williams, 23 September 1872, William E. Chand-

ler Papers, LC, vol. 31; William E. Chandler to Ulysses S. Grant, 24 September 1872, *PUSG,* 23:257n.

36. Charles Cowlam to William E. Chandler, 25 September 1872, William E. Chandler Papers, LC, vol. 32.

37. Charles Cowlam to William E. Chandler, 26 September 1872, William E. Chandler Papers, LC, vol. 32.

38. Charles Cowlam to William E. Chandler, 28 September 1872, William E. Chandler Papers, LC, vol. 32; *PUSG,* 23:253n.

39. Clement Hugh Hill to Charles Hale, 28 September 1872, RG 60, entry 80, Letters Sent by the Department of Justice to Executive Officers and to Members of Congress, NARA, microfilm reel 2, vol. B, 21.

40. Ron Chernow, *Grant* (New York: Penguin Press, 2017), 624, 728–739, quotations 728, 77; Ari Hoogenboom, *Outlawing the Spoils: A History of the Civil Service Reform Movement, 1865–1883* (Urbana: Univ. of Illinois Press, 1961), 61–63. Grant would later entrust his savings to the swindler Ferdinand Ward. See Geoffrey C. Ward, *A Disposition to Be Rich: How a Small-Town Pastor's Son Ruined an American President, Brought on a Wall Street Crash, and Made Himself the Best-Hated Man in the United States* (New York: Knopf, 2012), 127–271.

41. The *Jacksonville (Fla.) Courier* quoted in "The Removal of Conant and Bisbee," *Jacksonville (Fla.) Tri-Weekly Union,* 8 October 1872, 2.

42. *PUSG,* 23:257n, 256n, 260n.

43. John F. Rollins to William E. Chandler, 4 October 1872, William E. Chandler Papers, LC, vol. 32.

44. Edward M. Cheney to William E. Chandler, 3 and 4 October 1872, William E. Chandler Papers, LC, vol. 32.

45. In October 1871, Conant had arrested six men associated with the Ku Klux Klan in Clay County for "flogging and drawing from their homes two colored persons Samuel and Hannah Tutson" after a local grand jury had refused to indict the men earlier that year. Four of the six were later convicted in federal court for violating the Enforcement Act. Alva A. Knight to William E. Chandler, 6 October 1872, William E. Chandler Papers, LC, vol. 33; Sherman Conant to Amos T. Akerman, 23 October 1871, Letters Received by the Department of Justice from the State of Florida, 1871–1884, NARA, microfilm reel 1; Kidada E. William, "The Wounds That Cried Out: Reckoning with African Americans' Testimonies of Trauma and Suffering from Night Riding," in *The World the Civil War Made,* ed. Gregory P. Downs and Kate Masur (Chapel Hill: Univ. of North Carolina Press, 2015), 165; Ralph Peek, "Lawlessness in Florida, 1868–1871," *Florida Historical Quarterly* 40, no. 2 (October 1961): 170–172; Ralph L. Peek, "Curbing Voter Intimidation in Florida, 1871," *Florida Historical Quarterly* 43, no. 4 (April 1965): 344; "Testimony Taken by the Joint Select Committee to Inquire into the Condition of Affairs in the Late Insurrectionary States: Florida," 42nd Congress, 2nd Session, House Report 22, Part 13, Series no. 1541, 13 vols. (Washington, D.C.: Government Printing Office, 1872), 13:54–64.

46. Walter M. Walsh to George Henry Williams, 4 October 1872, Charles S. Park to Moses H. Hale, 5 October 1872, Alvin B. Clark to Moses H. Hale, 5 October 1872, all in NACP, RG

60, entry 350 Appointment Files for Judicial Districts, 1853–1905, box 212, Charles Conlan folder; *PUSG,* 23:257n, 256n, 260n.

47. Walter M. Walsh to George Henry Williams, 4 October 1872, Charles S. Park to Moses H. Hale, 5 October 1872, Alvin B. Clark to Moses H. Hale, 5 October 1872, Thomas W. Osborn to George Henry Williams, 8 October 1872, all in NACP, RG 60, entry 350 Appointment Files for Judicial Districts, 1853–1905, box 212, Charles Conlan folder.

48. Morris H. Alberger to William E. Chandler, 9 October 1872, William E. Chandler Papers, LC, vol. 33.

49. William K. Cessna to Ulysses S. Grant, Docketed as Received 12 October 1872, *PUSG,* 23:260n–261n.

50. William P. Dockray to Ulysses S. Grant, 6 October 1872, *PUSG,* 23:257n.

51. Edward M. Cheney to William E. Chandler, 7 October 1872, William E. Chandler Papers, LC, vol. 33.

52. Alva A. Knight to Ulysses S. Grant, 10 October 1872, *PUSG,* 23:258n.

53. Horatio Bisbee to Henry S. Sanford, 9 October 1872, Henry Shelton Sanford Papers, General Sanford Memorial Library, Sanford, Florida, microfilm reel 77, box 136, folder 2.

54. Charles Cowlam to William E. Chandler, 7 October 1872, William E. Chandler Papers, LC, vol. 33.

55. John S. Adams to Horace Porter, 5 October 1872, *PUSG,* 23:257n–258n; "General Directory," *Jacksonville (Fla.) Tri-Weekly Union,* 2 May 1872, 1.

56. Charles Cowlam to William E. Chandler, 8 October 1872, William E. Chandler Papers, LC, vol. 33.

57. Charles Cowlam to Harrison Reed, 8 October 1872, William E. Chandler Papers, LC, vol. 33.

58. Charles Cowlam to Clement Hugh Hill, 8 October 1872, Letters Received by the Department of Justice from the State of Florida, 1871–1884, NARA, microfilm reel 1.

59. "The Grant and Wilson Club," *Jacksonville (Fla.) Tri-Weekly Union,* 10 October 1872, 3; "Reception of Hon. J.T. Walls," *Jacksonville (Fla.) Tri-Weekly Union,* 17 October 1872, 3.

60. Edward M. Cheney to William E. Chandler, 11 October 1872, William E. Chandler Papers, LC, vol. 33.

61. Commission of Charles Cowlam, RG 59, Acceptances and Orders for Commissions, NACP, box 8; Alexander J. Falls to Robert S. Chew, 30 September 1872, Clement Hugh Hill to F. B. Basnett, 7 October 1872, B. H. Bristow to F. B. Basnett, 10 October 1872, Benjamin H. Bristow to Charles Cowlam, 11 October 1872, RG 60, Letters Sent by the Department of Justice: General and Miscellaneous, NARA, microfilm reel 14, vol. 1, 449, 452, 454, 455.

62. Harrison Reed to William E. Chandler, 24 October 1872, William E. Chandler Papers, LC, vol. 34.

63. Thomas W. Osborn to William E. Chandler, 18 October 1872, William E. Chandler Papers, LC, vol. 34; Thomas W. Osborn to William E. Chandler, 25 October 1872, William E. Chandler Papers, LC, vol. 34; "Republican Meeting in Leon," *Tallahassee Weekly Floridian,* 22 October 1872, 2; Summers, *The Press Gang,* 243; Meador, "Florida Political Parties, 1865–1877," 196–198, 231.

64. Larry Eugene Rivers and Canter Brown Jr., *Laborers in the Vineyard of the Lord: The Beginnings of the AME Church in Florida, 1865–1895* (Gainesville: Univ. Press of Florida, 2001), 75, 79–80; Brown, "Carpetbagger Intrigues, Black Leadership, and a Southern Loyalist Triumph," 282–288.

65. "Why Don't They Withdraw!" and an untitled article, *Tallahassee Weekly Floridian*, 22 October 1872, 2; Larry Eugene Rivers, *Father James Page: An Enslaved Preacher's Climb to Freedom* (Baltimore: Johns Hopkins Univ. Press, 2021), 173–221, especially 198–201, 207–209, 212; Brown, *Ossian Bingley Hart*, 252; Learotha Williams Jr., "'A Wider Field of Usefulness': The Life and Times of Jonathan Clarkson Gibbs c.1828–1874." (Ph.D. diss., Florida State University, 2003), 216–218.

66. "Purman," *Tallahassee Weekly Floridian*, 22 October 1872, 2.

67. Cantor Brown observes that the 1872 election was largely peaceful compared to the more turbulent election in 1870. Despite the tranquility that prevailed on election day, the weeks leading up to it produced several violent encounters. On September 15, a fight broke out between an African American Grant club and a white Greeley club in Pittsburg, in central Florida. Although the fight lasted only ten minutes, the combatants fired more than one hundred shots. Six African Americans were shot, and one white Greeley supporter had his skull fractured with a rock and was not expected to survive. Brown, *Ossian Bingley Hart*, 268–269; Shofner, *Nor Is It Over Yet*, 285; *Tallahassee Weekly Floridian*, 22 October 1872, 1–3; "Conflict Between White and Negro Clubs," *Jacksonville (Fla.) Tri-Weekly Union*, 21 September 1872, 1.

68. Harrison Reed to Ulysses S. Grant, 31 October 1872, Ulysses S. Grant to Harrison Reed, 1 November 1872, *PUSG*, 23:258n.

69. Malachi Martin to Jonathan C. Gibbs, 7 October 1872, FLA, S1325, box 4, folder 2; A. C. Lightburn to Jonathan C. Gibbs, 7 October 1872, FLA, S1325, box 4, folder 4; "The Trouble in Gadsden," *Jacksonville (Fla.) Tri-Weekly Union*, 24 October 1872, 2.

70. "Illegally Changing Election Precincts," *Jacksonville (Fla.) Tri-Weekly Union*, 26 October 1872, 2.

71. Alva A. Knight to William E. Chandler, 4 November 1872, William E. Chandler Papers, LC, vol. 35.

72. John Wallace believed the rumors of Reed selling out the Republican Party had been concocted by the Osborn faction as a way of discrediting the former governor and his allies to destroy Reed's senatorial prospects and ensure that carpetbag politicians would replace Reed's African American appointments. Wallace's recollections of postwar politics have offered ample fodder for critics of Reconstruction, but his remembrances should be treated with considerable skepticism. His sympathetic portrayal of Bloxham and almost constant criticism of his fellow Republicans has led some historians to question whether or not Wallace wrote the book at all, or if he merely stood in for a Democratic ghost writer during an election year. John Wallace, *Carpetbag Rule in Florida: The Inside Workings of Civil Government in Florida After the Close of the Civil War* (Jacksonville: Da Costa Printing and Publishing House, 1888), 221; James C. Clark, "John Wallace and the Writing of Reconstruction History," *Florida Historical Quarterly* 67, no. 4 (April 1989): 421–426; Harrison Reed to John Tyler Jr., 3 September 1872, John Tyler Jr. Papers, Group A, SWEM, box 5, folder 7.

73. Republican Ticket for Florida 1872, Campaign Broadside, FLA; Florida Election Official State Canvass, FLA, S1258, vol. 1, 70; "The Florida Election—Official State Canvass," *Jacksonville (Fla.) Tri-Weekly Union,* 17 December 1872, 2.

74. Thomas W. Osborn to William E. Chandler, 10 November 1872, William E. Chandler Papers, LC, vol. 35.

75. Horatio Bisbee to George H. Williams, 13 November 1872, Letters Received by the Department of Justice from the State of Florida, 1871–1884, NARA, microfilm reel 1.

76. David Yulee to Henry Stebbins, 28 November 1872, David Levy Yulee Papers, P. K. Yonge Library of Florida History and the Manuscripts Collections in the Department of Special Collections and Area Studies, George A. Smathers Libraries, University of Florida, box 8.

77. John Tyler Jr. to George H. Williams, 27 November 1872, Letters Received by the Department of Justice from the State of Florida, 1871–1884, NARA, microfilm reel 1.

78. Jonathan C. Greeley to Henry S. Sanford, 7 December 1872, Henry Shelton Sanford Papers, General Sanford Memorial Library, Sanford, Florida, microfilm reel 77, box 136, folder 10; Jonathan Daniels, *Prince of Carpetbaggers* (1958; reprint, Westport: Greenwood Press, 1974), 244.

79. Florida Election Official State Canvass, FLA, S1258, vol. 1, 70; Shofner, *Nor Is It Over Yet,* 286–288.

80. "Influx of Northern Visitors," *Jacksonville (Fla.) Tri-Weekly Union,* 14 May 1872, 3; Shofner, *Nor Is It Over Yet,* 263–264.

5. SWINDLER

1. "Personal," *New York Herald,* 3 June 1874, 2; "Personal," *New York Herald,* 9 August 1874, 1; "Personal," *New York Herald,* 20 September 1874, 1.

2. "A Strange History," *Detroit Free Press,* 12 December 1874, 1; "Rewards," *New York Daily Herald,* 2 January 1875, 1.

3. On the Granger movement, see Thomas A. Woods, *Knights of the Plow: Oliver H. Kelley and the Origins of the Grange in Republican Ideology* (Ames: Iowa State Univ. Press, 1991), 147–164; George H. Miller, *Railroads and the Granger Laws* (Madison: Univ. of Wisconsin Press, 1971), 161–168.

4. Sven Beckert, *The Monied Metropolis: New York City and the Consolidation of the American Bourgeoisie, 1850–1896* (Cambridge: Harvard Univ. Press, 2001), 145–171. On the emerging independent press, see Summers, *The Press Gang,* 59–76.

5. Gale Harris, "Bennett Building," New York City Landmarks Preservation Commission Report, 21 November 1995.

6. Nicolas Barreyre, "The Politics of Economic Crises: The Panic of 1873, the End of Reconstruction, and the Realignment of American Politics," *Journal of the Gilded Age and Progressive Era* 10, no. 4 (October 2011): 403–423; Richard White, *The Republic for Which It Stands: The United States During Reconstruction and the Gilded Age, 1865–1896* (New York: Oxford Univ. Press, 2017), 260–273; Christoph Nitschke, "Theory and History of Financial Crises: Explaining the Panic

of 1873," *Journal of the Gilded Age and Progressive Era* 17, no. 2 (April 2018): 221–240; George Templeton Strong, *The Diary of George Templeton Strong: The Postwar Years 1865–1875*, ed. Allan Nevins and Milton Halsey Thomas (New York: MacMillan, 1952), 493; New York Association for Improving the Condition of the Poor, *Thirty-First Annual Report for the Year 1874* (New York: New York Association for Improving the Condition of the Poor, 1874), 28–29.

7. "Patrons of Industry," *Rock Island Daily Argus*, 10 January 1874, 3.

8. "The Scythe," *Greensboro (N.C.) Patriot*, 24 September 1873, 2; "He Called Himself Cowlan—First Name Charles," *New York Semi-Weekly Tribune*, 13 November 1874, 7; Jonathan Periam, *The Groundswell: A History of the Origin, Aims, and Progress of the Farmers' Movement* (Cincinnati: Hannaford, 1874), 566.

9. "The Mysterious Order," *New York Daily Graphic*, 6 January 1874, 3; "'The Patrons of Industry.' A Fruitless Search for the Men Who Get the Money—A Secretary Who Cannot Be Found and an Associate Who is 'Out' When Wanted—The Profits Derived Through Post-Office Box 1839," *New York Daily Graphic*, 12 January 1874, 3; Strong, *The Diary of George Templeton Strong: The Postwar Years 1865–1875*, 498.

10. Periam, *The Groundswell*, 566–576, quotation 158.

11. The lodge in Bronson, Michigan, attracted around sixty-nine members. "The National Grange Headquarters, Washington, D.C.," *Atlanta Georgia Grange*, 1 January 1874, 1; "Patrons of Industry," *Los Angeles Herald*, 9 December 1873, 1; "Patrons of Industry," *Rock Island Daily Argus*, 10 January 1874, 3; "Dakota Items," *Sioux City Daily Journal*, 15 January 1874, 2; "Bronson Items," *Coldwater (Mich.) Republican*, 10 January 1874, 4; "Bronson Items," *Coldwater (Mich.) Republican*, 31 January 1874, 5; "Correspondence," *Coldwater (Mich.) Republican*, 18 April 1874, 1; Woods, *Knights of the Plow*, 150–151.

12. "An Auxiliary to the Granges," *Pioche (Nev.) Daily Record*, 11 November 1873, 3; "Patrons of Industry," *Los Angeles Herald*, 9 December 1873, 1; "The Patrons of Industry," *Camden (N.J.) Democrat*, 27 December 1873; "The Patrons of Industry," *Camden (N.J.) Democrat*, 3 January 1874, 2; "The Twin Orders," *Coldwater (Mich.) Republican*, 17 January 1874, 1; "The Two Orders," *Red Wing (Minn.) Grange Advance*, 14 January 1874, 5; H. J. Walker, "Look Out for Counterfeits," *Wichita City (Kans.) Eagle*, 12 March 1874, 3.

13. Ibid.

14. On the origins of the Labor Reform Party, see David A. Zonderman, *Uneasy Allies: Working for Labor Reform in Nineteenth-Century Boston* (Amherst: Univ. of Massachusetts Press, 2011), 156–164.

15. "An Auxiliary to the Granges," *Pioche (Nev.) Daily Record*, 11 November 1873, 3; "Patrons of Industry," *Los Angeles Herald*, 9 December 1873, 1; "The Patrons of Industry," *Camden (N.J.) Democrat*, 27 December 1873; "The Patrons of Industry," *Camden (N.J.) Democrat*, 3 January 1874, 2; "The Twin Orders," *Coldwater (Mich.) Republican*, 17 January 1874, 1; "The Two Orders," *Red Wing (Minn.) Grange Advance*, 14 January 1874, 5; H. J. Walker, "Look Out for Counterfeits," *Wichita City (Kans.) Eagle*, 12 March 1874, 3; "The Revolution Onward," *Camden (N.J.) Democrat*, 17 January 1874, 4.

16. Periam, *The Groundswell,* 572–573, 574; "Patrons of Industry," *Gilroy (Calif.) Advocate,* 22 November 1873, 2; "The Patrons of Industry," *Camden (N.J.) Democrat,* 27 December 1873; "The Patrons of Industry," *Camden (N.J.) Democrat,* 3 January 1874, 2.

17. Holly Jacklyn Blake, "Marie Howland—19th-Century Leader for Women's Economic Independence," *American Journal of Economics and Sociology* 74, no. 5 (November 2015): 878–1192, especially 1038–1042; Verena Adamik, *In Search of the Utopian States of America: Intentional Communities in Novels of the Long Nineteenth Century* (New York: Palgrave MacMillan, 2020), 123–162; Susan Lynch Foster, "Romancing the Cause: Fourierism, Feminism, and Free Love in Papa's Own Girl," *Utopian Studies* 8, no. 1 (1997): 31–54.

18. "The Sunday Meeting," *Philadelphia Inquirer,* 1 December 1873, 2; "The Mysterious Order," *New York Daily Graphic,* 6 January 1874, 3.

19. "'The Patrons of Industry.' A Fruitless Search for the Men Who Get the Money—A Secretary Who Cannot Be Found and an Associate Who is 'Out' When Wanted—The Profits Derived Through Post-Office Box 1839," *New York Daily Graphic,* 12 January 1874, 3.

20. No William E. Burlick appears in any of the New York City directories from this period, but a William E. Burlock and Co., one of the largest manufacturers of shirts in the country, operated nine blocks north of the Bennett Building at 332 Broadway. H. Wilson, *Trow's New York City Directory* (New York: Trow City Directory Company, 1873), 166.

21. "'The Patrons of Industry.' A Fruitless Search for the Men Who Get the Money—A Secretary Who Cannot Be Found and an Associate Who is 'Out' When Wanted—The Profits Derived Through Post-Office Box 1839," *New York Daily Graphic,* 12 January 1874, 3.

22. Ibid.

23. "Political and General Notes," *Worcester Massachusetts Weekly Spy,* 23 January 1874, 1; Marie Howland, "The New Secret Order," *New York Daily Graphic,* 23 January 1874, 3; Master, "'Sovereigns of Industry' vs. 'Patrons of Industry,'" *Jackson (Mich.) Daily Citizen,* 18 March 1874, 4; "Correspondence," *Coldwater (Mich.) Republican,* 18 April 1874, 1; "The New Flux of Frauds," *Des Moines Iowa State Register,* 11 April 1874, 2.

24. Beckert, *The Monied Metropolis,* 30–31, 154–157, 207–217; "The Balls," *New York Times,* 4 January 1874, 5; Mark Power Smith, "Séances in the City: The 'Operational Aesthetic' and 'Modern Spiritualism' in the Popular Culture of New York City, 1865–1870," *American Nineteenth Century History* 18, no. 1 (April 2017): 45–62. For bigamy as a theme in Victorian literature, see Maia McAleavey, *The Bigamy Plot: Sensation and Convention in the Victorian Novel* (Cambridge: Cambridge Univ. Press, 2015), 172–182; Ian Ward, *Sex, Crime and Literature in Victorian England* (Oxford: Hart Publishing, 2014), 53–80; Jeanne Fahnestock, "Bigamy: The Rise and Fall of a Convention," *Nineteenth-Century Fiction* 36, no. 1 (June 1981): 47–71.

25. H. Charles Ulman, *Lawyers' Record and Official Register of the United States* (New York: Barnes, 1872), 763; "Mr. Shafer's Fierce Threats," *New York Tribune,* 22 March 1887, 1; "Ira Shafer Dead," *New York Times,* 1 December 1896, 2; "Why Shafer Is Furious," *Chicago Tribune,* 23 March 1887, 3.

26. Revelations of Cowlam's past life arrived at the same time that another New York scandal was brewing. Henry Ward Beecher, the nation's preeminent preacher and the younger brother

of Harriet Beecher Stowe, stood accused of adultery and would soon face a scandalous civil trial. Carol Faulkner, *Unfaithful: Love, Adultery, and Marriage Reform in Nineteenth-Century America* (Philadelphia: Univ. of Pennsylvania Press, 2019), 146–146, 151–157; "A Strange History," *Detroit Free Press,* 12 December 1874, 1.

27. "A Strange History," *Detroit Free Press,* 12 December 1874, 1.

28. On the history of bounty brokers during the war, see Luskey, *Men Is Cheap,* 1–10.

29. "Cowlam," *Detroit Free Press,* 24 December 1874, 3.

30. The *Chicago Tribune* challenged the allegations surrounding Cowlam's time at the *Evening Post,* noting that this part of Cowlam's story "becomes unintelligible, accompanied by the explanation that it occurred in 1868." "A Startling Arrest: The Defaulting State Official's Money in a New York Banking Office," *New York Herald,* 19 October 1873, 9; "Personal," *Chicago Tribune,* 19 December 1874, 9; "Personal," *Chicago Tribune,* 24 December 1874, 5.

31. Measuringworth.com.

32. "A Gay Deceiver," *Madison (Wisc.) State Journal,* 12 January 1875, 2; "A Graceless Sinner," *Madison (Wisc.) Daily Democrat,* 15 January 1875, 1.

33. Beverly Schwartzberg, "'Lots of Them Did That': Desertion, Bigamy, and Marital Fluidity in Late-Nineteenth-Century America," *Journal of Social History* 37, no. 3 (spring 2004): 573–600; Rebecca Probert, *Double Trouble: The Rise and Fall of the Crime of Bigamy* (London: Selden Society, 2015), 27.

34. Friedman argues that the absolute number of bigamy cases was on the rise, but subsequent research has shown that the incidence of bigamy prosecutions was declining in the middle decades of the nineteenth century. Friedman, *Crime and Punishment in American History,* 199; Lawrence M. Friedman, *Personal Identity in the Modern World: A Society of Strangers* (Lanham, Md.: Rowman and Littlefield, 2022), 25–28; Tomas Cvrcek, "When Harry Left Sally: A New Estimate of Marital Disruption in the U.S., 1860–1948," *Demographic Research* 21 (2009), 719–758; Timothy J. Gilfoyle, "The Hearts of Nineteenth-Century Men: Bigamy and Working-Class Marriage in New York City, 1800–1890," *Prospects* 19 (October 1994): 135–160. On bigamy and the Canadian border, see Benjamin Hoy, "Policing Morality: Regulating Sexuality Across the Canada-United States Border," *Canadian Historical Review* 99, no. 1 (March 2018): 30–62.

35. Lawrence Friedman describes bigamy as a crime committed against middle-class sensibility. See Friedman, *Personal Identity in the Modern World,* 28; Ginger S. Frost, *Living in Sin: Cohabitating as Husband and Wife in Nineteenth-Century England* (Manchester: Manchester Univ. Press, 2008), 75–77; John Benson, *Respectability, Bankruptcy and Bigamy in Late Nineteenth- and Early Twentieth-Century Britain* (New York: Routledge, 2023), 1–6, 32–33, 89–91.

36. The scholarship on nineteenth-century American bigamy is sparse, and often embedded within studies of divorce or polygamy. See Schwartzberg, "'Lots of Them Did That,'" 576, 579; Hendrik Hartog, *Man and Wife in America: A History* (Cambridge: Harvard Univ. Press, 2000), 87–92; Guy N. Woolnough, "A Victorian Fraudster and Bigamist: Gentleman or Criminal?" *Criminology and Criminal Justice* 19, no. 4 (September 2019): 439–455.

37. Rebecca Probert, "Escaping Detection: Illegal Second Marriages and the Crime of Bigamy," *Journal of Genealogy and Family History* 6, no. 1 (2022): 27–33; Gilfoyle, "The Hearts of

Nineteenth-Century Men," 139; Frost, *Living in Sin,* 72–76, 87–88; David Cox, "'Trying to Get a Good One': Bigamy Offences in England and Wales, 1850–1950," *Plymouth Law and Criminal Justice Review* 4 (2012), 1–32; S. Colwell, "The Incidence of Bigamy in 18th and 19th Century England," *Family History* 11 (1980): 91–102.

38. Faulkner, *Unfaithful,* 63–64, 159–162; Van Nolan Jr., "Indiana: Birthplace of Migratory Divorce," *Indiana Law Journal* 26, no. 4 (summer 1951): 515–527, especially 527n.

39. "The Woman Question: Monroe vs. Monroe," *Chicago Tribune,* 12 January 1875, 8. On marital expectations and exits in the nineteenth century, see Hendrik Hartog, "Marital Exits and Marital Expectations in Nineteenth Century America," *Georgetown Law Review* 80, no. 1 (October 1991): 95–129.

40. U.S. Passport Applications, 1795–1925, NARA, microfilm reel 352, 01 Jun 1890–09 Jun 1890; "Americans Abroad," *New York Times,* 10 June 1871, 2; "Notices," *Detroit Free Press,* 6 August 1876, 3; Chancery Calendar, Wayne County, Circuit Court, Archives of Michigan, RG 85-34, vol. 59, #477; Superior Court Chancery Records, Wayne County, Circuit Court, Archives of Michigan, RG 85-34, vol. 69, 561, #477; "The Courts," *Detroit Free Press,* 12 November 1876, 1.

6. VETERAN

1. Vernon Seaman to William C. Endicott, 18 June 1886, Livingston Grahame Casefile, RG 94, Letters Received by the Adjutant General, Main Series, 1881–1889, NARA, Publication Number M689, microfilm reel 0459:3102.

2. *Report of Joint Special Committee to Investigate Chinese Immigration,* 44th Congress, 2nd Session (Washington, D.C.: Government Printing Office, 1877), 548; "Personal," *New Orleans Times-Democrat,* 15 March 1873, 2; "Angelenes in New York," *Los Angeles Herald,* 5 January 1881, 3; "That Recent Upheaval," *San Francisco Chronicle,* 16 November 1890, 18; "The Baptist Pastors," *New York Times,* 14 March 1882, 2; "To-Day's Examination," *San Francisco Examiner,* 1 August 1874, 3; "San Francisco Jots," *Los Angeles Herald,* 26 April 1878, 1; "Perjury," *San Francisco Chronicle,* 14 January 1879, 3; "Vernon Seaman's Offenses," *San Francisco Chronicle,* 16 January 1879, 3. Seaman lost the weight in the decade before his death. See "How Flesh Can Be Reduced," *San Francisco Chronicle,* 4 August 1889, 15.

3. Livingston Grahame Casefile, RG 94, Letters Received by the Adjutant General, Main Series, 1881–1889, NARA, Publication Number M689, microfilm reel 0459:3102.

4. Michael J. Sulick, *Spying in America: Espionage from the Revolutionary War to the Dawn of the Cold War* (Washington, D.C.: Georgetown Univ. Press, 2012), 67, 87–92; John H. Eicher and David J. Eicher, eds., *Civil War High Commands* (Stanford: Stanford Univ. Press, 2001), 59, 588; William James Flavin, "Lafayette C. Baker and the Union Secret Service" (Master's thesis, Emory University, 1973), 6–7; Lafayette C. Baker, *History of the United States Secret Service* (Philadelphia: Baker, 1867), 524–542. On the Baker-Turner Papers, see Mark E. Neely Jr., *The Fate of Liberty: Abraham Lincoln and Civil Liberties* (New York: Oxford Univ. Press, 1991), 118–120.

5. John Tweedale to Vernon Seaman, 24 July 1886, Livingston Grahame Casefile, RG 94, Letters Received by the Adjutant General, Main Series, 1881–1889, NARA, Publication Number

M689, microfilm reel 0459:3102; Case files of Investigations by Levi C. Turner and Lafayette C. Baker, 1861–1866, RG 94, entry 179, NARA, microfilm reel 1.

6. On the nervous disorders that afflicted upper-middle-class Americans in the Gilded Age, see Lears, *No Place of Grace*, 47–58; "Col. Livingstone Grahame. A Romantic Story from the Soldiers' Home," *Dayton (Ohio) Herald*, 22 October 1886, 2; "Restored to His Friends. A Story of an Insane Inmate of a Soldiers' Home," *Burlington (Vt.) Free Press*, 25 October 1886, 6; "The Pension Bureau," *Memphis Avalanche*, 24 October 1886, 1; "A Demented Soldier's Story," *Savannah Morning News*, 25 October 1886, 2; "Story of a Demented Soldier," *New York World*, 23 October 1886, 1.

7. Livingston Grahame Casefile, RG 94, Letters Received by the Adjutant General, Main Series, 1881–1889, NARA, Publication Number M689, microfilm reel 0459:3102.

8. James Boswell, *The Life of Samuel Johnson* (1791; reprint, New York: Penguin Classics, 1986), 182.

9. J. Matthew Gallman estimates the median age of enlistment at 23.5. Robert Fogel found that 43.5 percent of northern white men born the same year as Cowlam (1837) mustered into the Union army, compared to 33.6 percent of men in their late twenties, and around 20 percent of men in their thirties. Younger men were even more likely to serve. For men born the same year as his brother, George (1844), 66.4 percent served in the Union army. Gallman, *Defining Duty in the Civil War: Personal Choice, Popular Culture, and the Union Home Front* (Chapel Hill: Univ. of North Carolina Press, 2015), 8; Robert W. Fogel, "New Sources and New Techniques for the Study of Secular Trends in Nutritional Status, Health, Mortality, and the Process of Aging," *Historical Methods: A Journal of Quantitative and Interdisciplinary History* 26, no. 1 (winter 1993): 5–39. For veterans migrating in search of new opportunities, see Paul A. Cimbala, *Veterans North and South: The Transition from Soldier to Civilian after the American Civil War* (Santa Barbara: Praeger, 2015), 74–82; James Marten, *Sing Not War: The Lives of Union and Confederate Veterans in Gilded Age America* (Chapel Hill: Univ. of North Carolina Press, 2011), 54–61.

10. Gallman, *Defining Duty in the Civil War*, 7–17, 65–90, quotation 70. It is remarkable that contemporaries treated Cowlam as an object of pity rather than scorning him as a "malingerer" who had lied about his service to the Union. Sarah Handley-Cousins, *Bodies in Blue: Disability in the Civil War North* (Athens: Univ. of Georgia Press, 2019), 95–113; Jean Franzino, "Tales Told by Empty Sleeves: Disability, Mendicancy, and Civil War Life Writing," *American Literature* 94, no. 3 (September 2022): 420–422.

11. Theda Skocpol, *Protecting Soldiers and Mothers: The Political Origins of Social Policy in the United States* (Cambridge: Harvard Univ. Press, 1992), 105–111; William Marvel, "Johnny Ransom's Imagination," *Civil War History* 41, no. 3 (September 1995): 181–189; Brandi C. Brimmer, *Claiming Union Widowhood: Race, Respectability, and Poverty in the Post-Emancipation South* (Durham: Duke Univ. Press, 2020); Brandi C. Brimmer, "Black Women's Politics, Narratives of Sexual Immorality, and Pension Bureaucracy in Mary Lee's North Carolina Neighborhood," *Journal of Southern History* 80, no. 4 (November 2014): 827–858; Brandi C. Brimmer, "'Her Claim for Pension Is Lawful and Just': Representing Black Union Widows in Late-Nineteenth Century North Carolina," *Journal of the Civil War Era* 1, no. 2 (June 2011): 207–236; Donald R. Shaffer, "'I Do Not Suppose That Uncle Sam Looks at the Skin': African Americans and the

Civil War Pension System, 1865–1934," *Civil War History* 46, no. 2 (June 2000): 132–147; Carrie Kiewit, "A Study of Fraud in African-American Civil War Pensions: Augustus Parlett Lloyd, Pension Attorney, 1882–1909" (Master's thesis, University of Richmond, 1996). For the effects of class on pensions, see Russell L. Johnson, "'Great Injustice': Social Status and the Distribution of Military Pensions after the Civil War," *Journal of the Gilded Age and Progressive Era* 10, no. 2 (April 2011): 137–160.

12. Adam Domby describes the pensions afforded to false Confederates as a "form of patronage and political spoils" that shaped the way Americans remembered the war. The abundance of imposters and undeserving pensioners fueled the myth that Confederates rarely deserted. See Adam H. Domby, "Loyal Deserters and the Veterans Who Weren't," in *The War Went On: Reconsidering the Lives of Civil War Veterans*, ed. Brian Matthew Jordan and Evan C. Rothera (Baton Rouge: Louisiana State Univ. Press, 2020), 283–306; Adam H. Domby, *The False Cause: Fraud, Fabrication, and White Supremacy in Confederate Memory* (Charlottesville: Univ. of Virginia Press, 2020), 76–103, quotation 88; Richard A. Serrano, *Last of the Blue and Gray: Old Men, Stolen Glory, and the Mystery that Outlived the Civil War* (Washington, D.C.: Smithsonian Books, 2013), 27–42, 123–165; William Marvel, "The Great Imposters," *Blue and Grey Magazine* 8 (February 1991), 32–33. Willie McGee's life bears some similarities to Cowlam's. McGee fraudulently received the Medal of Honor without any evidence documenting his wartime claims of gallantry, successfully petitioned Andrew Johnson to reconsider his application for an officer's commission, convinced Ulysses S. Grant to pardon him for a murder conviction, initiated several bigamous marriages, and claimed falsely later in life to have survived Custer's last stand. Thomas Fox, *Drummer Boy Willie McGee, Civil War Hero and Fraud* (Jefferson, N.C.: McFarland, 2008).

13. Unfortunately, the National Archives destroyed the case files and other records from the National Soldiers' Home decades ago. Only a select number of randomly sampled case files survive for use in exhibits. Patrick J. Kelly, *Creating a National Home: Building the Veterans' Welfare State 1860–1900* (Cambridge: Harvard Univ. Press, 1997), 5, 110, 115–120, 140–142, quotation 128. On suspected imposters in the soldiers' homes, see James Marten, "Not a Veteran in the Poorhouse: Civil War Pensions and Soldiers' Homes," in *Wars Within a War: Controversy and Conflict Over the American Civil War*, ed. Joan Waugh and Gary W. Gallagher (Chapel Hill: Univ. of North Carolina Press, 2009), 215–217; Marten, *Sing Not War*, 159–198; Brian Matthew Jordan, "Veterans in New Fields: Directions for Future Scholarship on Civil War Veterans," in Jordan and Rothera, eds., *The War Went On*, 307; *Annual Report of the Board of Managers of the National Home for Disabled Volunteer Soldiers for the Fiscal Year Ending June 30, 1887*, House of Representatives, 50th Congress, 1st Session. Miscellaneous Document 86, 32.

14. James Marten, "Exempt from the Ordinary Rules of Life: Sources on Maladjusted Union Civil War Veterans," *Civil War History* 47, no. 1 (March 2001): 57–70; *Annual Report of the Board of Managers of the National Home for Disabled Volunteer Soldiers for the Fiscal Year Ending June 30, 1887*, 28–29, 75–76.

15. Neither Cowlam nor Grahame appear in the index to Benjamin Butler's letterbooks or in any of the relevant boxes among his papers. Benjamin F. Butler Papers, LC, boxes 46–51, 53–54, 58–61, 66–72, 201; Livingston Grahame Casefile, RG 94, Letters Received by the Adjutant General,

NOTES TO PAGES 136–138

Main Series, 1881–1889, NARA, Publication Number M689, microfilm reel 0459:3102. On the difficulty of ascertaining claims of loyalty and the Southern Claims Commission, see Susanna Michele Lee, *Claiming the Union: Citizenship in the Post–Civil War South* (Cambridge: Cambridge Univ. Press, 2014), 19–66; Erik Mathisen, *The Loyal Republic: Traitors, Slaves, and the Remaking of Citizenship in Civil War America* (Chapel Hill: Univ. of North Carolina Press, 2018), 1–12.

16. Livingston Grahame Casefile, RG 94, Letters Received by the Adjutant General, Main Series, 1881–1889, NARA, Publication Number M689, microfilm reel 0459:3102; Robert P. Watson, *Escape! The Story of the Confederacy's Infamous Libby Prison and the Civil War's Largest Jail Break* (Lanham, Md.: Rowman and Littlefield, 2021), 46–47.

17. William B. Feis, *Grant's Secret Service: The Intelligence War from Belmont to Appomattox* (Lincoln: Univ. of Nebraska Press, 2002), 198–199; "Restored to His Friends. A Story of an Insane Inmate of a Soldiers' Home," *Burlington (Vt.) Free Press*, 25 October 1886, 6; "A Demented Soldier's Story," *Savannah Morning News*, 25 October 1886, 2; "Story of a Demented Soldier," *New York World*, 23 October 1886, 1.

18. "Col. Livingstone Grahame. A Romantic Story from the Soldiers' Home," *Dayton (Ohio) Herald*, 22 October 1886, 2.

19. Angela M. Riotto, "Remembering 'That Dark Episode': Union and Confederate Ex-Prisoners of War and Their Captivity Narratives," in Jordan and Rothera, eds., *The War Went On*, 121–123, quotation 121–122. Brian Matthew Jordan notes that, "physically ravaged and emotionally devastated by their implausible past, ex-prisoners needed public understanding and meaningful recognition even more than other veterans." See Brian Matthew Jordan, *Marching Home: Union Veterans and Their Unending Civil War* (New York: Liveright, 2014), 131–150, 172–191, quotation 133–134; For examples of veterans who felt the world had passed them by, see Mary-Susan Grant, "Reimagined Communities: Union Veterans and the Reconstruction of American Nationalism," *Nations and Nationalism* 14, no. 3 (2008): 498–519.

20. "A Demented Soldier's Story," *Savannah Morning News*, 25 October 1886, 2; "Restored to His Friends. A Story of an Insane Inmate of a Soldiers' Home," *Burlington (Vt.) Free Press*, 25 October 1886, 6; "Story of a Demented Soldier," *New York World*, 23 October 1886, 1.

21. The firm consisted of brothers Howard Bunting, Robert S. Bunting, and Thomas Browne Bunting. Thomas was the only brother who had traveled to Guatemala. "Bunting-Spaulding-General," *Brooklyn Daily Eagle*, 18 February 1876, 3; "Miscellaneous," *New Orleans South-Western Presbyterian*, 17 January 1884, 7.

22. Early biographies of Barrios, published in an era of military rule in Guatemala, present him as a reformer and national hero. Paul Burgess described Barrios as the Guatemalan Lincoln. See Alice Raine, *Eagle of Guatemala: Justo Rufino Barrios* (New York: Harcourt, Brace, 1947), 148–219; Casimiro D. Rubio, *Biografía del General Justo Rufino Barrios, Reformador de Guatemala: Recopilación Histórica y Documentada* (Guatemala City: Tipographia Nacional, 1935), 5; Paul Burgess, *Justo Rufino Barrios: A Biography* (New York: Dorrance, 1926), xiv. More recent reconsiderations have tempered Barrios's reputation. See Jordan T. Merritts, "Presidents Miguel Garcia Granados and Justo Rufino Barrios in Reform Guatemala: 1871–1885" (Master's thesis, University of Arizona, 2012), 54–55; James Mahoney, *The Legacies of Liberalism: Path Dependence*

NOTES TO PAGES 138–143

and Political Regimes in Central America (Baltimore: Johns Hopkins Univ. Press, 2001), 117–124; Hector Perez-Brignoli, *A Brief History of Central America*, trans. Ricardo B. Sawrey and Susana Stettri de Sawrey (Berkeley: Univ. of California Press, 1989), 83–87. On the transition to liberalism in Guatemala, see Ralph Lee Woodward, *Rafael Carrera and the Emergence of the Republic of Guatemala, 1821–1871* (Athens: Univ. of Georgia Press, 1993), 331–348. For Americans who traveled to Mexico and Central America in search of riches, see John Mason Hart, *Empire and Revolution: The Americans in Mexico Since the Civil War* (Berkeley: Univ. of California Press, 2002), 131–166.

23. "Personal Notes," *San Francisco Daily Alta California*, 17 August 1880, 1; "Shipping Intelligence," *Portland Morning Oregonian*, 10 August 1880, 4; *Daily Star and Herald* (Panama City, Panama), 7 July 1885, 2.

24. "A New El Dorado," *Philadelphia Inquirer*, 14 August 1877, 3; Perley Poore, *Congressional Directory*, 43rd Congress, 1st Session (Washington, D.C.: Government Printing Office, 1873), 85.

25. "President Barrios, of Guatemala," *Chicago Tribune*, 10 December 1880, 5; "How the President of Guatemala Treated Women Who Disagreed with Him," *Chicago Tribune*, 6 December 1880, 5.

26. "President Barrios, of Guatemala," *Chicago Tribune*, 10 December 1880, 5; LeRoy P. Graf, ed, *The Papers of Andrew Johnson*, 16 vols. (Knoxville: Univ. of Tennessee Press, 1986), 7:398.

27. "Old John Brown," *Chicago Tribune*, 19 December 1880, 18; "Mr. Vest," *Chicago Tribune*, 17 December 1880, 4.

28. Louis DeCaro quotes Grahame's story authoritatively in *Freedom's Dawn: The Last Days of John Brown in Virginia* (London: Rowman and Littlefield, 2015), 51; "Old John Brown," *Chicago Tribune*, 19 December 1880, 18.

29. "Old John Brown," *Chicago Tribune*, 19 December 1880, 18; John Stauffer and Benjamin Soskis, *The Battle Hymn of the Republic: A Biography of the Song That Marches On* (New York: Oxford Univ. Press, 2013), 7–9.

30. For an example of Isabel Cowlam's photography, see "Camera Club Exhibit," *Washington (D.C.) Evening Star*, 31 March 1907, 10; "Akron Woman Literally Has Had 'Money to Burn,'" *Akron (Ohio) Beacon Journal*, 23 October 1930, 21; "Ups and Downs," *Elgin (Ill.) Daily Courier*, 9 August 1886, 4.

31. "Ups and Downs," *Elgin (Ill.) Daily Courier*, 9 August 1886, 4.

32. U.S. Copyright Office, Library of Congress, *Dramatic Compositions Copyrighted in the United States 1870 to 1916* (Washington, D.C.: Government Printing Office, 1918), 6 December 1880, copyright 35937; "Ups and Downs," *Elgin (Ill.) Daily Courier*, 9 August 1886, 4; "Story of a Demented Soldier," *New York World*, 23 October 1886, 1; "Restored to His Friends. A Story of an Insane Inmate of a Soldiers' Home," *Burlington (Vt.) Free Press*, 25 October 1886, 6; "A Demented Soldier's Story," *Savannah Morning News*, 25 October 1886, 2.

33. "Ups and Downs," *Elgin (Ill.) Daily Courier*, 9 August 1886, 4; Casstevens, *George W. Alexander and Castle Thunder*, 75–77, 88–96.

34. "She Rebelled," *Springfield (Ohio) Globe Republic*, 13 February 1886, 4; "Before the Mayor," *Springfield (Ohio) Globe Republic*, 17 February 1886, 3; "Wanted to Die," *Springfield (Ohio) Globe Republic*, 28 May 1886, 5.

35. "Wanted to Die," *Springfield (Ohio) Globe Republic,* 28 May 1886, 5; "Col. Livingstone Grahame. A Romantic Story from the Soldiers' Home," *Dayton (Ohio) Herald,* 22 October 1886, 2.

36. "Col. Livingstone Grahame. A Romantic Story from the Soldiers' Home," *Dayton (Ohio) Herald,* 22 October 1886, 2; "Restored to His Friends. A Story of an Insane Inmate of a Soldiers' Home," *Burlington (Vt.) Free Press,* 25 October 1886, 6; "The Pension Bureau," *Memphis Avalanche,* 24 October 1886, 1; "A Demented Soldier's Story," *Savannah Morning News,* 25 October 1886, 2; "Story of a Demented Soldier," *New York World,* 23 October 1886, 1.

EPILOGUE

1. A "Charles Cowlam" does appear in the city directory for 1887–1888; however, this was George B. Cowlam's son, Charles A. Cowlam, who died suddenly in 1887 at the age of eighteen. Sutton Publishing Company, *Madison, Vevay, Vernon, North Vernon, and Jefferson County Illustrated Directory 1887–88* (Dubuque, Iowa: Hugh and Hardie, 1887), 53; "The Late Charlie Cowlam," *Madison (Ind.) Daily Courier,* 2 December 1887, 4; "George Cowlam Arrived," *Madison (Ind.) Daily Courier,* 1 December 1887, 4; R. L. Polk, *Detroit City Directory for 1889* (Detroit: R. L. Polk, 1889), 415; "A Strange History," *Detroit Free Press,* 12 December 1874, 1.

2. Thomas Robisheaux, "Microhistory Today: A Roundtable Discussion," *Journal of Medieval and Early Modern Studies* 47, no. 1 (January 2017): 14.

3. On underage enlistments in the Civil War, see Frances M. Clarke and Rebecca Jo Plant, *Of Age: Boy Soldiers and Military Power in the Civil War Era* (New York: Oxford Univ. Press, 2023), 167–196; George B. Cowlam, 11th N.Y. Infantry, Compiled Military Service Record, NARA; pension file of George B. Cowlam, 11th N.Y. Infantry, NARA; Plum, *The Military Telegraph During the Civil War in the United States,* 2:79; George B. Cowlam, "It Was Abe: A Boy's Recollection of Lincoln," 13 September 1896, *Washington (D.C.) Morning Times,* 23.

4. George B. Cowlam, "It Was Abe: A Boy's Recollection of Lincoln," 13 September 1896, *Washington (D.C.) Morning Times,* 23.

5. Michael Burlingame and John R. Turner Ettlinger, eds., *Inside Lincoln's White House: The Complete Civil War Diary of John Hay* (Carbondale: Southern Illinois Univ. Press, 1997), 20; "The War for the Union. Military Display in Washington. The Fire Brigade," *New York Tribune,* 8 May 1861, 5.

6. Anna Gibson Holloway and Jonathan W. White, *"Our Little Monitor": The Greatest Invention of the Civil War* (Kent, Ohio: Kent State Univ. Press, 2018), 68–69; Plum, *The Military Telegraph During the Civil War in the United States,* 1:139–140; John Emmet O'Brien, *Telegraphing in Battle: Reminiscences of the Civil War* (Scranton: Reader Press, 1910), 58, 62–65; George B. Cowlam, 11th N.Y. Infantry, Compiled Military Service Record, NARA; pension file of George B. Cowlam, 11th N.Y. Infantry, NARA; George B. Cowlam to Thomas Thompson Eckert, 13 March 1861, James William Eldridge Collection, The Huntington Library, San Marino, California, box 12; "Death of Col. Geo. B. Cowlam," *New York Times,* 12 March 1901, 9; "Death of Colonel C.B. Cowlam," *Fort Wayne (Ind.) Daily News,* 12 March 1901, 4.

7. Joshua Wolff describes George as a former employee of Western Union who had been fired for fraud, and "appears under shadowy circumstances in several places in [William] Orton's letterbooks." In another example of morally questionable behavior, George offered a testimonial for a Dr. Lighthill's cure of deafness and discharges of the ear in July 1866. In the endorsement he described experiencing a cold fifteen years before that had caused him to lose three-fourths of his hearing, which was now fully restored thanks to Lighthill's remedy. It seems strange to think that George could have been a telegraph operator with hearing so impaired. Joshua D. Wolff, *Western Union and the Creation of the American Corporate Order, 1845–1893* (Cambridge: Cambridge Univ. Press, 2013), 220n; "Cure of Deafness and Discharges from the Ear," *Chicago Tribune*, 6 July 1866, 1; William Orton to John M. S. Williams and William Orton to Thomas T. Eckert, 27 February 1874, William Orton to Anson Stager, 5 March 1874, Western Union Telegraph Company Records, National Museum of American History, Series 4, box 200A, vol. 13, 127–130, 146–147.

8. George Cowlam to Benjamin Butler, 26 September–16 October 1868, Benjamin F. Butler Papers, LC, box 46.

9. George Cowlam to Benjamin Butler, 26 September–16 October 1868, Benjamin F. Butler Papers, LC, box 46; David Montgomery, *Beyond Equality: Labor and the Radical Republicans 1862–1872* (1967; reprint, Urbana: Univ. of Illinois Press, 1981), 364–365; "Letter from Gen. Butler," 1 October 1868, *Boston Daily Evening Traveller*, 2; "Excitement in the House," *Buffalo Commercial*, 9 April 1872, 3.

10. Butler also joined Francis W. Kellogg and William Aldrich in recommending the youngest Cowlam sister, Isabel, for employment in the Treasury Department in 1873. Biography of Treasury Employees 1835–1912, RG 56, entry 218: Records of the Division of Appointments, NACP, Registers and Lists of Treasury Employees, 9:175–176, 11:418–419, 424–425, 12:406–409.

11. *Report of the Select Committee of the House of Representatives, Appointed Under the Resolution of January 6, 1873 To Make Inquiry in Relation to the Affairs of the Union Pacific Railroad Company, the Crédit Mobilier of America, and Other Matters Specified in Said Resolution and in Other Resolutions Referred to Said Committee* (Washington, D.C.: Government Printing Office, 1873), 410–416, quotation 413. On the Crédit Mobilier scandal, see Maury Klein, *Union Pacific: Birth of a Railroad, 1862–1893* (New York: Doubleday, 1987), 285–305.

12. George B. Cowlam to James A. Garfield, 26 October 1880, 16 November 1880, 4 December 1880, 6 January 1881, 16 February 1881, James A. Garfield Papers, Series 4: General Correspondence, LC, vols. 100, 110, 114, 121, 130, quotation from the letter of 16 February 1881. George published the argument he presented to Garfield as "The South's Opportunity," *Louisville Commercial*, 16 February 1881. George B. Cowlam, *The Undeveloped South: Its Resources, and the Importance of Their Development as a Factor in Determining the Future Prosperity and Growth of Wealth in the United States* (Louisville: Courier Journal Job Printing Company, 1887), 3–31, especially 26–28; George B. Cowlam, "The Industrial Future of the South," in *The Industrial Future of the South Prize Essays* (Richmond: Norfolk & Western Railroad, 1891), 1–6. See also C. Vann Woodward, *Origins of the New South, 1877–1913* (Baton Rouge: Louisiana State Univ. Press, 1951), 122; Natalie J. Ring, "The Problem South: Region, Race, and 'Southern Readjustment,' 1880–1930" (Ph.D. diss., University of California, San Diego, 2003), 96–97.

13. The contracts found in the court case file describe Cowland as a mining engineer "of Denver, Colorado," and he appears in the Denver city directories for 1892 and 1893. Various mining publications published long after Cowland's death contain recollections variously describing him as either English or Australian. A "Charles Cowland" born in Notting Hill, London, in 1850 appears in the 1891 British census with the occupation mine owner and mining engineer. *Wiser v. Lawler*, 189 U.S. 260 (1903); Arizona Supreme Court. Territorial Records, Civil Cases: 644–651 (1899), Arizona State Library; *Wiser v. Lawler*, NARA, RG 267, entry 21, Appellate Case Files for the United States Supreme Court, case file 18287; "15 Per Cent, Guaranteed," *Lancaster (Pa.) News-Journal*, 15 October 1892, 4.

14. "A Long Trip to Be Married," *Philadelphia Inquirer*, 10 November 1894, 1.

BIBLIOGRAPHY

MANUSCRIPT COLLECTIONS

Archives of Michigan, Lansing, Michigan
Chancery Calendar, Wayne County, Circuit Court, RG 85-34.
Superior Court Chancery Records, Wayne County, Circuit Court, RG 85-34.
The People v. Charles Cowlam, Criminal Calendar, Calhoun County, RG 2017-111.

Arizona State Library, Phoenix, Arizona
Arizona Supreme Court, Territorial Records, Civil Cases: 644–651.

Bentley Historical Collection, University of Michigan, Ann Arbor, Michigan
First Baptist Church Records, 1830–1920 and 1956, Saline, Michigan.

College of William & Mary, Earl Gregg Swem Library, Special Collections Research Center, Williamsburg, Virginia
John Tyler Jr. Papers.

Devonshire Collection Archives, Chatsworth House, Bakewell, United Kingdom
Papers of Spencer Compton Cavendish, 8th Duke of Devonshire (1833–1908).

Georgia Archives, Morrow, Georgia
Martin V. Brantley v. State of Georgia, A-03652, Georgia Supreme Court Case Files, RG 092-01-001.

Huntington Library, San Marino, California
James William Eldridge Collection.

Library and Archives of Canada, Ottawa, Ontario, Canada
John A. MacDonald Fonds, MG26-A.

Library of Congress, Manuscript Division, Washington, D.C.
Benjamin F. Butler Papers.
James A. Garfield Papers.

Records of the Confederate States of America.
William E. Chandler Papers.

Library of Virginia, Richmond, Virginia
Records of the Virginia Penitentiary, APA 131.
State Government Records Collection, Governor John Letcher Papers.

National Archives and Records Administration, Atlanta, Georgia
United States v. Albert S. Bigelow and Others, U.S. District Court of Georgia, Southern District, Savannah Division, Mixed Case Files 1866–1900.
United States v. One Pipe of Cherries and Bitters and Other Property, J.N. Muller, Claimant, U.S. District Court of Georgia, Southern District, Savannah Division.
United States v. One Pipe of Cherries and Bitters and Other Property, J.N. Muller, Claimant, U.S. District Court of Georgia, Southern District, Savannah Division, General Minutes, 1869–1871.

National Archives and Records Administration, College Park, Maryland
RG 56, entry 218, Registers and Lists of Treasury Employees.
RG 58, entry 317-A, Internal Revenue Secret Service Record, 1865–1881.
RG 59, entry 897, General Pardon Records, Pardons and Remissions.
RG 59, entry 902, Requisitions for Pardons.
RG 59, Acceptances and Orders for Commissions, M-T645.
RG 60, entry 9-A, Letters Received by the Attorney General. 1809–1870: Federal Government Correspondence.
RG 60, entry 80, Letters Sent by the Department of Justice to Executive Officers and to Members of Congress.
RG 60, entry 350 Appointment Files for Judicial Districts, 1853–1905.
RG 60, Letters Sent by the Department of Justice: General and Miscellaneous, M-699.
RG 60, Letters Sent by the Department of Justice to Executive Officers and to Members of Congress, M-702.
RG 60, Letters Received by the Department of Justice from the State of Florida, 1871–1884, M-1327.
RG 87, entry A1/E.1-A, Name Index to Registers of Reports.
RG 87, entry A-1 51, Record of Secret Service Operatives Employed 1865–1871.
RG 204, entry 1a, Pardon Case Files, 1853–1946.

National Archives and Records Administration, Washington, D.C.
RG 59, Letters of Application and Recommendation During the Administration of U.S. Grant, 1869–1877, M698.

RG 92, entry NM-81 404, Card List of Employees Working on Telegraph Lines and Wages Earned, 1861–65.
RG 92, entry NM-81 405, List of Names of Military Telegraph Operators, 1863–65.
RG 94, Letters Received by the Adjutant General, Main Series, 1881–1889, M689.
RG 94, entry 179, Case Files of Investigations by Levi C. Turner and Lafayette C. Baker, 1861–1866, M797.
RG 109, entry 183, Miscellaneous Records, Manuscript 939.
RG 109, Papers of and Relating to Military and Civilian Personnel, 1874–1899.
RG 109, Reports on Prisoners Brought Before Commissioners Vowles and Sands, Richmond, Virginia, 1864, chapter IX, vol. 229.
RG 110, NM-65, part 1, entry 32, Correspondence, Reports, and Other Records Relating to Telegraph Employees, 1861–66.
RG 110, NM-65, part 1, entry 95, Accounts of Secret Service Agents, 1861–1870.
RG 267, entry 21, Appellate Case Files for the United States Supreme Court.

P. K. Yonge Library of Florida History and the Manuscripts Collections in the Department of Special Collections and Area Studies, George A. Smathers Libraries, University of Florida, Gainesville, Florida
David Levy Yulee Papers.
Miscellaneous Manuscripts.

Private Collection
Pardon of Charles Cowlam, 28 May 1861.
William H. Seward to John Letcher, 28 May 1861.

Sanford Memorial Library, Sanford, Florida
Henry Shelton Sanford Papers.

Smithsonian National Museum of American History, Washington, D.C.
Western Union Telegraph Company Records.

Southern Historical Collection, Wilson Library, University of North Carolina at Chapel Hill, Chapel Hill, North Carolina
Edward M. L'Engle Papers.
Rice, Thompson, and Winbourne Family Papers, 1838–1972.

State Library and Archives of Florida, Tallahassee, Florida
RG 101, Territorial and State Governors, S577, State Governors' Incoming Correspondence, 1857–1888.

BIBLIOGRAPHY

RG 151, Office of the Secretary of State, S1325, Secretary of the Territory and Secretary of State Incoming Correspondence, 1831–1917.

RG 156, Election Return Canvassing Results, Florida Election Official State Canvass, S1258.

DIGITAL DATABASES

Ancestry.com
Fold3.com
FamilySearch.com
Newspapers.com
ReadEx

PRINTED PRIMARY SOURCES

Annual Report of the Board of Managers of the National Home for Disabled Volunteer Soldiers for the Fiscal Year Ending June 30, 1887. House of Representatives. 50th Congress, 1st Session. Miscellaneous Document 86.

Annual Reports of Officers, Boards and Institutions of the Commonwealth of Virginia Part 5. Richmond, Va.: Ritchie, 1858.

Baker, Lafayette C. *History of the United States Secret Service.* Philadelphia: Baker, 1867.

Beaumont, Gustave de., and Alexis de Tocqueville. *On the Penitentiary System in the United States, and Its Application in France: The Complete Text.* Translated by Emily Katherine Ferkaluk. 1833. Reprint, Cham, Switzerland: Palgrave Macmillan, 2018.

Boyd, Andrew. *Boyd's Washington and Georgetown Directory of Washington, Containing also a Business Directory of Washington, Georgetown and Alexandria.* Washington, D.C.: Hudson Taylor, 1864.

Boyd, William H. *Boyd's Directory of Washington, Georgetown, and Alexandria.* Washington, D.C.: Boyd, 1871.

Brown, William W. *The American Fugitive in Europe: Sketches of Places and People Abroad.* Boston: Jewett, 1855.

Burlingame, Michael, and John R. Turner Ettlinger, eds. *Inside Lincoln's White House: The Complete Civil War Diary of John Hay.* Carbondale: Southern Illinois Univ. Press, 1997.

CIS Index to Presidential Executive Orders and Proclamations: Part I: April 30, 1789 to March 4, 1921 George Washington to Woodrow Wilson. Washington, D.C.: Congressional Information Service, 1987.

Congressional Globe.

Constitution of the Confederate States of America.

BIBLIOGRAPHY

Constitution of Georgia.

Cowlam, George B. "The Industrial Future of the South." In *The Industrial Future of the South Prize Essays*. Richmond: Norfolk & Western Railroad, 1891.

———. *The Undeveloped South: Its Resources, and the Importance of Their Development as a Factor in Determining the Future Prosperity and Growth of Wealth in the United States*. Louisville: Courier Journal Job Printing Company, 1887.

Crist, Lynda Lasswell, et al., eds. *The Papers of Jefferson Davis*. 14 vols. Baton Rouge: Louisiana State Univ. Press, 1971–2015.

Cushman, Henry Wyles. *A Historical and Biographical Genealogy of the Cushmans: The Descendants of Robert Cushman the Puritan from the Year 1617 to 1855*. Boston: Little, Brown, 1855.

Denoon, Samuel D. *Annual Report of the Board of Directors of the Penitentiary Institution, Year Ending September 30, 1862*, Document no. VI. Richmond, Va., 1862.

———. *Annual Report of the Board of Directors of the Penitentiary Institution, Year Ending September 30, 1863*, Document no. IX. Richmond, Va., 1863.

Edwards, William C., and Edward Steers Jr., eds., *The Lincoln Assassination: The Evidence*. Urbana: Univ. of Illinois Press, 2009.

Gordon, Peter, ed. *The Red Earl: The Papers of the Fifth Earl Spencer 1835–1910*. 2 vols. Northampton: Northamptonshire Record Society, 1981.

Graf, LeRoy P., ed. *The Papers of Andrew Johnson*. 16 vols. Knoxville: Univ. of Tennessee Press, 1986.

Glyndon, Howard. *Notable Men in "The House": A Series of Sketches of Prominent Men in the House of Representatives, Members of the Thirty-Seventh Congress*. New York: Baker and Goodwin, 1862.

Jones, J. B. *A Rebel War Clerk's Diary: At the Confederate States Capital*, vol. 2, *August 1863–April 1865*, edited by James I. Robertson Jr. 1866. Reprint, Lawrence: Univ. Press of Kansas, 2015.

Kidd, J. H. *Personal Recollections of a Cavalryman with Custer's Michigan Cavalry Brigade in the Civil War*. Ionia, Mich.: Sentinel Printing Company, 1908.

Morgan, Charles S. *Annual Report of the Board of Directors of the Penitentiary Institution, 1857*, Document no. XIII. Richmond, Va., 1857.

———. *Annual Report of the Board of Directors of the Penitentiary Institution, Year Ending September 30, 1858*, Document no. XIII. Richmond, Va., 1858.

New York Association for Improving the Condition of the Poor. *Thirty-First Annual Report for the Year 1874*. New York: New York Association for Improving the Condition of the Poor, 1874.

Patrick, Rembert W., ed. *The Opinions of the Confederate Attorneys General, 1861–1865*. Buffalo: Dennis, 1950.

BIBLIOGRAPHY

Pendleton, James F. *Annual Report of the Board of Directors of the Penitentiary Institution, Year Ending September 30, 1859,* Document no. XIII. Richmond, Va., 1859.

———. *Annual Report of the Board of Directors of the Penitentiary Institution, Year Ending September 30, 1860,* Document no. III. Richmond, Va., 1860.

———. *Annual Report of the Board of Directors of the Penitentiary Institution, Year Ending September 30, 1861,* Document no. XIII. Richmond, Va., 1861.

Periam, Jonathan. *The Groundswell: A History of the Origin, Aims, and Progress of the Farmers' Movement.* Cincinnati: Hannaford, 1874.

Polk, R. L. *Detroit City Directory for 1889.* Detroit: R. L. Polk, 1889.

Poore, Perley. *Congressional Directory.* 43rd Congress, 1st Session. Washington, D.C.: Government Printing Office, 1873.

Prosecuting Attorneys. "Annual Report of the Attorney General." In *Joint Documents of the State of Michigan for the Year 1853,* document 6. Lansing, Mich.: Peck, 1854.

Reid, William D. *Death Notices of Ontario.* Lambertville, N.J.: Clearfield, 1997.

Report of Joint Special Committee to Investigate Chinese Immigration. 44th Congress, 2nd Session. Washington, D.C.: Government Printing Office, 1877.

Report of the Select Committee of the House of Representatives, Appointed Under the Resolution of January 6, 1873 To Make Inquiry in Relation to the Affairs of the Union Pacific Railroad Company, the Credit Mobilier of America, and Other Matters Specified in Said Resolution and in Other Resolutions Referred to Said Committee. Washington, D.C.: Government Printing Office, 1873.

Simon, John Y., ed. *The Papers of Ulysses S. Grant.* 31 vols. Carbondale: Southern Illinois Univ. Press, 1967–2009.

Strong, George Templeton. *The Diary of George Templeton Strong: The Postwar Years 1865–1875,* edited by Allan Nevins and Milton Halsey Thomas. New York: MacMillan, 1952.

Sutton Publishing Company. *Madison, Vevay, Vernon, North Vernon, and Jefferson County Illustrated Directory 1887–88.* Dubuque, Iowa: Hugh and Hardie, 1887.

Thoreau, Henry David. *Walden,* edited by Jeffrey S. Cramer. 1854. Reprint, New Haven: Yale Univ. Press, 2004.

"Testimony Taken by the Joint Select Committee to Inquire into the Condition of Affairs in the Late Insurrectionary States: Florida." 42nd Congress, 2nd Session, House Report 22, Part 13, Series no. 1541. 13 vols. Washington, D.C.: Government Printing Office, 1872.

The ABC Court Directory and Fashionable Guide for 1871. London: Effingham Wilson, 1871.

Ulman, H. Charles. *Lawyers' Record and Official Register of the United States.* New York: Barnes, 1872.

BIBLIOGRAPHY

U.S. Copyright Office, Library of Congress. *Dramatic Compositions Copyrighted in the United States 1870 to 1916*. Washington, D.C.: Government Printing Office, 1918.

U.S. War Department, comp. *War of the Rebellion: A Compilation of the Official Records of the Union and Confederate Armies*. 128 vols. Washington D.C.: Government Printing Office, 1880–1901.

Wilson, H. *Trow's New York City Directory*. New York: Trow City Directory Company, 1873.

NEWSPAPERS

Akron (Ohio) Beacon Journal
Ann Arbor Signal of Liberty
Atlanta Georgia Grange
Augusta (Ga.) Daily Constitutionalist
Baltimore Sun
Belfast (Ireland) News-Letter
Boston Daily Evening Traveller
Boston Morning Journal
Brooklyn Daily Eagle
Buffalo Commercial
Burlington (Vt.) Free Press
Camden (N.J.) Democrat
Charleston (S.C.) Mercury
Charlotte (N.C.) Democrat
Chicago Tribune
Chicago Times
Cincinnati Semi-Weekly Gazette
Coldwater (Mich.) Republican
Daily Columbus (Ga.) Enquirer
Daily Milwaukee News
Daily Star and Herald (Panama City, Panama)
Dayton (Ohio) Herald
Des Moines Iowa State Register
Detroit Free Press
Elgin (Ill.) Daily Courier
Fort Wayne (Ind.) Daily News
Freeman's Journal (Dublin, Ireland)
Gilroy (Calif.) Advocate

Greensboro (N.C.) Patriot
Guardian (London, UK)
Jackson (Mich.) Daily Citizen
Jacksonville (Fla.) Tri-Weekly Union
Libertyville (Ill.) Lake County Independent
Lancaster (Pa.) Inquirer
Lancaster (Pa.) News-Journal
Lancaster (UK) Gazette
Louisville Commercial
Los Angeles Herald
Macon Georgia Journal and Messenger
Macon Georgia Weekly Telegraph, Journal and Messenger
Madison (Ind.) Daily Courier
Madison (Wisc.) Daily Democrat
Madison Wisconsin State Journal
Manchester (UK) Guardian
Memphis Avalanche
Montgomery (Ala.) Daily Confederation
Nashville Union and American
New Orleans South-Western Presbyterian
New Orleans Times-Democrat
New York Daily Graphic
New York Herald
New York Irish American
New York Telegrapher
New York Times
New York Tribune
New York World
Norfolk Day Book
North-Eastern Daily Gazette (Middlesbrough, UK)
Philadelphia Inquirer
Pioche (Nev.) Daily Record
Portland Morning Oregonian
Red Wing (Minn.) Grange Advance
Richmond (Va.) Dispatch
Richmond (Va.) Examiner
Rock Island (Ill.) Daily Argus
Rome (Ga.) Weekly Courier

Sacramento Daily Union
San Francisco Chronicle
San Francisco Daily Alta California
San Francisco Examiner
Savannah Daily Advertiser
Savannah Morning News
Sioux City Daily Journal
Springfield (Ohio) Globe Republic
Tallahassee Weekly Floridian
Times (London, UK)
Vicksburg Whig
Washington (D.C.) Evening Star
Washington (D.C.) Morning Times
Wichita City (Kans.) Eagle
Wilmington (N.C.) Tri-Weekly Commercial
Wilmington (N.C.) Journal
Windsor Vermont Journal
Worcester Massachusetts Weekly Spy

SECONDARY SOURCES

Adamik, Verena. *In Search of the Utopian States of America: Intentional Communities in Novels of the Long Nineteenth Century*. New York: Palgrave MacMillan, 2020.

Amlund, Curtis A. *Federalism in the Southern Confederacy*. Washington, D.C.: Public Affairs Press, 1966.

Andrew, Christopher. *Secret Service: The Making of the British Intelligence Community*. London: Sceptre, 1986.

Angell, Stephen W. *Bishop Henry McNeal Turner and African-American Religion in the South*. Knoxville: Univ. of Tennessee Press, 1992.

Ash, Stephen V. *Rebel Richmond: Life and Death in the Confederate Capital*. Chapel Hill: Univ. of North Carolina Press, 2019.

Arnade, Peter, and Elizabeth Colwill. "Crime and Testimony: Life Narratives, Pardon Letters, and Microhistory." *Journal of Medieval and Early Modern Studies* 47, no. 1 (January 2017): 147–166.

Augst, Thomas. *The Clerk's Tale: Young Men and Moral Life in Nineteenth-Century America*. Chicago: Univ. of Chicago Press, 2003.

Ayers, Edward L. *Vengeance and Justice: Crime and Punishment in the Nineteenth-Century American South*. New York: Oxford Univ. Press, 1984.

Bailey, Hugh C. "Alabama and West Florida Annexation." *Florida Historical Quarterly* 35, no. 3 (January 1957): 219–232.

Baker, Bruce E. "Fires on Shipboard: Sandbars, Salvage Fraud, and the Cotton Trade in New Orleans in the 1870s." *Journal of Southern History* 86, no. 3 (August 2020): 601–624.

Baldasty, Gerald J. *The Commercialization of the News in the Nineteenth Century*. Madison: Univ. of Wisconsin Press, 1992.

Balleisen, Edward J. *Fraud: An American History from Barnum to Madoff*. Princeton: Princeton Univ. Press, 2017.

———. "A Profusion of Microhistories: The Historiography of American Business Fraud." October 2017. https://sites.duke.edu/suckersandswindlers/files/2017/10/Historical-Scholarship-on-Business-Fraud-10-3-17.pdf.

Balogh, Brian. *A Government Out of Sight: The Mystery of National Authority in Nineteenth-Century America*. Cambridge: Cambridge Univ. Press, 2009.

Barnes, Charles E. "Battle Creek as a Station on the Underground Railway." In *Historical Collections: Collections and Researches Made by the Michigan Pioneer and Historical Society*. 40 vols. Lansing: Wynkoop Hallenbeck Crawford, 1912.

Barr, Chris, David R. Bush, et al. "Civil War Incarceration in History and Memory: A Roundtable." *Civil War History* 63, no. 3 (September 2017): 295–319.

Barreyre, Nicolas. "The Politics of Economic Crises: The Panic of 1873, the End of Reconstruction, and the Realignment of American Politics." *Journal of the Gilded Age and Progressive Era* 10, no. 4 (October 2011): 403–423.

Beckert, Sven. *The Monied Metropolis: New York City and the Consolidation of the American Bourgeoisie, 1850–1896*. Cambridge: Harvard Univ. Press, 2001.

Beilein, Joseph M., Jr. *A Man by Any Other Name: William Clarke Quantrill and the Search for American Manhood*. Athens: Univ. of Georgia Press, 2023.

Bell, John. *Confederate Seadog: John Taylor Wood in War and Exile*. Jefferson, N.C.: McFarland, 2002.

Bell, Richard. "Peepholes, Eels, and Pickett's Charge: Doing Microhistory Then and Now." *Journal of the Civil War Era* 12, no. 3 (September 2022): 362–387.

———. *We Shall Be No More: Suicide and Self-Government in the Newly United States*. Cambridge: Harvard Univ. Press, 2012.

Bensel, Richard F. *Yankee Leviathan: The Origins of Central State Authority in America, 1859–1877*. Cambridge: Cambridge Univ. Press, 1990.

Benson, John. *Respectability, Bankruptcy and Bigamy in Late Nineteenth- and Early Twentieth-Century Britain*. New York: Routledge, 2023.

Bergmann, Johannes Dietrich. "The Original Confidence Man." *American Quarterly* 21, no. 3 (August 1969): 560–577.

Bjelopera, Jerome P. *City of Clerks: Office and Sales Workers in Philadelphia, 1870–1920.* Urbana: Univ. of Illinois Press, 2005.

Blake, Holly Jacklyn. "Marie Howland—19th-Century Leader for Women's Economic Independence." *American Journal of Economics and Sociology* 74, no. 5 (November 2015): 878–1192.

Blevins, Cameron. *Paper Trails: The US Post and the Making of the American West.* New York: Oxford Univ. Press, 2021.

Boswell, James. *The Life of Samuel Johnson.* 1791. Reprint, New York: Penguin Classis, 1986.

Bowen, Heath J. "Your Obedient Servant: Government Clerks, Officeseeking, and the Politics of Patronage in Antebellum Washington City." Ph.D. diss., Michigan State University, 2011.

Bowes, John P. *Land Too Good for Indians: Northern Indian Removal.* Norman: Univ. of Oklahoma Press, 2016.

Brimmer, Brandi C. "Black Women's Politics, Narratives of Sexual Immorality, and Pension Bureaucracy in Mary Lee's North Carolina Neighborhood." *Journal of Southern History* 80, no. 4 (November 2014): 827–858.

———. *Claiming Union Widowhood: Race, Respectability, and Poverty in the Post-Emancipation South.* Durham: Duke Univ. Press, 2020.

———. "'Her Claim for Pension Is Lawful and Just': Representing Black Union Widows in Late-Nineteenth Century North Carolina." *Journal of the Civil War Era* 1, no. 2 (June 2011): 207–236.

Brown, Canter, Jr. "Carpetbagger Intrigues, Black Leadership, and a Southern Loyalist Triumph: Florida's Gubernatorial Election of 1872." *Florida Historical Quarterly* 72, no. 3 (January 1994): 277–278.

———. *Ossian Bingley Hart: Florida's Loyalist Reconstruction Governor.* Baton Rouge: Louisiana State Univ. Press, 1997.

Brown, Richard D. "Microhistory and the Post-Modern Challenge." *Journal of the Early Republic* 23, no. 1 (spring, 2003): 1–20.

Broxmeyer, Jeffrey D. "Bringing the 'Ring' Back In: The Politics of Booty Capitalism." *Journal of the Gilded Age and Progressive Era* 19 (2020): 235–245.

———. *Electoral Capitalism: The Party System in New York's Gilded Age.* Philadelphia: Univ. of Pennsylvania Press, 2020.

Brumfield, Dale M. *Virginia State Penitentiary: A Notorious History.* Charleston, S.C.: History Press, 2017.

Brummer, Sidney D. "The Judicial Interpretation of the Confederate Constitution." *Lawyer and Banker and Southern Bench and Bar Review* 8, no. 6 (December 1915): 387–409.

Burgess, Paul. *Justo Rufino Barrios: A Biography.* New York: Dorrance, 1926.
Butler, Clayton J. *True Blue: White Unionists in the Deep South during the Civil War and Reconstruction.* Baton Rouge: Louisiana State Univ. Press, 2022.
Calhoun, Frederick S. *The Lawmen: United States Marshals and Their Deputies, 1789–1989.* Washington, D.C.: Smithsonian Institution Press, 1989.
Caplan, Jane, and John Torpey, eds. *Documenting Individual Identity: The Development of State Practices in the Modern World.* Princeton: Princeton Univ. Press, 2001.
Carlson, Robert D. "Breach of Faith: Conscription in Confederate Georgia." Ph.D. diss., Emory University, 2009.
Carr, Marty. "A Fourth of July Celebration, 1840." *Family History Capers.* Genealogical Society of Washtenaw County, Michigan, 10, no. 4 (spring 1987): 79–82.
Casstevens, Frances H. *George W. Alexander and Castle Thunder.* Jefferson, N.C.: McFarland, 2004.
Chernow, Ron. *Grant.* New York: Penguin Press, 2017.
Churchill, Robert H. *The Underground Railroad and the Geography of Violence in Antebellum America.* Cambridge: Cambridge Univ. Press, 2020.
Cimbala, Paul A. *Veterans North and South: The Transition from Soldier to Civilian after the American Civil War.* Santa Barbara: Praeger, 2015.
Clark, James C. "John Wallace and the Writing of Reconstruction History." *Florida Historical Quarterly* 67, no. 4 (April 1989): 409–427.
Clarke, Frances M., and Rebecca Jo Plant. *Of Age: Boy Soldiers and Military Power in the Civil War Era.* New York: Oxford Univ. Press, 2023.
Cleland, Charles E. *Rites of Conquest: The History and Culture of Michigan's Native Americans.* Ann Arbor: Univ. of Michigan Press, 1992.
Cloyd, Benjamin G. *Haunted by Atrocity: Civil War Prisons in American Memory.* Baton Rouge: Louisiana State Univ. Press, 2010.
Cohen, Thomas V. "The Macrohistory of Microhistory." *Journal of Medieval and Early Modern Studies* 47, no. 1 (January 2017): 53–73.
Cole, Simon A. *Suspect Identities: A History of Fingerprinting and Criminal Identification.* Cambridge: Harvard Univ. Press, 2001.
Colwell, S. "The Incidence of Bigamy in 18th and 19th Century England." *Family History* 11 (1980): 91–102.
Cook, James W. *The Arts of Deception: Playing with Fraud in the Age of Barnum.* Cambridge: Harvard Univ. Press, 2001.
Coulter, Merton E. "Henry M. Turner: Georgia Negro Preacher-Politician During the Reconstruction Era." *Georgia Historical Quarterly* 48, no. 4 (December 1964): 389–394.

Cox, David. "'Trying to Get a Good One': Bigamy Offences in England and Wales, 1850–1950." *Plymouth Law and Criminal Justice Review* 4 (2012): 1–32.

Cresswell, Stephen. *Mormons and Cowboys, Moonshiners and Klansmen: Federal Law Enforcement in the South and West, 1870–1893.* Tuscaloosa: Univ. of Alabama Press, 1991.

Cronon, William. *Nature's Metropolis: Chicago and the Great West.* New York: Norton, 1991.

Cumming, Carman. *Devil's Game: The Civil War Intrigues of Charles A. Dunham.* Urbana: Univ. of Illinois, 2004.

Currie, David P. "Through the Looking-Glass: The Confederate Constitution in Congress, 1861–1865." *Virginia Law Review* 90, no. 5 (September 2004): 1257–1399.

Cvrcek, Tomas. "When Harry Left Sally: A New Estimate of Marital Disruption in the U.S., 1860–1948." *Demographic Research* 21 (2009): 719–758.

Daniels, Jonathan. *Prince of Carpetbaggers.* 1958. Reprint, Westport: Greenwood Press, 1974.

Davidson, Carlisle G. "A Profile of Hicksite Quakerism in Michigan, 1830–1860." *Quaker History* 59, no. 2 (autumn 1970): 106–112.

Davis, Natalie Zemon. *Fiction in the Archives: Pardon Tales and Their Tellers in Sixteenth-Century France.* Stanford: Stanford Univ. Press, 1987.

———. *The Return of Martin Guerre.* Cambridge: Harvard Univ. Press, 1983.

Davis, William C. *Inventing Loreta Velasquez: Confederate Soldier Impersonator, Media Celebrity, and Con Artist.* Carbondale: Southern Illinois Univ. Press, 2016.

Davis, William W. *The Civil War and Reconstruction in Florida.* New York: Colombia University, 1913.

DeCaro, Louis. *Freedom's Dawn: The Last Days of John Brown in Virginia.* London: Rowman and Littlefield, 2015.

DeCredico, Mary A. *Confederate Citadel: Richmond and Its People at War.* Lexington: Univ. Press of Kentucky, 2020.

DeGrave, Kathleen. *Swindler, Spy, Rebel: The Confidence Woman in Nineteenth-Century America.* Columbia: Univ. of Missouri Press, 1995.

DeRosa, Marshall L. *The Confederate Constitution of 1861: An Inquiry into American Constitutionalism.* Colombia: Univ. of Missouri Press, 1991.

Domby, Adam H. *The False Cause: Fraud, Fabrication, and White Supremacy in Confederate Memory.* Charlottesville: Univ. of Virginia Press, 2020.

Dorris, Jonathan Truman. *Pardon and Amnesty under Lincoln and Johnson: The Restoration of the Confederates to Their Rights and Privileges, 1861–1898.* Chapel Hill: Univ. of North Carolina Press, 1953.

———. "President Lincoln's Clemency." *Journal of the Illinois State Historical Society* 20, no. 4 (January 1928): 547–568.

Downs, Gregory P., and Kate Masur, eds. *The World the Civil War Made*. Chapel Hill: Univ. of North Carolina Press, 2015.

Ducharme, Michel. "Closing the Last Chapter of the Atlantic Revolution: The 1837–38 Rebellions in Upper and Lower Canada." *Proceedings of the American Antiquarian Society* 116, no. 2 (October 2006): 413–430.

Dukova, Anastasia. *A History of the Dublin Metropolitan Police and Its Colonial Legacy*. London: Palgrave MacMillan, 2016.

Eicher, John H., and David J. Eicher, eds. *Civil War High Commands*. Stanford: Stanford Univ. Press, 2001.

Ellis, Franklin. *History of Livingston County, Michigan: With Illustrations and Biographical Sketches of Its Prominent Men and Pioneers*. Philadelphia: Everts and Abbott, 1880.

Ewing, Cortez A. M. "Florida Reconstruction Impeachments: Impeachment of Governor Harrison Reed." *Florida Historical Quarterly* vol. 36, no. 4 (April 1958): 299–318.

Fahnestock, Jeanne. "Bigamy: The Rise and Fall of a Convention." *Nineteenth-Century Fiction* 36, no. 1 (June 1981): 47–71.

Faulkner, Carol. *Unfaithful: Love, Adultery, and Marriage Reform in Nineteenth-Century America*. Philadelphia: Univ. of Pennsylvania Press, 2019.

Feis, William B. *Grant's Secret Service: The Intelligence War from Belmont to Appomattox*. Lincoln: Univ. of Nebraska Press, 2002.

Fish, Peter G. *Federal Justice in the Mid-Atlantic South: United States Courts from Maryland to the Carolinas, 1836–1861*. Durham: Carolina Academic Press, 2015.

Flavin, William James. "Lafayette C. Baker and the Union Secret Service." Master's thesis, Emory University, 1973.

Fogel, Robert W. "New Sources and New Techniques for the Study of Secular Trends in Nutritional Status, Health, Mortality, and the Process of Aging." *Historical Methods: A Journal of Quantitative and Interdisciplinary History* 26, no. 1 (winter 1993): 5–39.

Foner, Eric. *Free Soil, Free Labor, Free Men: The Ideology of the Republican Party Before the Civil War*. 1970. Reprint, New York: Oxford Univ. Press, 1995.

———. *Reconstruction: America's Unfinished Revolution, 1863–1877*. New York: HarperCollins, 1988.

Foote, Lorien. *The Yankee Plague: Escaped Union Prisoners and the Collapse of the Confederacy*. Chapel Hill: Univ. of North Carolina Press, 2016.

Forret, Jeff, and Bruce E. Baker, eds. *Southern Scoundrels: Grifters and Graft in the Nineteenth Century*. Baton Rouge: Louisiana State Univ. Press, 2021.

Foster, Susan Lynch. "Romancing the Cause: Fourierism, Feminism, and Free Love in *Papa's Own Girl*." *Utopian Studies* 8, no. 1 (1997): 31–54.

Fox, Thomas. *Drummer Boy Willie McGee, Civil War Hero and Fraud*. Jefferson, N.C.: McFarland, 2008.

Franzino, Jean. "Tales Told by Empty Sleeves: Disability, Mendicancy, and Civil War Life Writing." *American Literature* 94, no. 3 (September 2022): 399–438.

Friedman, Lawrence M. *Crime and Punishment in American History*. New York: Basic Books, 1993.

———. *Personal Identity in the Modern World: A Society of Strangers*. Lanham, Md.: Rowman and Littlefield, 2022.

Friend, Jack. *West Wind, Flood Tide: The Battle of Mobile Bay*. Annapolis: Naval Institute Press, 2004.

Frost, Ginger S. *Living in Sin: Cohabitating as Husband and Wife in Nineteenth-Century England*. Manchester: Manchester Univ. Press, 2008.

Gallman, J. Matthew. *Defining Duty in the Civil War: Personal Choice, Popular Culture, and the Union Home Front*. Chapel Hill: Univ. of North Carolina Press, 2015.

Gardner, Washington. *History of Calhoun County, Michigan: A Narrative Account of Its Historical Progress, Its People, and Its Principal Interests*. 2 vols. Chicago: Lewis, 1913.

Gilfoyle, Timothy J. "The Hearts of Nineteenth-Century Men: Bigamy and Working-Class Marriage in New York City, 1800–1890." *Prospects* 19 (October 1994): 135–160.

———. *A Pickpocket's Tale: The Underworld of Nineteenth-Century New York*. New York: Norton, 2006.

Ginzburg, Carlos. "Microhistory: Two or Three Things That I Know About It." *Critical Inquiry* 20, no. 1 (autumn 1993): 10–35.

Glickstein, Jonathan A. *Concepts of Free Labor in Antebellum America*. New Haven: Yale Univ. Press, 1991.

Golden, J. J. "The Protestant Influence on the Origins of Irish Home Rule, 1861–1871." *English Historical Review* 128, no. 535 (December 2013): 1483–1516.

Goldman, Robert M. *"A Free Ballot and a Fair Count": The Department of Justice and the Enforcement of Voting Rights in the South, 1877–1893*. 1990. Reprint, New York: Fordham Univ. Press, 2001.

Grainger, Brett Malcolm. *Church in the Wild: Evangelicals in Antebellum America*. Cambridge: Harvard Univ. Press, 2019.

Grant, Susan-Mary. "Reimagined Communities: Union Veterans and the Reconstruction of American Nationalism." *Nations and Nationalism* 14, no. 3 (2008): 498–519.

Grasso, Christopher. *Teacher, Preacher, Soldier, Spy: The Civil Wars of John R. Kelso*. New York: Oxford Univ. Press, 2021.

Gray, Michael P., ed. *Crossing the Deadlines: Civil War Prisons Reconsidered*. Kent, Ohio: Kent State Univ. Press, 2018.

Gray, Susan E. *The Yankee West: Community Life on the Michigan Frontier.* Chapel Hill: Univ. of North Carolina Press, 1996.

Grendi, Edoardo. "Ripensare la microstoria?" *Quaderni Storici* 86, no. 2 (August 1994): 539–549.

Halttunen, Karen. *Confidence Men and Painted Women: A Study of Middle-Class Culture in America, 1830–1870.* New Haven: Yale Univ. Press, 1982.

Hamilton, J. G. de Roulhac. "The State Courts and the Confederate Constitution." *Journal of Southern History* 4, no. 4 (November 1938): 425–448.

Handley-Cousins, Sarah. *Bodies in Blue: Disability in the Civil War North.* Athens: Univ. of Georgia Press, 2019.

Harris, Gale. "Bennett Building." New York City Landmarks Preservation Commission Report. 21 November 1995.

Hart, John Mason. *Empire and Revolution: The Americans in Mexico Since the Civil War.* Berkeley: Univ. of California Press, 2002.

Hartog, Hendrik. *Man and Wife in America: A History.* Cambridge: Harvard Univ. Press, 2000.

———. "Marital Exits and Marital Expectations in Nineteenth Century America." *Georgetown Law Review* 80, no. 1 (October 1991): 95–129.

Hedley, James. *A Sketch of the Canadian Telegraph System, Its Rise and Development.* Toronto: Roddy and Nurse, 1883.

Hemphill, C. Dallett. *Siblings: Brothers and Sisters in American History.* New York: Oxford Univ. Press, 2011.

Henkin, David M. *The Postal Age: The Emergence of Modern Communications in Nineteenth-Century America.* Chicago: Univ. of Chicago Press, 2006.

Hobart and Mather. *Biographical Review of Calhoun County, Michigan: Containing Historical, Biographical and Genealogical Sketches of Many of the Prominent Citizens of To-day and Also of the Past.* Chicago: Hobart and Mather, 1904.

Hodes, Martha. *Mourning Lincoln.* New Haven: Yale Univ. Press, 2015.

Holland, Bernard. *The Life of Spencer Compton, Eighth Duke of Devonshire.* 2 vols. London: Longmans, Green, 1911.

Holloway, Anna Gibson, and Jonathan W. White. *"Our Little Monitor": The Greatest Invention of the Civil War.* Kent, Ohio: Kent State Univ. Press, 2018.

Holzer, Harold, et al., eds. *The Lincoln Assassination: Crime and Punishment, Myth and Memory.* New York: Fordham Univ. Press, 2010.

Hoogenboom, Ari. *Outlawing the Spoils: A History of the Civil Service Reform Movement, 1865–1883.* Urbana: Univ. of Illinois Press, 1961.

Hopkins, Timothy. *The Kelloggs in the Old World and the New.* 3 vols. San Francisco: Sunset Press and Photo Engraving Co., 1903.

BIBLIOGRAPHY

Howe, Daniel W. *What Hath God Wrought: The Transformation of America, 1815–1848.* New York: Oxford Univ. Press, 2007.

Hoy, Benjamin. "Policing Morality: Regulating Sexuality Across the Canada-United States Border." *Canadian Historical Review* 99, no. 1 (March 2018): 30–62.

Hunt, William R. *Front-Page Detective: William J. Burns and the Detective Profession, 1880–1930.* Bowling Green, Ky.: Bowling Green State Univ. Popular Press, 1990.

Hurst, Michael. "Ireland and the Ballot Act of 1872." *Historical Journal* 8, no. 3 (1965): 326–352.

Huston, James L. *The British Gentry, the Southern Planter, and the Northern Family Farmer: Agriculture and Sectional Antagonism in North America.* Baton Rouge: Louisiana State Univ. Press, 2015.

Jackson, Patrick. *The Last of the Whigs: A Political Biography of Lord Hartington, Later Eighth Duke of Devonshire (1833–1908).* London: Associated Univ. Presses, 1994.

Jenkins, Brian. *The Fenian Problem: Insurgency and Terrorism in a Liberal State, 1858–1874.* Montreal: McGill-Queens Univ. Press, 2008.

John, Richard R. *Spreading the News: The American Postal System from Franklin to Morse.* Cambridge: Harvard Univ. Press, 1995.

Johnson, Paul E. *A Shopkeeper's Millennium: Society and Revivals in Rochester, New York, 1815–1837.* Twenty-Fifth Anniversary ed. 1978. Reprint, New York: Hill and Wang, 2004.

Johnson, Paul E., and Sean Wilentz. *The Kingdom of Matthias: A Story of Sex and Salvation in 19th-Century America.* New York: Oxford Univ. Press, 1994.

Johnson, Russell L. "'Great Injustice': Social Status and the Distribution of Military Pensions after the Civil War." *Journal of the Gilded Age and Progressive Era* 10, no. 2 (April 2011): 137–160.

Jordan, Brian Matthew. *Marching Home: Union Veterans and Their Unending Civil War.* New York: Liveright, 2014.

Jordan, Brian Matthew, and Evan C. Rothera, eds. *The War Went On: Reconsidering the Lives of Civil War Veterans.* Baton Rouge: Louisiana State Univ. Press, 2020.

Kamerling, Henry. *Capital and Convict: Race, Region, and Punishment in Post–Civil War America.* Charlottesville: Univ. of Virginia Press, 2017.

Kaczorowski, Robert J. *The Politics of Judicial Interpretation: The Federal Courts, Department of Justice, and Civil Rights, 1866–1876.* New York: Fordham Univ. Press, 2005.

Keehn, David C. *Knights of the Golden Circle: Secret Empire, Southern Secession, Civil War.* Baton Rouge: Louisiana State Univ. Press, 2013.

Kehoe, Thomas J., and Jeffrey E. Pfeifer, eds. *History and Crime: A Transdisciplinary Approach.* Bingley: Emerald Publishing, 2021.

Kelly, Patrick J. *Creating a National Home: Building the Veterans' Welfare State, 1860–1900*. Cambridge: Harvard Univ. Press, 1997.

Kennedy, Padraic C. "The Secret Service Department: A British Intelligence Bureau in Mid-Victorian London, September 1867 to April 1868." *Intelligence and National Security* 18, no. 3 (autumn 2003): 100–127.

Keshen, Jeff. "Cloak and Dagger: Canada West's Secret Police, 1864–1867." *Ontario History* 79, no. 4 (December 1987): 353–381.

Keve, Paul W. *The History of Corrections in Virginia*. Charlottesville: Univ. Press of Virginia, 1986.

Kiewit, Carrie. "A Study of Fraud in African-American Civil War Pensions: Augustus Parlett Lloyd, Pension Attorney,1882–1909." Master's thesis, University of Richmond, 1996.

Kilday, Anne-Marie, and David Nash, eds. *Law, Crime and Deviance Since 1700: Micro-Studies in the History of Crime*. London: Bloomsbury, 2017.

Kimmel, Stanley. *Mr. Lincoln's Washington*. New York: Coward-McCann, 1957.

Kinchen, Oscar A. *Confederate Operations in Canada and the North*. North Quincy, Mass.: Christopher, 1970.

Klaus, Ian. *Forging Capitalism: Rogues, Swindlers, Frauds, and the Rise of Modern Finance*. New Haven: Yale Univ. Press, 2014.

Klein, Christopher. *When the Irish Invaded Canada: The Incredible True Story of the Civil War Veterans Who Fought for Ireland's Freedom*. New York: Doubleday, 2019.

Klein, Maury. *Union Pacific: Birth of a Railroad, 1862–1893*. New York: Doubleday, 1987.

Klement, Frank L. *Dark Lanterns: Secret Political Societies, Conspiracies, and Treason Trials in the Civil War*. Baton Rouge: Louisiana State Univ. Press, 1984.

Klingman, Peter D. *Josiah Walls: Florida's Black Congressman of Reconstruction*. 1976. Reprint, Gainesville: Univ. Press of Florida, 2017.

Konnikova, Maria. *The Confidence Game: The Psychology of the Con and Why We Fall for It . . . Every Time*. New York: Viking, 2016.

Kutzler, Evan A. *Living by Inches: The Smells, Sounds, Tastes, and Feeling of Captivity in Civil War Prisons*. Chapel Hill: Univ. of North Carolina Press, 2019.

Larabee, Ann. *The Dynamite Fiend: The Chilling Tale of a Confederate Spy, Con Artist, and Mass Murderer*. New York: Palgrave Macmillan, 2005.

Lause, Mark A. *Free Labor: The Civil War and the Making of an American Working Class*. Urbana: Univ. of Illinois Press, 2015.

———. *Free Spirits: Spiritualism, Republicanism, and Radicalism in the Civil War Era*. Champaign: Univ. of Illinois Press, 2016.

Lawson, Linda. "Advertisements Masquerading as News in Turn-of-the-Century American Periodicals." *American Journalism* 5, no. 2 (spring 1988): 81–96.

Lears, T. J. Jackson. *No Place of Grace: Antimodernism and the Transformation of American Culture, 1880–1920.* Chicago: Univ. of Chicago Press, 1981.

Lee, Susanna Michele. *Claiming the Union: Citizenship in the Post–Civil War South.* Cambridge: Cambridge Univ. Press, 2014.

Leonard, Elizabeth D. *Lincoln's Avengers: Justice, Revenge, and Reunion after the Civil War.* New York: Norton, 2004.

Lepore, Jill. "Historians Who Love Too Much: Reflections on Microhistory and Biography." *Journal of American History* 88, no. 1 (June 2001): 129–144.

Levinson, Sanford, ed. *Nullification and Secession in Modern Constitutional Thought.* Lawrence: Univ. Press of Kansas, 2016.

Lindberg, Gary H. *The Confidence Man in American Literature.* New York: Oxford Univ. Press, 1982.

Lofland, Lyn H. *A World of Strangers: Order and Action in Urban Public Space.* New York: Basic Books, 1973.

Lowry, Thomas P. *The Story the Soldiers Wouldn't Tell: Sex in the Civil War.* Mechanicsburg, Pa.: Stackpole Books, 1994.

Lucey, Seán D. *Land, Popular Politics and Agrarian Violence in Ireland: The Case of County Kerry, 1872–86.* Dublin: Univ. College Dublin Press, 2011.

Luskey, Brian P. *Men Is Cheap: Exposing the Frauds of Free Labor in Civil War America.* Chapel Hill: Univ. of North Carolina Press, 2020.

———. *On the Make: Clerks and the Quest for Capital in Nineteenth-Century America.* New York: New York Univ. Press, 2010.

Luskey, Brian P., and Wendy A. Woloson, eds. *Capitalism by Gaslight: Illuminating the Economy of Nineteenth-Century America.* Philadelphia: Univ. of Pennsylvania Press, 2015.

Magnússon, Sigurður Gylfi, and István M. Szijártó. *What Is Microhistory?: Theory and Practice.* Abingdon: Routledge, 2013.

Mahoney, James. *The Legacies of Liberalism: Path Dependence and Political Regimes in Central America.* Baltimore: Johns Hopkins Univ. Press, 2001.

Marten, James. "Exempt from the Ordinary Rules of Life: Sources on Maladjusted Union Civil War Veterans." *Civil War History* 47, no. 1 (March 2001): 57–70.

———. *Sing Not War: The Lives of Union and Confederate Veterans in Gilded Age America.* Chapel Hill: Univ. of North Carolina Press, 2011.

Marvel, William. "The Great Imposters." *Blue and Grey Magazine* 8 (February 1991): 32–33.

———. "Johnny Ransom's Imagination." *Civil War History* 41, no. 3 (September 1995): 181–189.

Mathisen, Erik. *The Loyal Republic: Traitors, Slaves, and the Remaking of Citizenship in Civil War America.* Chapel Hill: Univ. of North Carolina Press, 2018.

McAleavey, Maia. *The Bigamy Plot: Sensation and Convention in the Victorian Novel.* Cambridge: Cambridge Univ. Press, 2015.

McCaffery, Peter. *When Bosses Ruled Philadelphia: The Emergence of the Republican Machine, 1867–1933.* University Park: Penn State Univ. Press, 1993.

McPherson, James M. "Grant or Greeley? The Abolitionist Dilemma in the Election of 1872." *American Historical Review* 71, no. 1 (October 1965): 43–61.

Meador, John Allen. "Florida Political Parties, 1865–1877." Ph.D. diss., University of Florida, 1964.

Merritts, Jordan T. "Presidents Miguel Garcia Granados and Justo Rufino Barrios in Reform Guatemala: 1871–1885." Master's thesis, University of Arizona, 2012.

Mihm, Stephen. "Clerks, Classes, and Conflicts." *Journal of the Early Republic* 26, no. 4 (winter 2006): 605–615.

———. *A Nation of Counterfeiters: Capitalists, Con Men, and the Making of the United States.* Cambridge: Harvard Univ. Press, 2007.

Miller, George H. *Railroads and the Granger Laws.* Madison: Univ. of Wisconsin Press, 1971.

Miller, Wilbur R. *Revenuers and Moonshiners: Enforcing Federal Liquor Law in the Mountain South, 1865–1900.* Chapel Hill: Univ. of North Carolina Press, 1991.

Montgomery, David. *Beyond Equality: Labor and the Radical Republicans 1862–1872.* 1967. Reprint, Urbana: Univ. of Illinois Press, 1981.

Morn, Frank. *The Eye That Never Sleeps: A History of the Pinkerton National Detective Agency.* Bloomington: Indiana Univ. Press, 1982.

Mull, Carol E. *The Underground Railroad in Michigan.* Jefferson, N.C.: McFarland, 2010.

Natale, Simone. *Supernatural Entertainments: Victorian Spiritualism and the Rise of Modern Media Culture.* University Park: Penn State Univ. Press, 2016.

Neely, Mark E., Jr. *The Fate of Liberty: Abraham Lincoln and Civil Liberties.* New York: Oxford Univ. Press, 1991.

———. *Southern Rights: Political Prisoners and the Myth of Confederate Constitutionalism.* Charlottesville: Univ. of Virginia Press, 1999.

Nicoletti, Cynthia. "William Henry Trescot, Pardon Broker." *Journal of the Civil War Era* 11, no. 4 (December 2021): 478–506.

Nitschke, Christoph. "Theory and History of Financial Crises: Explaining the Panic of 1873." *Journal of the Gilded Age and Progressive Era* 17, no. 2 (April 2018): 221–240.

Nolan, Van, Jr. "Indiana: Birthplace of Migratory Divorce." *Indiana Law Journal* 26, no. 4 (summer 1951): 515–527.

Ó Cathaoir, Brendán. "The Kerry 'Home Rule' By-Election, 1872." *Journal of the Kerry Archaeological and Historical Society* 3 (1970): 154–177.

BIBLIOGRAPHY

Obert, Jonathan. "The Coevolution of Public and Private Security in Nineteenth-Century Chicago." *Law and Social Inquiry* 43, no. 3 (summer 2018): 827–861.

———. "A Fragmented Force: The Evolution of Federal Law Enforcement in the United States, 1870–1900." *Journal of Policy History* 29, no. 4 (October 2017): 640–675.

O'Brien, John E. *Telegraphing in Battle: Reminiscences of the Civil War.* Scranton: Reader Press, 1910.

Parnaby, Andrew, and Gregory S. Kealey. "The Origins of Political Policing in Canada: Class, Law, and the Burden of Empire." *Osgoode Hall Law Journal* 41, no. 2/3 (summer 2003): 211–240.

Peek, Ralph L. "Curbing Voter Intimidation in Florida, 1871." *Florida Historical Quarterly* 43, no. 4 (April 1965): 333–348.

———. "Lawlessness in Florida, 1868–1871." *Florida Historical Quarterly* 40, no. 2 (October 1961): 164–185.

Perez-Brignoli, Hector. *A Brief History of Central America,* translated by Ricardo B. Sawrey and Susana Stettri de Sawrey. Berkeley: Univ. of California Press, 1989.

Peters, John O. *From Marshall to Moussaoui: Federal Justice in the Eastern District of Virginia.* Petersburg, Va.: Dietz Press, 2013.

Pettit, Michael. *The Science of Deception: Psychology and Commerce in America.* Chicago: Univ. of Chicago Press, 2013.

Pickenpaugh, Roger. *Captives in Blue: The Civil War Prisons of the Confederacy.* Tuscaloosa: Univ. of Alabama Press, 2013.

Plum, William R. *The Military Telegraph During the Civil War in the United States.* 2 vols. Chicago: Jansen, McClurg, 1882.

Porter, Bernard. *The Origins of the Vigilant State: The London Metropolitan Police Special Branch Before the First World War.* 1987. Reprint, Woodbridge, UK: Boydell Press, 1991.

Probert, Rebecca. *Double Trouble: The Rise and Fall of the Crime of Bigamy.* London: Selden Society, 2015.

———. "Escaping Detection: Illegal Second Marriages and the Crime of Bigamy." *Journal of Genealogy and Family History* 6, no. 1 (2022): 27–33.

Pula, James S. *For Liberty and Justice: The Life and Times of Wladimir Krzyżanowski.* Chicago: Polish American Congress Charitable Foundation, 1978.

Quinlivan, Patrick., and Paul Rose. *The Fenians in England 1865–1872: A Sense of Insecurity.* London: John Calder, 1982.

Raine, Alice. *Eagle of Guatemala: Justo Rufino Barrios.* New York: Harcourt, Brace, 1947.

Richardson, Joe M. *The Negro in the Reconstruction of Florida, 1865–1877.* Tallahassee: Florida State Univ. Press, 1965.

Riddleberger, Patrick W. "The Break in the Radical Ranks: Liberals vs Stalwarts in the Election of 1872." *Journal of Negro History* 44, no. 2 (April 1959): 136–157.

Ring, Natalie J. "The Problem South: Region, Race, and 'Southern Readjustment,' 1880–1930." Ph.D. diss, University of California, San Diego, 2003.

Rivers, Larry E. *Father James Page: An Enslaved Preacher's Climb to Freedom.* Baltimore: Johns Hopkins Univ. Press, 2021.

Rivers, Larry E., and Canter Brown Jr. *Laborers in the Vineyard of the Lord: The Beginnings of the AME Church in Florida, 1865–1895.* Gainesville: Univ. Press of Florida, 2001.

Robinson, William M., Jr. *Justice in Grey: A History of the Judicial System of the Confederate States of America.* Cambridge: Harvard Univ. Press, 1941.

Robisheaux, Thomas. "Microhistory Today: A Roundtable Discussion." *Journal of Medieval and Early Modern Studies* 47, no. 1 (January 2017): 7–52.

Rockman, Seth. *Scraping By: Wage Labor, Slavery, and Survival in Early Baltimore.* Baltimore: Johns Hopkins Univ. Press, 2009.

Roscoe, Theodore. *The Web of Conspiracy: The Complete Story of the Men Who Murdered Abraham Lincoln.* Englewood Cliffs, N.J.: Prentice Hall, 1959.

Rubio, Casimiro D. *Biografía del General Justo Rufino Barrios, Reformador de Guatemala: Recopilación Histórica y Documentada.* 1935.

Ruckman, P. S., Jr., and David Kincaid. "Inside Lincoln's Clemency Decision Making." *Presidential Studies Quarterly* 29, no. 1 (March 1999): 84–99.

Samito, Christian G. *Becoming American Under Fire: Irish Americans, African Americans, and the Politics of Citizenship During the Civil War Era.* Ithaca: Cornell Univ. Press, 2009.

Sanders, Charles W., Jr. *While in the Hands of the Enemy: Military Prisons of the Civil War.* Baton Rouge: Louisiana State Univ. Press, 2005.

Schrauwers, Albert. *"Union Is Strength": W.L. Mackenzie, the Children of Peace, and the Emergence of Joint Stock Democracy in Upper Canada.* Toronto: Univ. of Toronto Press, 2009.

Schwartzberg, Beverly. "'Lots of Them Did That': Desertion, Bigamy, and Marital Fluidity in Late-Nineteenth-Century America." *Journal of Social History* 37, no. 3 (spring 2004): 573–600.

Seeman, Erik R. *Speaking with the Dead in Early America.* Philadelphia: Univ. of Pennsylvania Press, 2019.

Sellers, Charles. *The Market Revolution: Jacksonian America, 1815–1846.* New York: Oxford Univ. Press, 1991.

Senior, Hereward. *The Last Invasion of Canada: The Fenian Raids, 1866–1870.* Toronto: Dundurn Press, 1991.

Serrano, Richard A. *Last of the Blue and Gray: Old Men, Stolen Glory, and the Mystery that Outlived the Civil War*. Washington, D.C.: Smithsonian Books, 2013.

Shaffer, Donald R. "'I Do Not Suppose That Uncle Sam Looks at the Skin': African Americans and the Civil War Pension System, 1865–1934." *Civil War History* 46, no. 2 (June 2000): 132–147.

Shofner, Jerrell H. *Nor Is It Over Yet: Florida in the Era of Reconstruction, 1863–1877*. Gainesville: Univ. Press of Florida, 1974.

———. "Political Reconstruction in Florida." *Florida Historical Quarterly* 45, no. 2 (October 1966): 145–170.

Singerman, David Roth. "Science, Commodities, and Corruption in the Gilded Age." *Journal of the Gilded Age and Progressive Era* 15, no. 3 (July 2016): 278–293.

Skocpol, Theda. *Protecting Soldiers and Mothers: The Political Origins of Social Policy in the United States*. Cambridge: Harvard Univ. Press, 1992.

Slap, Andrew L. *The Doom of Reconstruction: The Liberal Republicans in the Civil War Era*. New York: Fordham Univ. Press, 2006.

Smith, Mark Power. "Séances in the City: The 'Operational Aesthetic' and 'Modern Spiritualism' in the Popular Culture of New York City, 1865–1870." *American Nineteenth Century History* 18, no. 1 (April 2017): 45–62.

Smith, Michael Thomas. *The Enemy Within: Fears of Corruption in the Civil War North*. Charlottesville: Univ. of Virginia Press, 2011.

Smith, Phillip Thurmond. *Policing Victorian London: Political Policing, Public Order, and the London Metropolitan Police*. Westport: Greenwood Press 1985.

Snay, Mitchell. *Fenians, Freedmen, and Southern Whites: Race and Nationality in the Era of Reconstruction*. Baton Rouge: Louisiana State Univ. Press, 2007.

Sommerville, Diane Miller. *Aberration of Mind: Suicide and Suffering in the Civil War–Era South*. Chapel Hill: Univ. of North Carolina Press, 2018.

Speer, Lonnie R. *Portals to Hell: Military Prisons of the Civil War*. Mechanicsburg, Pa.: Stackpole Books, 1997.

Springer, Paul J., and Glenn Robins. *Transforming Civil War Prisons: Lincoln, Lieber, and the Politics of Captivity*. New York: Routledge, 2015.

Stanley, Amy Dru. *From Bondage to Contract: Wage Labor, Marriage, and the Market in the Age of Slave Emancipation*. Cambridge: Cambridge Univ. Press, 1998.

Stauffer, John, and Benjamin Soskis. *The Battle Hymn of the Republic: A Biography of the Song That Marches On*. New York: Oxford Univ. Press, 2013.

Stedman, Laura, and George Milbry Gould. *Life and Letters of Edmund Clarence Stedman*. New York: Moffat, Yard, 1910.

Steers, Edward. *Blood on the Moon: The Assassination of Abraham Lincoln*. Lexington: Univ. Press of Kentucky, 2001.

Steinfeld, Robert J. *Coercion, Contract, and Free Labor in the Nineteenth Century.* New York: Cambridge Univ. Press, 2001.

Sternhell, Yael A. *Routes of War: The World of Movement in the Confederate South.* Cambridge: Harvard Univ. Press, 2012.

Still, Bayrd. "Patterns of Mid-Nineteenth Century Urbanization in the Middle West." *Mississippi Valley Historical Review* 28, no. 2 (September 1941): 187–206.

Strom, Sharon H. *Fortune, Fame, and Desire: Promoting the Self in the Long Nineteenth Century.* Lanham, Md.: Rowman and Littlefield, 2016.

Sulick, Michael J. *Spying in America: Espionage from the Revolutionary War to the Dawn of the Cold War.* Washington, D.C.: Georgetown Univ. Press, 2012.

Summers, Mark W. *The Ordeal of the Reunion: A New History of Reconstruction.* Chapel Hill: Univ. of North Carolina Press, 2014.

———. *The Plundering Generation: Corruption and the Crisis of the Union, 1849–1861.* New York: Oxford Univ. Press, 1987.

———. "The Press Gang: Corruption and the Independent Press in the Grant Era." *Congress and the Presidency* 17, no. 1 (spring 1990): 29–44.

———. *The Press Gang: Newspapers and Politics, 1863–1878.* Chapel Hill: Univ. of North Carolina Press, 1994.

Tidwell, William A. *April '65: Confederate Covert Action in the American Civil War.* Kent, Ohio: Kent State Univ. Press, 1995.

———. *Come Retribution: The Confederate Secret Service and the Assassination of Lincoln.* Jackson: Univ. Press of Mississippi, 1988.

Thayne, Stanley J. "Walking on Water: Nineteenth-Century Prophets and a Legend of Religious Imposture." *Journal of Mormon History* 36, no. 2 (spring 2010): 160–204.

Thomas, Benjamin P. *Abraham Lincoln: A Biography.* 1952. Reprint, Carbondale: Southern Illinois Univ. Press, 2008.

Thomas, Don. "How They Got Away with Murder." https://reasonlincoln.co m/wp-content/uploads/2017/09/New-How-They-Got-Away-with-Murder.pdf.

Thompson, Margaret S. "Ben Butler versus the Brahmins: Patronage and Politics in Early Gilded Age Massachusetts." *New England Quarterly* 55, no. 2 (June 1982): 163–186.

———. "Corruption—or Confusion? Lobbying and Congressional Government in the Early Gilded Age." *Congress and the Presidency* 10, no. 2 (autumn 1983): 169–193.

———. *The "Spider Web": Congress and Lobbying in the Age of Grant.* Ithaca: Cornell Univ. Press, 1985.

Thornley, David. "The Irish Conservatives and Home Rule, 1869–73." *Irish Historical Studies* 11, no. 43 (March 1959): 200–222.

Thornton, T. D. *My Adventures with Your Money: George Graham Rice and the Golden Age of the Con Artist.* New York: St. Martin's Press, 2015.

Towne, Stephen E. *Surveillance and Spies in the Civil War: Exposing Confederate Conspiracies in America's Heartland.* Athens: Ohio Univ. Press, 2015.

Tuchinsky, Adam-Max. *Horace Greeley's New-York Tribune: Civil War-Era Socialism and the Crisis of Free Labor.* Ithaca: Cornell Univ. Press, 2009.

Unterman, Katherine. "Boodle Over the Border: Embezzlement and the Crisis of International Mobility, 1880–1890." *Journal of the Gilded Age and Progressive Era* 11, no. 2 (April 2012): 151–189.

———. *Uncle Sam's Policemen: The Pursuit of Fugitives Across Borders.* Cambridge: Harvard Univ. Press, 2015.

Van Driel, Hugo. "Financial Fraud, Scandals, and Regulation: A Conceptual Framework and Literature Review." *Business History* 61, no. 8 (November 2019): 1259–1299.

Wallace, John. *Carpetbag Rule in Florida: The Inside Workings of Civil Government in Florida After the Close of the Civil War.* Jacksonville: Da Costa Printing and Publishing House, 1888.

Walker, David. "The Humbug in American Religion: Ritual Theories of Nineteenth-Century Spiritualism." *Religion and American Culture* 23 (winter 2013): 30–74.

Ward, Geoffrey C. *A Disposition to Be Rich: How a Small-Town Pastor's Son Ruined an American President, Brought on a Wall Street Crash, and Made Himself the Best-Hated Man in the United States.* New York: Knopf, 2012.

Ward, Ian. *Sex, Crime and Literature in Victorian England.* Oxford: Hart Publishing, 2014.

Watson, Robert P. *Escape! The Story of the Confederacy's Infamous Libby Prison and the Civil War's Largest Jail Break.* Lanham, Md.: Rowman and Littlefield, 2021.

Waugh, Joan, and Gary W. Gallagher, eds. *Wars Within a War: Controversy and Conflict Over the American Civil War.* Chapel Hill: Univ. of North Carolina Press, 2009.

Williams, Timothy J., and Evan A. Kutzler, eds. *Prison Pens: Gender, Memory, and Imprisonment in the Writings of Mollie Scollay and Wash Nelson, 1863–1866.* Athens: Univ. of Georgia Press, 2018.

Whitaker, Reginald, Gregory S. Kealey, and Andrew Parnaby. *Secret Service: Political Policing in Canada from the Fenians to Fortress America.* Toronto: Univ. of Toronto Press, 2012.

White, G. E. "Recovering the Legal History of the Confederacy." *Washington and Lee Law Review* 68, no. 2 (spring 2011): 467–556.

White, Jonathan. "The Presidential Pardon Records of the Lincoln Administration." *Journal of the Abraham Lincoln Association* 39, no. 2 (summer 2018): 55–65.

———, ed. *To Address You as My Friend: African Americans' Letters to Abraham Lincoln.* Chapel Hill: Univ. of North Carolina Press, 2021.

White, Richard. "Information, Markets, and Corruption: Transcontinental Railroads in the Gilded Age." *Journal of American History* 90, no. 1 (June 2003): 19–43.

———. *The Republic for Which It Stands: The United States During Reconstruction and the Gilded Age, 1865–1896.* New York: Oxford Univ. Press, 2017.
Wiebe, Robert H. *The Search for Order 1877–1920.* New York: Hill and Wang, 1967.
Wilentz, Sean. *Chants Democratic: New York City and the Rise of the American Working Class, 1788–1850.* Twentieth Anniversary ed.. New York: Oxford Univ. Press, 2004.
Williams, Learotha, Jr. "'A Wider Field of Usefulness': The Life and Times of Jonathan Clarkson Gibbs c.1828–1874." Ph.D. diss., Florida State University, 2003.
Wilson, David A. *Canadian Spy Story: Irish Revolutionaries and the Secret Police.* Montreal: McGill-Queen's Univ. Press, 2022.
———, ed. *Irish Nationalism in Canada.* Montreal: McGill-Queens Univ. Press, 2009.
———. *Thomas D'Arcy McGee*, vol. 2, *The Extreme Moderate, 1857–1868.* Montreal: McGill-Queens Univ. Press, 2011.
Wolff, Joshua D. *Western Union and the Creation of the American Corporate Order, 1845–1893.* Cambridge: Cambridge Univ. Press, 2013.
Woods, Thomas A. *Knights of the Plow: Oliver H. Kelley and the Origins of the Grange in Republican Ideology.* Ames: Iowa State Univ. Press, 1991.
Woodward, C. Vann. *Origins of the New South, 1877–1913.* Baton Rouge: Louisiana State Univ. Press, 1951.
Woodward, Ralph Lee. *Rafael Carrera and the Emergence of the Republic of Guatemala, 1821–1871.* Athens: Univ. of Georgia Press, 1993.
Woolnough, Guy N. "A Victorian Fraudster and Bigamist: Gentleman or Criminal?" *Criminology and Criminal Justice* 19, no. 4 (September 2019): 439–455.
Zakim, Michael. *Accounting for Capitalism: The World the Clerk Made.* Chicago: Univ. of Chicago Press, 2018.
———. "The Business Clerk as Social Revolutionary; or, a Labor History of the Nonproducing Classes." *Journal of the Early Republic* 26, no. 4 (winter 2006): 563–603.
Zombek, Angela M. *Penitentiaries, Punishment, and Military Prisons: Familiar Responses to an Extraordinary Crisis During the American Civil War.* Kent, Ohio: Kent State Univ. Press, 2018.
———. "Transcending Stereotypes: A Study of Civil War Military Prisons in the Context of Nineteenth-Century Penitentiaries and Penal Development at the Ohio, Virginia, and D.C. Penitentiaries and at Camp Chase, Castle Thunder, and Old Capitol Military Prisons." Ph.D. diss., University of Florida, 2012.
Zonderman, David A. *Uneasy Allies: Working for Labor Reform in Nineteenth-Century Boston.* Amherst: Univ. of Massachusetts Press, 2011.

INDEX

Note: Charles Cowlam is abbreviated CC.

3rd Michigan Cavalry, 65
4th New York Cavalry, 132
11th New York Infantry (Ellsworth's Zouaves), 35, 135, 146–147
14th Regiment of the Irish Republican Army, 56
21st New York Infantry, 132
Adams, John S., 100, 102–103
African Americans, 4, 25, 45, 61, 64, 119, 120, 133, 140; in Florida, 85–88, 92, 96, 99, 101, 104–109 passim, 111, 177n45, 179n67, 179n72
African Methodist Episcopal (A.M.E.) Church, 96, 106
Alberger, Morris H., 100
Alcantara, Susana, 139
Alder, Monroe J., 61, 169n25
Alexander, George, 44
Allen, George S., 23
Allen, John, 22
Anderson, Samuel Lee, 73
Andersonville prison, 133
antislavery, 19, 30, 139, 140, 144, 174n5
Armstrong, William J., 130
Aten, Isaac, 36–37
Atkinson, Edward, 148

Baker, Lafayette C., 130–131
Banks, Nathaniel P., 67

Barrios, Justo Rufino, 137–139, 140, 141, 187n22
Basnett, F. B., 97, 98, 101–104 passim, 176n33
Bates, Edward, 14–15, 17, 18, 30, 31
Battle Creek, Michigan, x, 19, 21–22, 27, 29, 123–124, 146, 176n30
Battle of Mobile Bay, 34, 41
Beaumont, Gustave de, 6–7
Beecher, Henry Ward, 182n26
Benjamin, Judah P., 46, 49
Bennett, James Gordon, Jr., 114
Bennett Building, 112, 114, 119–120, 137, 182n20
Bernard, Hewitt, 55
bigamy, 5, 7, 12, 112–113, 121–128, 183n34–36, 186n12
Bigelow, Albert S., 60, 169n25
Bingham, John, 130
Black, John C., 131, 136
blackmail. *See* extortion
Blair, Francis, 31
Bloxham, William D., 89, 93, 94–95, 101, 102, 104, 105, 109–110, 179n72
Bock, Max, 130
Bonham, Milledge, 40
Booth, John Wilkes, 48, 49
Bowles Brothers, 66, 69, 70, 124
Brant, Joseph, 20
Brantley, Martin V., 37–38
Brennan, Matthew T., 120
Brooks, James, 149

INDEX

Brown, J. H., 117, 119, 121
Brown, John, 139–141
Brown, John Henry, 147
Buchanan, James, 18, 23, 24, 26–30, 35
Bunting, Thomas Browne, 137–138, 141
Bunting Brothers, 137, 187n21
Bureau of Pensions, 12, 32, 126, 131, 133–134, 144
Burke, Thomas Henry, 73
Burlick, William E. (alias for CC), 3, 119–121, 182n20. *See also* Cowlam, Charles
Burnett, Henry L., 49
Butler, Benjamin F., 7, 97, 137, 186n15, 190n10; and George Cowlam, 69, 135, 148–149, 150, 172n47

Cabell, Edward Carrington, 86–87
Call, Wilkinson, 93, 101, 176n33
Cannon, Kate, 48
capitalism, 8–9, 115, 117, 156n16
Career, Alezandro, 18
carpetbaggers, 7, 85, 87, 88, 101, 106, 111, 179n72
Cass, Lewis, 29
Castle Thunder, 44–45, 50, 135, 142
Cavendish, Frederick, 73
Cavendish, Spencer Compton (Marquess of Hartington), 64–71, 73–74
Central America. *See* Latin America
Central Branch soldiers' home. *See* National Home for Disabled Volunteer Soldiers
Cessna, William K., 100
Chandler, William E., 91, 95, 96–98, 101, 102–103, 105–106, 108–109, 125, 172n47
Chandler, Zachariah, 31–32
Cheney, Edward M., 98–99, 100–101, 104
Chicago, 2–3, 19, 21, 116, 121, 127, 146; CC in, 50, 55, 125, 128, 141, 167n3; Fenians movements in, 55, 57, 58; great fire, 69–70
Chicago Evening Post, 58, 124, 183n30
Chicago Tribune, 138–139, 141, 167n2
City of Brooklyn (steamer), 64

City of Panama (steamer), 138
Civil War, 6–7, 8, 65, 66, 91, 131, 137, 141, 146, 157n17. *See also* Cowlam, Charles; Davis, Jefferson; Lincoln, Abraham; loyalty and disloyalty, pardons; prisons; secession; veterans
Clark, Horace F., 149
Clark, Mrs. E. A. J. *See* Sands, Mrs. M. A.
clerks, 9, 33, 40, 42, 72, 104, 172n47; congressional committees, 52, 64, 68–69, 138, 148, 150, 170n29; county clerks, 90, 108; pardon office 14, 17, 18; pension bureau, 32, 126, 130; Post Office Department, 3, 37; Treasury Department, 62; War Department, 131, 132
Cole, J. S., 143
Conant, Sherman, 95, 96, 97–104, 107, 177n45
con artists, ix–x, 2–3, 8–10, 54, 98, 122, 127, 133, 157n18. *See also* Cowlam, Charles
Confederate Army, 4, 33–34, 39–41, 45, 91
Confederate constitutionalism, 32, 36–38, 163n6, 164n11
Confederate Secret Service Bureau, 4, 33, 34, 42, 43, 46, 47, 49–50, 56, 123
Confidence Man, The (Melville), 1, 10, 14, 33, 51, 85, 112, 129, 145
confidence men. *See* con artists
Conover, Simon B., 91, 110
Cooke, John Kearns, 23
corruption, 2, 5, 9, 60, 70, 88, 89, 149, 156n15, 157n17
Cosgrove, James F., 56
counterfeit currency, 4, 23, 36, 38, 60, 61
Cowlam, Charles (father of CC), 19–21, 160n20
Cowlam, Charles, 3, 6–10, 12–13, 150–151, 183n30, 185n9; early life and family, 18–22, 26–31, 50, 64, 123, 128, 144–150 passim, 169n17; arrested for mail robbery, 3, 22–24; in Virginia State Penitentiary, 24–25, 38–

220

INDEX

39; pardoned by Abraham Lincoln, ix, 3, 10, 14–15, 18, 26–32; pardoned by Jefferson Davis, 3–4, 10, 34–36; narratives of wartime exploits, 39–47, 65–66, 68, 123–124, 135–137, 142–143; and Lincoln assassination investigation, 4, 11, 33–34, 47–50, 68; as Canadian informant, 4, 11, 52–59, 68, 74, 169n12; as revenue detective, 4, 11, 59–64, 66, 70, 74; in United Kingdom, 4, 11, 64, 66, 67, 68–74, 124; in Florida, 4–5, 11–12, 87–88, 91, 92–95, 97–107, 109–111, 124, 176n30; as editor of the *Scythe*, 5, 12, 112, 113, 114–116, 120–121; bigamist, 5, 12, 112–113, 121–122, 125–127; author of *Perpetual Motion*, 142; in soldiers' home, 5, 12, 131–135 passim; as Charles Cushman, 3, 22, 24; as William E. Burlick, 3, 119–121, 182n20; as Charles Harry Cowland, 125; as Livingston Grahame, 3, 129–132, 137–144. *See also* Cowlam & Co.; Cowlan Brothers; Order of the Patrons of Industry; *specific topics*

Cowlam, Charles A. (nephew of CC), 189n1
Cowlam, Elizabeth (sister of CC), x, 21, 47, 50
Cowlam, Elizabeth Amelia Cushman (first wife of CC's father), 20
Cowlam, Elsie (half-sister of CC), 20, 30, 159n14
Cowlam, George B. (brother of CC), 50, 123, 128, 131, 144, 145, 149–150, 167n2, 189n1, 190n7, 190n12; author of works of Southern boosterism, 150; early life, 21, 27, 28, 146, 162n40, 169n17; Civil War service, 35, 135, 146, 147–148, 185n9; as clerk, 64, 69, 138, 170n29, 172n47; as source of information, 58, 74, 113, 136, 138, 142, 148–149, 150; memories of Abraham Lincoln, 146–147. *See also under* Butler, Benjamin F.; telegraph operators
Cowlam, Isabella "Belle" "Isabel" (sister of CC), 21, 28–29, 31, 128, 141, 144, 190n10

Cowlam, Isabella Hays (mother of CC), 20
Cowlam, Mariette "Minnie" (sister of CC), 21, 28–29, 31, 160n19
Cowlam, Mary Ives (wife of CC), 50, 64, 112, 127–128, 145
Cowlam, Mary S. (née McGregory; wife of George B. Cowlam), 50, 64, 146
Cowlam, Sarah "Sammie" (sister of CC), 14, 20, 26–31, 70, 127–128, 160n19
Cowlam & Co., 167n3, 168n6
Cowlan Brothers, 51–52, 58
Cowland, Charles Harry (alias for CC), 125. *See also* Cowlam, Charles
CSS *Tallahassee*, 44
CSS *Virginia*, 147
Cushman, Charles (alias for CC), 3, 22, 24. *See also* Cowlam, Charles
Cushman, Henry Josiah, 20, 21, 29

Daniel, John M., 43
Davis, Jefferson, 42, 44, 46, 66; pardon of CC, 3–4, 8, 10, 11, 15–16, 34–37, 39, 123
Day, Samuel T., 89, 94
Dayton, Ohio, 5, 12, 129, 131, 134, 138, 141, 146
Democratic Party, 30, 149, 174n5; anti-Tammany Democrats, 122, 129; in Florida, 12, 86–96, 98–103, 105, 107–110, 179n72
detectives, 9, 10, 23, 42, 44, 95, 109, 124, 170n29; Lincoln assassination, 4, 11, 33–34, 39, 40, 43–50 passim, 52, 59, 131, 136; in Canada, 54, 168n9, 169n12; internal revenue 3–4, 11, 59–64, 71, 74, 88, 101, 123, 128; United Kingdom, 4, 11, 65, 67, 68, 70–74, 171n43
Detroit, 3, 19, 54, 55, 57, 112, 128, 145; CC in, 33, 46, 48, 50
Detroit Free Press, 123, 128, 145
Dickson, William G., 60, 62
District of Columbia. *See* Washington, District of Columbia
Dublin, Ireland, 64, 67, 70, 71, 72–73

221

INDEX

Dublin Castle, 67, 73
Dublin Metropolitan Police, 71
Dyer, Alexander B., 58

Edmunds, Samuel Page, 60, 169n25
Ellsworth, Elmer E., 35, 146
Emmons, Jedediah Philo Clark, 175n11
Endicott, William C., 129–130
Engel, Benjamin, 130
Enos, Jacob D., 88, 104
Enterprise (schooner), 18
espionage, 4, 34, 49–50, 67, 131, 135–137, 142
extortion, 4, 62–64, 99

Farragut, David, 41
Fay, Hugh, 72
Fenian Brotherhood, 53–59, 64, 67, 72–74, 168n11, 169n12
Fisher, Mrs. Lida E., 143–144
Fitch, Henry S., 59–60
forgery, 33, 35, 38, 40, 45, 172n52
Fort Sumter, 14, 31, 146
Foster, John A., 33, 47, 48–49
Frank R. Sherwin and Co., 69, 124
Fraud, 5, 7, 10, 60, 62, 74, 151, 186n12, 190n7; electoral fraud, 86–87, 96, 99, 107–109; fraudulent secret society, 12, 113–121; bigamy frauds, 121–128; pension fraud, 130, 133–134
free labor, 1–2, 21, 115, 153n1
Free Soil Party, 19, 174n5
Fremont, John C., 30
French, S. Bassett, 15
Friedman, Lawrence, 7, 126, 183n34–35
Fry, James B., 33, 48–49
Fry, William H., 45

Garfield, James A., 149
George (brig), 60
Gibbs, Jonathan Clarkson, 94, 96, 100, 105, 108

Gilded Age, 3, 6, 12, 122, 126
Gladstone, William, 64
Glen Cove (steamer), 24
Goodrich, Thomas, 42
Goodrich, Washington, 42
Gould, John H., 63, 170n31
Grahame, Livingston (alias for CC), 3, 129–132, 137–144. *See also* Cowlam, Charles
Granger movement. *See* National Grange of the Order of Patrons of Husbandry
Grant, Ulysses S., 94, 111, 149, 177n40, 186n12; and 1872 election, 88, 96, 107, 109, 110, 176n30; appointments in Florida, 4, 8, 12, 90–92, 97–105, 176n33; and CC's wartime stories, 124, 136, 142
Grant and Wilson Club, 101, 103, 179n67
Greeley, Horace, 88, 96, 97, 101–102, 105, 176n30, 179n67
Greeley, Jonathan C., 109–110
Gregory, John Munford, 23
Guatemala, 12, 131, 137–139, 140, 187n21–22
Guillot, Faustin, 17–18

Hale, Moses H., 99–100
Halyburton, James D., 23–24, 35, 39
Harris, Iverson L., 38
Harris, Marian, 61
Harrison, William Henry, 30
Hart, Ossian Bingley, 92, 110
Hartington, Lord. *See* Cavendish, Spencer Compton
Hay, John, 147
Henderson, Edmund, 71
Hill, Bennett Hoskin, 33, 47, 48–49
Hill, Clement Hugh, 98
Hoeg, Halstead H., 94
Holmes, David E., 130
Holt, Joseph, 49
home rule (Ireland), 67, 71–72
Honduras (steamer), 138
Horton, Alice, 151

INDEX

Hotes, Nate, ix, xii
Howland, Marie, 118
Hunt, Thomas G., 33
Hussey, Erastus, 19, 29

Industrial Future of the South, The (George Cowlam), 150
Ingraham, Timothy, 47
Internal Revenue Service, 4, 11, 59–64, 71, 74, 88, 101, 120, 123, 128, 132
Irish nationalism, 11, 53, 55, 67, 72, 171n36, 173n56. *See also* Fenian Brotherhood; home rule (Ireland)
Izard, Henry, 58, 146
Izard, James, 162n40

Jacksonville, Florida, 61, 93, 98–105 passim, 107, 109, 110, 176n33
Jay Cooke and Company, 114–115
Johnson, Andrew, 65, 139, 186n12
Johnson, John, 22
Johnson, Samuel, 132
Jones, Allen, 106
Jones, Charles W., 93, 109
Jones, Robert F., 107
journalists, 9, 12, 51, 57, 68, 85, 110, 113, 118–121, 139, 141; CC as journalist, 58, 66, 68, 69, 95, 105, 113–121, 124; newspaper editors, 9, 41, 52, 88, 91, 114, 118, 122, 138
Juarez, Benito, 139

Kalamazoo, Michigan, 46, 52, 54–58
Kasiski, Friedrich, 49
Keehn, David, 43
Kellogg, Alexander Hamilton, 30
Kellogg, Charles Carroll, 30
Kellogg, Francis William, 14, 29–32, 64–69
Kellogg, George Ward, 30, 32
Kellogg, John Harvey, 19
Kellogg, John R., 31
Kellogg, John Sidney "J. S.," 32

Kelly, John, 122
Keyes, Wade, 34–35
Kingsmill, George R., 58
Knight, Alva A., 99, 101, 103, 108
Knights of the Golden Circle, 43, 50, 116
Krzyżanowski, Włodzimierz, 61–62, 63
Ku Klux Klan, 62, 98, 99, 177n45

Labor Reform Party, 117
Lake, Henry Atwell, 71–72, 74
Latin America, xi, 43, 137–139, 141. *See also* Guatemala
Lawler, John, 150–151
Lee, Robert E., 39
Letcher, John, x, 3–4, 15, 26, 39
Libby Prison, 7, 135–137
Liberal Republicans, 88, 92–93, 174n5
Liberty Party, 19
Lincoln, Abraham, 7, 65–66, 166n38, 187n22; pardon of CC, ix, x, 3, 8, 10, 15, 26, 30–33, 35, 41, 68; other uses of the pardon power, 10, 15–18, 36–38; assassination rumors and conspiracies, 42–43, 50; assassination investigation, 4, 11, 33, 39–40, 43–44, 46–48, 52, 59, 68, 131, 136–137; George Cowlam's reminiscences of, 146–147
Lincoln, Tad, 147
Littlefield, Milton, 110, 174n6
local knowledge, 7–8, 10, 12, 87, 98, 111
Lochrane, Osborne Augustus, 37–38
London, United Kingdom, 64, 67, 69, 73, 141
London Metropolitan Police, 67, 71
loyalty and disloyalty: to the Confederacy, 4, 10, 43, 45, 134; to the Union, 4, 11, 34, 132, 135. *See also* Southern Unionists
Lynch, Mary, 72

Macdonald, John A., 53, 54, 55, 59, 169n12
Maguire, James L., 23
mail robbery, 3, 14, 17, 22–24, 26, 36–38, 87–88, 103, 123

223

INDEX

Manhattan. *See* New York City
Marvin, William, 18
McCabe, John, 72
McClellan, George B., 39, 147
McCubbin, Samuel, 44
McCulloch, Hugh, 148
McGee, Thomas D'Arcy, 53–54, 68, 168n7
McGregory, Mary. *See* Cowlam, Mary S.
McMicken, Gilbert, 54–59, 68, 168–169n11–12
Meacham, Robert, 92
Melville, Herman, 1, 10, 14, 33, 51, 85, 112, 129, 145
microhistory, 5–6, 145, 155n8, 157n21
Military District of Michigan, 33, 47–49
Milton, John L., 41–42
Mobile, Alabama, 34, 40–42, 65
Mohawks, 20
Monroe, Elisha Lyman Cole, 69–70, 127–128
Morantes, Beciente A., 18
Morgan, Charles S., 14, 18, 24, 25–26, 124
Mosely, Morgan, 37
Muller, John Nicholas, 62–64, 99
Munger, Alvin B., 93
Murphy, Patrick, 57
Murtry, Lizzie, 48, 166n38
Myers, Henry, 24

National Detective Police, 131
National Grange of the Order of Patrons of Husbandry, 5, 12, 113, 115, 116, 117, 118
National Home for Disabled Volunteer Soldiers, 5, 8, 12, 129, 131, 134–135, 137, 141, 143–145
Negley, James S., 149
New York City, 35, 43, 61, 74, 114, 121–123, 127, 129, 146, 150, 182n26; CC in 5, 12, 64, 66, 69, 97, 112–128 passim, 137–138
New York Daily Graphic, 118–121
New York Herald, 112, 114, 122, 141
Niblack, Silas L., 93

Norfolk, Virginia, 23, 24, 29, 34–35, 45, 47, 136, 143

Olcott, Henry Steel, 47, 49, 166n36
O'Neill, Harriet, 73
O'Neill, John, 55, 57, 169n12
Ontario, Canada, 19, 20, 27, 55, 146
Order of the Advocates of Justice, 121
Order of the Patrons of Industry, 113, 115–118, 121. *See also* Order of the Advocates of Justice; Sovereigns of Industry
Osborn, Thomas W., 86, 88–89, 91–92, 102, 103, 110, 175n15, 175n17, 179n72; and reports of CC's meddling in Florida politics, 95, 100, 105–106, 109. *See also* Osborn Ring
Osborn Ring, 88–89, 90, 91, 93, 95, 96, 104, 106
O'Sullivan, William Henry, 73

Panic of 1837, 20
Panic of 1873, 12, 114, 121
pardons, 25–26, 37–38, 39, 106, 157n21, 186n12. *See also* Davis, Jefferson; pardon of CC; Lincoln, Abraham; pardon of CC; Lincoln, Abraham; other uses of the pardon power
Park, Charles S., 100
Parker, Ely S., 97–98
Parkersburg, West Virginia, 14, 22
Patrick, Marsena R., 131, 135
patronage, 4, 8, 12, 52, 105, 111, 186n12
Patrons of Industry. *See* Order of the Patrons of Industry
Pearce, Charles, 96, 106
Peninsula House, 42, 43, 50
Periam, Jonathan, 115
Perpetual Motion (CC under alias Livingston Grahame), 142
Plainwell, Michigan, 46–47, 50
Pollard, Edward A., 43
Poppleton, Andrew J., 149

224

INDEX

Porter, Horace, 103, 105
Portsmouth, Virginia, 3, 14, 22–23, 26, 29, 35
Post Office Department, 14, 17, 22–24, 26, 27, 29, 36–37, 61, 87, 110. *See also* clerks: Post Office Department; mail robbery
Potawatomi, 20
prisoners of war, 11, 15, 39, 44, 45, 136, 137
prisons, 6, 10, 15, 22, 24, 39, 133; conditions, 24–26, 38–39, 44–45; escapes, 22, 25, 44, 135–137, 142, 144. *See also* Castle Thunder; Libby Prison; Virginia State Penitentiary
Pulitzer, Joseph, 122
Purman, William J., 90–92, 105–107, 109, 175n13, 175n17

Quartermaster's Department: Confederate, 33, 40, 45, 50; Union, 45, 130, 149

Randall, Edwin M., 100
Random, William R., 107–108
Ray, James M., 96
Reconstruction, 3, 4, 7, 8, 65, 68, 114, 139, 150, 171n36, 179n72; CC as revenue detective, 11, 59–64; Florida politics in, 85–111
Red Rangers, 22, 123
Reed, Harrison, 11–12, 85–96, 100–111, 113, 125; appointments and removals, 87, 90–91, 97, 103, 105, 107–109, 175n11, 175n17, 176n33, 179n72; impeachment proceedings against, 85, 89–90, 106, 174n6
Reed, Roland, 142
Republican Party, 1, 8, 18, 30, 32, 146–147, 149, 174n5; in Florida, 5, 11–12, 85–111, 113, 176n33, 179n72
Republican State Executive Committee (Florida), 88, 90, 95, 96, 98, 100, 104, 105
Richmond, Virginia, 4, 14, 24, 33–34, 39–45, 66, 143, 165n13. *See also* Castle Thunder; Libby Prison; Virginia State Penitentiary
"Ring." *See* Osborn Ring
Ringo, Daniel, 17

Robinson, Alexander H., 60, 169n25
Rollins, Edward A., 60, 70, 172n52

Saline, Michigan, 18, 19, 21, 131
Salter, George W., 132
Sands, Johnson H., 45
Sands, Mrs. M. A., 46–47, 50, 166n30
Savannah, Georgia, 59–64, 99–100, 175n11
Scanlan, Michael, 55
Schenck, Robert C., 66–69, 172n47
Schmitz, Philip, 151
Schurman, James H. A., 61
Schuyler, Hartley and Graham, 58
Scott, John, 40
Scythe. See under Cowlam, Charles
Seaman, Vernon, 129–131, 184n2
secession, 3, 10, 15–18, 31, 32, 35–38, 43, 48, 164n11
Second Great Awakening, 2, 20
secret societies, 5, 12, 43, 50, 113–121, 122
Seven Stars Gold Mining Company, 151
Seward, William H., x, 31, 43, 50, 136, 147
Shafer, Ira, 112, 122–124, 145
Sheridan, Phillip H., 100
Sherman, William T., 42, 100
Smith, Frances, 64
smuggling. *See* whiskey
Southern Claims Commission, 134, 187n15
Southern Unionists, 10, 85, 92, 96, 134
Sovereigns of Industry, 121
spiritualism, 19, 27, 166n36
St. Albans Raid, 43–44
St. George's Society of Chicago, 58
Stanton, Edwin M., 47, 49, 65, 68, 136–137
Stearns, Marcellus L., 92, 106, 107–108, 110
Stewart, Leonard H., 27
Stowe, Harriet Beecher, 182n26
Strong, George Templeton, 114–115
Stuart, Charles E., 14, 29
suicide, 14, 24, 26, 28, 143
Sullivan, Alexander Martin, 72

INDEX

Summerville, William, 45
swindlers. *See* con artists

Tallahassee, Florida, 93, 100, 105, 107–110 passim
Taylor, Tazewell, 23
telegraph operators, 9, 11, 52; George Cowlam as, 27, 35, 58, 74, 135, 146–150, 162n40, 190n7
Thoreau, Henry David, 2
Tocqueville, Alexis de, 6
Treasury Department, 61, 62, 90, 99, 141, 144, 148, 170n31, 190n10; CC as revenue detective, 4, 8, 64, 66, 70, 132. *See also* Internal Revenue Service
Treaty of Chicago, 20, 160n17
Truth, Sojourner, 19
Turner, Henry McNeal, 61
Tyler, John, Jr., 90–97, 100, 109

Underground Railroad, 19, 29
Undeveloped South, The (George Cowlam), 150
Upper Canada Rebellion, 20
U.S. Military Telegraph Corps, 135, 147
U.S. Secret Service, 65, 129–130, 135, 137, 169n20
USS *Michigan*, 57
USS *Monitor*, 147

Vest, George Graham, 139
veterans, 7, 124, 132, 135, 185n9, 187n19; imposters, 12, 133–134, 186n12. *See also* Cowlam, Charles: as Livingston Grahame; National Home for Disabled Volunteer Soldiers
Virginia State Penitentiary, 14, 18, 22, 24–25, 26, 34, 38–39, 45, 124, 140

Waddell, Lloyd D., 60
Walls, Josiah T., 92–93, 103–104
Walsh, Walter M., 99
War Department: Confederate, 40, 91; Union, 129, 131–132, 136. *See also* clerks: War Department; Quartermaster's Department
Ward, Sam, 148
Warner, Hulbert Harrington, 151
Washington, District of Columbia, 31–32, 51, 58, 64, 69, 115, 124, 128, 131, 144; communication between Florida Republicans and Republicans in, 87, 96, 97–98, 101–104, 106, 109, 111, 112; George Cowlam in, 58, 64, 69, 146–147, 148, 149; and Lincoln assassination investigation, 4, 33, 47–49
Waukegan, Illinois, 21, 141
Webster, Alfonzo C., 142
Welles, Gideon, 147
Wells, Edward W., 150–151
Wells, Henry H., 47
Whelan, Patrick James, 54–55, 168n7
Whig Party, 1, 30, 86, 96, 174n5
whiskey, 4, 34, 59–63, 70, 170n29
White, Jonathan, ix, xi
Wiley, John F., 24
Williams, George H., 175n15
Williams, William J., 61, 169n25
Willson, John A., 16–17
Wilson, Henry, 67, 69, 104, 109
Windsor, Ontario, 54–56, 68
Wise, Henry A., 140
Wood, John Taylor, 44
Woodhams, Edwin, 50
Woodhams, Elizabeth Cowlam. *See* Cowlam, Elizabeth
Wyatt, John W., 105

Young, John, 68, 172n46
Yulee, David, 109